TRUE
INDIE

DON COSCARELLI

TRUE INDIE

TRUE INDIE

Life and Death in Filmmaking

ST. MARTIN'S PRESS 🚏 NEW YORK

www.stmartins.com

Designed by Steven Seighman

The Library of Congress Cataloging-in-Publication Data is available upon request.

ISBN 978-1-250-19324-7 (hardcover)
ISBN 978-1-250-19326-1 (ebook)

Our books may be purchased in bulk for promotional, educational, or business use. Please contact your local bookseller or the Macmillan Corporate and Premium Sales Department at 1-800-221-7945, extension 5442, or by email at MacmillanSpecialMarkets@macmillan.com.

First Edition: October 2018

10 9 8 7 6 5 4 3 2 1

This book is lovingly dedicated to my wife,
Shelley, and my children, Andrew and Chloe.

CONTENTS

PROLOGUE:

So You Want to Be an Indie Filmmaker?

I t was my first car chase. I'd grown up watching some great ones. The Mustang vs. the Charger in *Bullitt*. The Pontiac vs. the New York subway train in *The French Connection*. For me, it would be a 1971 Plymouth 'Cuda vs. a "driverless" 1968 Cadillac hearse. We had no stunt drivers, just some eager student filmmakers willing to drive from our crew. We had no city permits, but we did have a dead-end road out in the hills of Thousand Oaks, California, which we figured would be empty during our late-night shoot. Did I mention we would be blowing off a shotgun from the 'Cuda and crashing the hearse into a tree at the end of the chase? How the hell did I ever think I'd be able to pull this scene off with no stunt team and no budget? This is how we made *Phantasm*. Welcome to indie filmmaking!

The traditional image idolizes the indie filmmaker as edgy, hip, and cool. Certainly once Quentin Tarantino burst onto the film scene in the early nineties, this image drew a huge flock of wannabes to the indie world. He made it look so damn easy. But all those wannabes quickly found out it's not. Indie filmmaking is damn hard.

Making a no-budget indie film is like going to war. But you're not General MacArthur storming the beaches with a force of a hundred thousand soldiers. Instead, you're more like a small squad of Vietcong guerillas behind enemy lines, trying to complete an impossible mission using guile and your wits, the odds stacked against you. It's risky, difficult, and dangerous. I can swear to it. I've been there.

In addition to writing and directing *Phantasm,* I also did the cinematography. I had no choice. We couldn't afford a thousand dollars a week for a low-budget director of photography. We could barely afford meals for our dedicated crew. My mom handled that. We sweet-talked camera purveyor Panavision into providing us a state-of-the-art Panaflex film camera package for peanuts. Let's make a movie!

To shoot that car chase required some serious risk taking, myself included. Most of the stunt driving was handled by our go-to camera grip on the show, George W. Singer Jr. He had no previous film experience but came on board my first film as a background extra, and never left. George was a surfer—fearless, compact, and hard-core.

We shot that Plymouth muscle car from every angle. Sometimes we'd put the $75,000 Panaflex camera right on the centerline of the asphalt and George would race the 'Cuda straight at it, aiming for it, then swerve away at the last instant. It made for, as George would say, "One bitchin' shot!"

We also hung that camera off the side of the speeding Plymouth for the actor close-ups. We had no camera mount, so we stole a food tray from a carhop drive-in restaurant. One of us would hang on to it during shots, hoping that flimsy little tray wouldn't break loose on the hairpin turns.

The challenge was filming that shotgun. When one of the actors pops up through the sunroof of the speeding 'Cuda and fires his twelve-gauge pump shotgun into that hearse, there was only one way to get the shot. I had to get in the car's trunk with that forty-pound Panaflex rig strapped to my shoulder while we raced along and actor Bill Thornbury fired the weapon point blank at me. Of course we were using blank cartridges. What we didn't know then, but what a well-known TV actor found out later and paid for with his life, was that those blank cartridges blow a lot of dangerous wadding and flaming debris out of the gun barrel at a high muzzle velocity. You certainly wouldn't want to be closer to a blank-loaded gun than about ten feet if it were aimed at you. Crammed in the trunk of our feature car, I was less than two feet away. Ignorance is bliss.

Common sense told me I needed some kind of protection. One of my loyal crew members, Roberto Quezada, would be crouched in the trunk beside me, with two jobs—to read the light meter and to keep one hand on that Panaflex camera. There was no room in the trunk for a piece of transparent Plexiglas protection like they would have on a real movie. Wrapping me in a furniture pad wouldn't cut it: racing at high speed the wind would blow it right off. "We got any aluminum foil?"

My producer pal Paul Pepperman wrapped my head in aluminum foil as I put on my thick parka and zipped it up to my neck. Our camera assistant, Marc Schwartz, offered up his small camera pad and gaffer taped it over the left side of my face. The right side would be left bare: I had to look into the eyepiece and figured the Panaflex camera would protect my face. Marc slid a glass blank in over the lens to protect it from getting fried. At least the lens would be safe. We were ready to roll.

Bill was given the loaded pump shotgun. We only had four blank shells. We had just the one take to get the shot. George revved the engine, threw it in gear, and the muscle car took off. I yelled, "Go!" and, like an action star, Thornbury hurled off that sunroof, and as the wind whipped the thing by me, I was almost decapitated. Bill popped up, aimed the shotgun at camera and fired. BLAM, BLAM, BLAM, BLAM! I have to admit I winced from the sound of the discharge, but witnessed several fiery blasts blow right by camera. We got the shot and I screamed, "Cut, cut, cut!"

George skidded the 'Cuda to a stop by our truck and Marc ran up and yanked the Panaflex away from me to safety. George leaped out of the driver's seat to help me and stopped dead in his tracks. "Dude, your face is on fire."

BIKE SAFETY WEEK

My parents, Donald and Kate Coscarelli, bought their first home for nineteen thousand dollars in a massive new development on the northern tip of Orange County, California. When my family moved in, three thousand homes were under construction along with four new elementary schools in this huge subdivision called Rossmoor. The Korean War was over, war hero Ike Eisenhower was capably president, and it was several years before John Kennedy would be assassinated and several years more before Vietnam would define my generation. It was the late fifties: all the dads were gainfully employed, the moms had beautiful brand-new homes, and we kids had this seemingly perfect landscape to thrive and grow. This was where I grew up and the possibilities for the future appeared limitless.

I met my first best friend on the day I moved into the neighborhood when I was four years old. His name was Darwin Horn and he was bigger, stronger, and a year older. I was like a young Tom Sawyer to his Huck Finn and we did everything together. Rossmoor was our playground and we roamed that suburb far and wide. Everybody called him Little Dar, because his father had the same name. Little Dar and Big Dar. I looked up to Little Dar as he taught me a lot about boy things like fishing, stargazing, and skin diving, but I *really* looked up to Big Dar. He was unlike the other dads, because Big Dar's day job was as a United States Secret Service agent. Decades later I would fondly memorialize both Little Dar and Big Dar in my films *The Beastmaster* and *Kenny & Company* respectively.

Big Dar had been a football star at Pepperdine, then became a beat cop in the LAPD. Now he worked for the Treasury Department as a Secret Service agent and carried a .38 Special revolver in a shoulder holster. He had spent three years protecting President Eisenhower and had been recently transferred to Southern California to their forgery and counterfeiting unit. I liked Big Dar because he was kind and funny and was never condescending to us kids. Sometimes, with a twinkle in his eye, he would give Little Dar and me what he called "government assignments." He would come home from work and tell us to get the fireplace going. Then he would hand us a big box filled with counterfeit twenties and hundred-dollar bills. It was then our job to burn this "cash" in the fireplace. As a kid it was so empowering, almost thrilling, to be incinerating thousands of "dollars" in service of our country.

All was not idyllic in Rossmoor. Situated on the border of notoriously arch-conservative Orange County, it was in close proximity to fringe right-wing political groups, including the infamous John Birch Society. The Cold War was at its height and fear of Communism was rife throughout the country. During this tumultuous time my father decided to run for the local school board on a comparatively benign platform that the schools needed better funding. With my loyal younger sister Anne, Little Dar, and his younger sister Diane, we combed the neighborhood delivering campaign brochures out of our little red wagon to all three thousand homes in Rossmoor. It was a big job, but it paid off. My dad won and was promptly elevated to the position of school board president.

Frequently the Birch Society members would swarm and disrupt the school board meetings, demanding all Communist teachers and administrators be rooted out and fired. My dad never carried a gun like Big Dar, but when aroused by injustice, he could be fearless. It would fall to my dad to confront these crazies and many times he was forced to bring in the sheriff to restore order.

Ralph Domino was an inspiring elementary school teacher who drew the wrath of the anti-Communist fringe over, of all things, bike safety. It was Bike Safety Week and Mr. Domino challenged his sixth-grade students to create clever artwork that might connect with their classmates. One of his sharper students painted a cute poster image of a smiling Soviet leader,

Nikita Khrushchev, riding a bicycle with a big shiny medal on his chest. The poster tagline read, "He received an award for bike safety, so can you!" The Birch Society freaked out when they heard of this poster and demanded the school board fire Ralph Domino for teaching Communist propaganda. I can proudly say that, in the face of furious protest, my dad and a few other courageous members of the school board voted down these wackos and Ralph was able to keep his job. I was ultimately the beneficiary as I had the honor and great fortune to be able to spend an entire year in the classroom with this brilliant and gifted teacher. I was proud to later memorialize Ralph in my film *Kenny & Company* with actor Reggie Bannister portraying a teacher much like him.

SALTPETER AND SUGAR

As I was about to start middle school, my family made plans to move into another suburban housing development, this time in Long Beach, California. It was only a short five miles from our previous house, but it was an immense disruption in my life. I had to leave all the good friends I had grown up with and was forced to enroll in a new middle school where I knew absolutely nobody. In retrospect, this relocation may be one of the key reasons why I became a filmmaker.

We were the first family to move into this new development on the north side of what was to become known as Bixby Hill. Construction on the south side of the hill wasn't planned for a few more years, so it was pretty much wilderness over there. Having moved away from my friends, I was a lonely kid, and after school I would wander around the construction zone and goof around by myself. One-by-one neighbors started to slowly move into the development and I quickly met a group of kids who would go on to become my partners-in-crime in some amazing adventures on Bixby Hill. Bruce "Bruno" Malasky was a brilliant mind, extremely curious with an early love of computer programming and photography. Craig Mitchell was the strong silent type—a solid football player with a creative streak that belied his quiet nature. Then there were the Frankenfeld boys. Three brothers, Eric, Paul, and Phil, who were eager, creative, and smart. We started running as a pack, playing street football together and getting into all kinds of trouble.

These kids were my loyal cohorts as we teamed up on a series of ever more ambitious "projects" using the immense resources at hand. First up was an audacious attempt to build a large wooden boat. We "requisitioned" lumber from the construction zone, and dragged it into Craig's family garage. Inside, we built ourselves a fourteen-foot, flat-bottom boat utilizing all of Craig's father's "off-limits" power tools. This craft turned out amazingly well, and we had grand plans to take our boat down to the ocean and use it for fishing. But there was one technical flaw. We hadn't figured out how to seal the gaps between the planks of wood. One night I had a genius breakthrough and came up with a brilliant plan in which we would jam paper into the gaps and then fill them over with white Elmer's glue. This process seemed to solve the problem nicely and our boat really looked ship-shape!

For our maiden voyage, we slid the boat into a neighborhood swimming pool. This would be our "shakedown cruise." Whoops! Elmer's glue turned out to be completely water-soluble and within minutes the gaps between the planks were melting and water was streaming into the boat. The youngest Frankenfeld brother had to bail out overboard as our boat went straight to the bottom. It took a couple of hours but we finally managed to drag the waterlogged craft out of the pool and across the street, where we unceremoniously dumped it in the empty field. For the next few days our beached boat sat there as a jarring testament to the folly of our grand plans. A couple of days later, our abandoned boat suddenly disappeared. We never saw it again and we never found out who took it, or for what purpose. For months afterward we were fixated on wild speculations of whether the boat-nappers were using it to smuggle contraband from offshore freighters or how they just might have drowned at sea during their first voyage in it.

We continued our path toward ever-larger and more elaborate projects, including some serious experimentation with model rockets, kites, and hot air balloons. Our rockets were genuinely dangerous, de facto pipe bombs actually, stuffed with every red-blooded American boy's rocket fuel of choice, paper match heads. We'd tear them out of packs of matches by the hundreds and stuff them into pipes purloined from the construction zone. A kid we knew, using the same materials, accidentally blew up his garage with one of these devices, which finally motivated us to migrate to a different recipe.

Bruno was the scientific mind of our bunch and had read an article about military rocket engines and patiently explained to us that if we could get our hands on some potassium nitrate, then we could mix it with sugar and have a genuine rocket fuel. Leave it to Bruno to know that potassium nitrate's common name was saltpeter and that pharmacies sold it by the can for various geriatric medicinal uses. What followed was a tag team process where our crew would split up and then enter the same drugstore alone and "innocently" buy canisters of saltpeter with the excuse our grandparents needed it for unknown reasons. This explanation always seemed to shut down any questions by the druggist. Our obsession with saltpeter came to a spectacular and terrifying end one day. Upon ignition, the body tube of one of our rockets cracked apart and a burning mass of our "rocket fuel" landed right on the arch of my shoe. I managed to kick the flaming shoe off my foot before this chemical inferno could scorch my skin, but our rocket fuel burned right through my jettisoned shoe from arch to sole and pretty much put an end to not only a nice pair of Converse sneakers but also our experimentation with such unstable stuff.

I had always liked photography and, with my friends' help, constructed a darkroom in my parents' garage from requisitioned lumber. (Again, courtesy of Phase Two of Bixby Hill's development.) I did a lot of experimentation with black and white negative film, although since I couldn't afford a photographic enlarger, I was forced to substitute a slide projector in its place. The resulting imagery from this contraption was pretty bizarre, although some untrained eyes called it "artistic."

My mom and dad had always been avid shutterbugs and used to torture my sister and me every Christmas morning with their 8 mm camera rig with its four blinding spotlights. One day I borrowed my parents' camera and showed it to my gang. Without a second thought we decided then and there to make a movie. Production began immediately on *Ways of the West*, a ridiculously ambitious Western epic. It was probably not the best subject for a first film, but we had lots of kids to star, our beloved field for the backdrop, and even a working archery kit with bow and arrow.

Again, we relied on Bruno to teach us the technology. Bruno had actually read a book about moviemaking techniques and taught us some important concepts about cinematic flow of action. It was a lightbulb moment that day when Bruno explained that for the action in a film to make sense filmically, if a character exited frame camera left, then on the very next cut the character must enter frame from camera right. When we cut this stuff together and watched the action flow it was just like the movies we watched in theaters! This was the beginning of our experimentation with the language of film. In later projects we would investigate techniques used by our favorite filmmakers such as cross-cutting, flashbacks, and that most powerful tool of all—the close-up.

Ways of the West was not a good movie. In fact, we never did finish it. But it had the most awesome stunt by a local kid named Nathan Heit, who took an arrow to the chest and then performed a radical tumble to the bottom of a steep hill. We would rewatch Nate's spectacular stunt over and over and it began to dawn on us that the possibility of us making a thrilling movie might just be within our grasp. You were a stud, Nate!

When I was in ninth grade I badgered my parents to drive me up to Hollywood Boulevard to see a science fiction film I had been eagerly anticipating. Director Stanley Kubrick's *2001: A Space Odyssey* was playing at the Hollywood Pacific Theater in 70 mm Cinerama and it literally blew my young mind. It was the first moment I perceived that film could be art and the first film I had ever seen that left the audience with more questions than answers. I left the theater dazzled and puzzled. I liked that feeling.

One day I came up with a brilliant idea, which would turn out to be one of the best academic moves of my entire middle school tenure. I asked one of our teachers if we could submit a short documentary movie as a substitute for the ten-page written report required for our English class. Surprisingly, our teacher was thrilled with the idea. Right there was an important lesson. I learned that everybody, even a stodgy middle school teacher, is dazzled with the glamour of movies. I guess she was enchanted with the idea of being elevated from an ignored middle school teacher right up to the status of an "Executive Producer"—truly heady stuff! And so started our epic, *The Fish Movie*.

A slight detour first . . . at that time in my life I actually believed that I was destined to devote my life to science and to pursue a career in marine biology and oceanography. Growing up on the eastern border of Long Beach, adjoining nearby Seal Beach, I developed a strong love of the ocean and all things aquatic. A short distance away was Alamitos Bay, where I first learned to sail at the municipal Leeway Junior Sailing Club. I was an avid swimmer and sailor and a huge fan of the great oceanic adventurer of the day, film-maker Jacques-Yves Cousteau. Maybe the true highlight of my high school life was the day Craig's father wrangled us a tour of the *Calypso,* Cousteau's research vessel, which happened to be docked for a few days in the port of Long Beach. In fact, the day we were on board, who should saunter by us but the dashing Captain Cousteau himself! We breathlessly introduced our-selves and the Captain was kind enough to indulge us with a photo.

Craig and I were both also avid scuba divers, a passion that transferred to an obsession with aquariums. Together we had hand-built several of them. So, when it came time to find a subject for our documentary short project, it was a no-brainer to make a movie about something we loved. Fish.

The Fish Movie was a five-minute overview of aquariums with some nice shots of colorful fish and a terrific stop-motion animated title sequence cre-ated by Bruno. The first time we screened it, our teacher flipped out. She loved it! She liked it so much she would pull all three of us out of our other classes and have us screen *The Fish Movie* for every one of her other classes. Obviously we were onto something here, and pretty soon we were not only doing our own school movies every semester, we were also helping friends to produce their own projects. And no matter how bad the movies turned out, we always received a grade of A on them!

THE YMCA IS WHERE IT'S AT!

n tenth grade, Craig and I received an offer we couldn't refuse. Through a family friend we were introduced to a producer who worked in educational films. He was looking for a low-cost alternative for one of his projects and offered to hire us to help him with it. The film was a 16 mm educational short for Disney entitled *Man's Remarkable Hands.* Our task would be to shoot dozens of shots of human hands doing various tasks for use in the documentary.

For days on end, after school and on weekends, Craig and I were shooting shots of various hands—hands opening doors, hands writing letters, hands cooking. It was hard work but it was also a hell of a lot of fun. Our deal with the producer called for us to shoot the scenes and then give the exposed film stock over to him for processing.

One day we received a phone call with some terrible news. The developed film had come back from the processing lab; our producer viewed it and to his dismay the resulting image was too dim. He could barely see the hands! Something must have gone wrong with our light meter (or we didn't know how to use the damn thing correctly). This was a huge disappointment: it was our first professional gig and we didn't want to let our producer down. We immediately offered to reshoot all the scenes to his satisfaction at no charge. The guy was very nice about it but told us that despite the fact that he really liked us, it was time for us to part company. He paid us everything owed, but it sealed the end of our first professional gig. In hindsight he probably was kicking himself for getting in business with fifteen-year-old kids.

So, minus a professional reference from Disney, Craig and I were brainstorming how as tenth graders we could get a movie job, especially without having any professional work to demonstrate our talents with. So, leave it to me to come up with what I thought was another brilliant idea.

I was convinced that Craig and I could make decent, fully professional 16 mm films for practically nothing (especially now that we had learned how to use our light meter). So, I speculated, what if we went to a random company and offered to shoot them a TV commercial for free? With our teenage efficiency, we could probably shoot a thirty-second spot for around a hundred bucks. We just needed that hundred bucks.

My father knew nothing about the movie business, but he had a strong entrepreneurial spirit. Banking on that spirit, I proposed to him that if he staked Craig and me to the hundred dollars necessary, there might be a good return if we could get established making commercials. A couple years before, he had gifted me a little green sign that I taped up over my bedroom door, which read, "THINK BIG!" So my closing argument was that we were just trying to "Think Big." I don't know for sure what motivated him, but my dad went for it and handed over a nice crisp hundred-dollar bill.

With our financing secured, Craig and I immediately set to work sending out solicitation letters to various businesses and organizations with an offer to let us make them a TV commercial for free. After a few weeks with no response, we finally received a nibble. It was the Greater Los Angeles YMCA and they loved the idea of getting a TV commercial for nothing.

After school, Craig and I drove up from Long Beach all the way into downtown Los Angeles and met with their creative ad director at the YMCA corporate offices. I think the ad director and his team were a bit dismayed when in walked two teenagers, although I guess the tantalizing offer of a free TV commercial was enough to overcome their trepidations. He told us that they needed an anti-drug commercial to run on local TV stations in both thirty- and sixty-second versions. He gave us a rough idea what they wanted, which had to include their brilliant new slogan, "The YMCA is where it's at."

Back in Long Beach, we assembled a team of friends and students to help us produce our first, of what we hoped would be many, epic commercials. We coaxed one of my sister Anne's friends to play the starring role of the strung-out dope dealer stumbling down a dark Long Beach alley and popping pills. For the prop Seconal pills we substituted Red Hots, a popular candy at the time, which to us looked just like the real pharmaceuticals. We then contrasted our druggie with shots of other friends, hanging out, tossing a football, and generally having drug-free teenage fun. The tagline, which my ever-creative mother came up with, was "TURN OFF DRUGS. TURN ON TO PEOPLE." Not very subtle but both spots ended with a blazing "THE YMCA IS WHERE IT'S AT!"

We submitted the finished spots to the powers-that-be at the YMCA. Then, nothing, nada, zilch. Craig and I were dismayed and honestly, our feelings were hurt. We had worked hard to produce the spots to their specifications, followed their storyline and used their damn tagline. We even exposed the film perfectly, and visually the spots looked great. A few long weeks went by and I finally wrote to the Y asking if they might have interest in us doing some paid, albeit very economical, work for them. They quickly responded in the negative, that they didn't have any budget and weren't looking for any producers. My father was out his hundred bucks and we had no future work. Another one of my "great" ideas bit the dust.

A few weeks later, a funny thing happened. Friends started seeing our commercial on TV. It was playing on all the local channels. We saw it dozens of times. Our friends who starred became mini-celebrities around Long Beach. *The YMCA was where it was at,* all right—but not for future professional film work for Craig and me.

LESSONS FROM THE ZOETROPE FILM BOOK

Back in the day, when public schools weren't underfunded, we actually had a for-real cinema class at my local high school, Woodrow Wilson Long Beach. For an hour a day my film pals and I could watch film, shoot film, cut film, and the best part—it counted as an English class!

One day while some short films were being shown, our film teacher, Jane Townley, summoned Craig, animator/classmate Kathy Miller, and me up to her desk. This was unusual and I wondered how much trouble we were in. Instead she asked if we might have interest in participating in an outside project related to cinema. Yes, that was very interesting. Ms. Townley informed us that a local filmmaker and Cal State Long Beach professor had invited her to nominate her best filmmakers for a "mystery" filmmaking project he was creating.

Ms. Townley said we should go meet with the man and he would reveal all. Nowadays that type of scenario would be considered a pretty creepy proposition, especially coming from a teacher, but at the time it sounded damn exciting! We eagerly agreed and, "cut to" a few days later, found ourselves at this man's apartment down on Ocean Boulevard.

The mystery filmmaker's name was Dr. August Coppola. His younger brother, filmmaker Francis Ford Coppola, had commissioned him with putting together the first print publication of their fledgling multimedia company, which they were calling American Zoetrope. As August explained it to us, their plan was to create a new magazine/comic book dedicated to young filmmakers, entitled *The Zoetrope Film Book*. We would be tasked with interviewing a working filmmaker and writing up a story from our "youthful" perspective that described what we learned. An actual Zoetrope movie producer, one Christopher Pearce, was on hand to set up the meeting and drive us to the interview. What a stimulating change from our humdrum high school existence—working with real Hollywood producers and meeting real movie directors. This sounded freakin' great!

Sitting in August Coppola's modest upstairs apartment while listening to the details of the assignment, I couldn't help but notice three elementary school boys racing wildly around. These were the Coppola kids, and little did I know that the six-year-old Nic Coppola, the one jumping over the furniture and the guests, would one day grow up to be an Academy Award winner, now known as Nicolas Cage. If only I'd said something like, "Hey kid. Here's my number. Hold on to it for ten years." In retrospect I wish I would have introduced myself, but then I guess it's pretty useless to try to curry favor with a six-year-old.

The next week we all met up at Chris Pearce's motel and he took us in his rental car over to the interview. We arrived at a light industrial section of Canoga Park, about forty miles distant from our hometown of Long Beach. The filmmaker who had volunteered for the interview was Douglas Trumbull, then directing his first feature. He was hard at work creating the visual effects for his modestly budgeted science fiction film *Silent Running*.

This was particularly exciting for me because I was very aware that Douglas Trumbull was a pioneer of the "new" cutting-edge visual effects and had collaborated with the great Stanley Kubrick to create many of the magnificent visual effects in my favorite film of all time, *2001: A Space Odyssey*. Trumbull's *Silent Running* was also set in outer space, but instead of ambiguous starbabies, his movie had an ecological theme, telling a story about a disillusioned astronaut, played by Bruce Dern, protecting orbiting greenhouse pods.

Once inside Trumbull's warehouse studio we were dazzled by what we saw. The place was chock-full of camera gear, lighting equipment, and dozens of highly detailed spaceship models. There were even some small robot suits named Huey and Dewey that were designed to be brought to life and given personality by little people who could puppet them from inside. A few years later another filmmaker within the Coppola orbit would alter the course of history and make a huge impact on twentieth-century popular culture using this same technique in his own science fiction saga. Craig and I were in heaven. This is exactly what we wanted to be doing!

Doug Trumbull was just a supernice guy and gave us an extended tour of his facility, and a quick education on the current state-of-the-art in visual effects. To our eyes, Mr. Trumbull was a mature, seasoned film director, but I now realize that at the time he was basically just a kid too.

At only twenty-eight years old, Douglas Trumbull was in the forefront of using the recently developed "front projection" process, an innovative compositing technique to put actors into different environments. Today, of course, such visual effects are easily done by computer, but back then they achieved a realism that had never been seen before. Trumbull and director Stanley Kubrick had refined the front projection process, using it extensively in *2001* to great success (most notably on the "Dawn of Man" sequence). With great patience he explained to us how it worked.

We were also shown a room packed with boxes of plastic model kits, mostly cars, planes, and spaceships. Doug told us that to create the detail on their elaborate *Silent Running* spaceship models, the Trumbull team would "kit bash" literally hundreds of model kits, in a sense scavenging for parts, using the ones that would look like real rocket parts when stuck on their much bigger spaceship miniatures. A car model might provide exhaust pipes or intake manifolds which, when glued onto the surface of their "hero" models, added all kinds of realistic texture to their surfaces, a low-tech way to achieve high-budget results.

After the tour we sat down with Mr. Trumbull for the interview. I'm afraid to report that we asked him some fairly inane questions. I just couldn't stop pestering him about *2001* and what it was like working with Stanley Kubrick. I don't think Doug was that interested in revisiting the past, but he patiently answered all our questions all the same. He even asked about the kinds of movie projects we were working on, which was extremely flattering.

On the drive home, Zoetrope's Chris Pearce called the day a success.

Now it was our task to write up our lengthy interview and submit it. A couple of weeks later we proudly handed in our finished article to Ms. Townley, which she forwarded to the Coppolas up north in San Francisco.

Will it dash your dreams if I report that we never heard a word back from August Coppola, Chris Pearce, or anybody from American Zoetrope ever again? In fact, all these years later, trying a word search on the web, there is absolutely no trace of the "Zoetrope Film Book." It's as if the project went into witness protection. I did manage to find a single reference to it in an old October 1971 issue of *American Cinematographer* magazine about American Zoetrope, which quotes Pearce as saying they were planning "a kind of comic book called the *Zoetrope Film Book,* which will be a monthly paperback on film-making for high school students. It is a very innovative type of project and was initiated by Francis's brother, Dr. August Coppola, who is a professor at Long Beach State University." Why was such a worthy project abandoned so quickly? My guess is that while writing the screenplay for *The Godfather* and producing George Lucas's *American Graffiti,* among other activities, Francis Ford lost focus on their little film magazine for young filmmakers and it slipped through the Hollywood cracks and disappeared.

At the time of the interview I did not realize that I had learned some immensely valuable lessons at Trumbull's warehouse studio, several of which I would soon be embracing wholeheartedly when making my film *Phantasm.* For one, I learned that you don't need to shoot on a Hollywood studio lot to make a movie; a warehouse out in the distant San Fernando Valley would work just fine. And I also learned that visual effects did not necessarily require a lot of money, but rather true creativity and ingenuity. The support of a Hollywood studio was not really necessary, especially when some kid's model kits can be cleverly repurposed. (Thanks for the tips, Doug!)

AND YOU SHALL BE A MAN

nvigorated from the Trumbull studio tour, Craig and I went back to work to finish a 16 mm short film project we had shot the previous summer. Our big problem was that the recording of our audio had been botched, so we delayed editing and seriously considered abandoning the film.

Our little movie had been designed as a slice-of-life story about a father and son wandering the woods while hunting rabbits. Our original intention was that by the end of the hunt there would be this cute little rabbit that was the victim, and the boy's sober reaction as he came to the understanding that this nice day out in the forest with his dad must end with the little creature's death. I had a similar experience at age seven when I was out on a fishing boat with some family friends and was charged with killing some captured fish that were still alive. It probably explains my transition later in life to eating vegetarian, which I practice to this day.

Filming had taken place in a wilderness area on the road to Lake Elsinore. The shoot went well, the actors were surprisingly good, and we even had a real dead rabbit that Craig's cat had dragged home a few months previously. (We didn't tell my mom about it; we just covered it in plastic wrap and hid it in her freezer for several months tucked back behind a carton of ice cream.)

During editing, those damaged sound tapes became a huge problem. This was really the first time in my movie career in which I had to do meaningful editing on a film, and during this process I came to understand exactly what this editing process was all about. Film editing is at its essence a puzzle. All the material, the visuals and audio, are brought into a room and the editor needs to solve the puzzle by piecing together these bits of information and finding a way to tell a story with them. It's not necessarily easy, but every time you solve a problem in the editing room, there is this really satisfying sensation, which is just like clicking that last piece of cardboard puzzle into place. We just had to find a solution to this audio jigsaw puzzle.

The origin of motion pictures was just that—motion and pictures. Those first films were the silent movies. Audio came later. The early filmmaking geniuses told their stories visually with composition and cutting. These great silent filmmakers—from F. W. Murnau to Buster Keaton and Charlie Chaplin—told their stories without dialog . . . why the heck couldn't we?!

Craig and I hit on an easy solution in which the father would narrate our entire film. He would prattle on about what a fine time they had in the woods, completely oblivious to his son's distress at the death of the rabbit. We should have stopped right there, but we were young and we just took it to a whole nother level by ending the film on the courthouse steps as the father is surrounded by reporters peppering him with questions about why his son became a mass murderer. I think in our young minds we saw the chance to make an artistic connection between the American culture of guns and the dark underside of gun violence. However, as I write this story today I cannot believe we actually took this half-baked creative leap with our story. Our little movie was instantly transformed from a simple father-son meditation into a political polemic. My mother tried to put a poetic spin on it by suggesting the title *And You Shall Be a Man, My Son*, which was a riff from the classic Rudyard Kipling poem "If."

When *And You Shall Be a Man, My Son* was completed we screened it for my parents. They loved it so much that, without even asking us, my mom immediately scheduled two consecutive dinner parties for her friends at our house, with the entertainment being the novelty of Craig and me screening *And You Shall Be a Man, My Son* and us taking questions from the partygoers. It would be our first Q&A session after a screening.

The audience comprised many of my parents' friends and neighbors, all middle-age and mostly conservative Long Beach folks. What really surprised us was that after the screening ended they had absolutely no interest at all in asking us about our cinematography or the use of narration or even where we found the dead rabbit. They immediately challenged us about our political intent and peppered us with hostile questions about what was this subversive anti-gun message we were trying to convey. Craig and I were knocked for a loop. We were sixteen years old, we didn't have a subversive message! We just wanted to portray a kid's response to a dead rabbit and the bad audio had caused us to go a little overboard with our narration!

Craig and I stuttered out some pretty lame answers to the questions, which only seemed to enrage the audience further. Luckily, the father of my high school pal Kim Everson was in attendance. Lynn Everson was probably a more staunch, right-wing Republican than anybody in the room. He was a solidly built veteran of the merchant marine and had single-handedly made a small fortune in the butcher supply business. Lynn was a sharp cookie and could see that we were in way over our heads. He dramatically rose to his feet, surveyed the room, and said, "I think Don and Craig here made a damn fine little film. I may not agree with everything in it but I say we give these kids a hand." And thanks to Mr. Everson's merciful gesture, Craig and I received our first applause ever for making a film.

After the screening debacle we submitted *And You Shall Be a Man, My Son* into a local student film competition, which was run in affiliation with KCET, the Los Angeles public television station. To our immense surprise *And You Shall Be a Man, My Son* won a prize.

This was our first real success as filmmakers and the attention was surprising and gratifying. This might have been the first moment where we entertained the idea that this filmmaking thing could be a career to pursue. Our local newspaper, the *Long Beach Press Telegram*, even ran a profile on Craig and me and our filmmaking exploits.

I soon found myself up in Hollywood, appearing on TV and meeting the competition jury, which included *Los Angeles Times* film critic Charles Champlin, and accepting the KCET award from none other than a noted Hollywood movie director. Michael Wadleigh had recently directed the movie *Woodstock,* which was a huge artistic and commercial success for Warner Bros. Michael was the epitome of the cool, seventies independent film director who was rewriting the rules of Hollywood. After the television taping, Craig and I latched onto Michael and bombarded him with questions about filmmaking, cameras, and technique. Michael was an affable guy and indulged us with some fascinating behind-the-scenes stories from the filming of *Woodstock*. He was happy to give us a detailed overview of how they shot and edited his massive documentary. (Before he directed movies, Martin Scorsese was one of Wadleigh's editors on *Woodstock*.) Then Michael got into some of the more compelling aspects of the shoot and revealed how singer Janis Joplin was so drunk onstage that night that they had to edit her completely out of the movie.

At the end of the day Michael even offered us his phone number, telling us he owned a bunch of Éclair 16 mm film cameras which were left over from *Woodstock* and that we were more than welcome to borrow one anytime, whenever we needed it for a project. Much like Doug Trumbull, Craig and I were dazzled by Michael Wadleigh, a truly independent filmmaker. Again, here was a young director, making his own movies, doing the kind of thing Craig and I wanted to do. We were determined to follow in Michael's footsteps and we quickly hatched a plan to use one of his Éclair cameras for another of our epic productions.

A few weeks later we called Michael at his number and left a message saying hi and that we wanted to take him up on his offer to borrow an Éclair camera for a weekend. There was no response. A week later, we called him again and left another message. We never did hear back from him. I now know that promises are tossed around casually in Hollywood, but my sixteen-year-old self really wanted to borrow that damn camera!

A FEATURE FILM BEFORE WE'RE TWENTY?

While editing was underway on *And You Shall Be a Man, My Son*, Craig had been drafted by Ms. Townley to assist classmate Kathy Miller on an animated project she was making entitled *The Egg*. Since Craig and I had shot *And You Shall Be a Man, My Son* on 16 mm film, Ms. Townley figured Craig would have the expertise to assist Kathy with her 16 mm film. Kathy was a very artistic teen illustrator and her movie was intended as a cute little stop-motion animation of a chick pecking its way out of an eggshell. I'm probably not properly conveying Kathy's talent or the charm of her movie very well, but there's a reason.

Craig spent over a month helping Kathy film each of the animation cells she drew. Around the same time a letter arrived in the mail. It was a solicitation to enter *And You Shall Be a Man, My Son* in the largest high school film festival in California. Without a second thought we mailed off a print of our movie with our entrance fee. We were both thrilled to promptly receive a response informing us that the judges had accepted our film and that the awards ceremony would be a month hence up in Mill Valley, north of San Francisco. It turned out that Kathy's film, *The Egg*, had been accepted also but her parents were not too keen on her taking an overnight trip with us, by plane without a chaperone, so she would not be attending. At sixteen years old we were completely stoked to be traveling on our own, by jet, as genuine filmmakers invited to a real film festival.

Upon landing, Craig and I took a taxi from SFO to Mill Valley and arrived at our dumpy little motel. We planned to get to the festival early, convinced we would win and that this night would be the crowning glory of our young filmmaking careers. In fact, we did arrive an hour early at the high school that was hosting the event. We paid the cabbie and he drove away as we climbed the stairs to the auditorium. The door was locked. There was no one around. It was Saturday night and we were in front of an empty high school. WTF?! We ran down the street to a gas station and managed to figure out that we had misread the instructions and the event was actually being held at another high school, all the way across town, eight full miles away. So Craig and I did the only thing we could, we started to run. With visions of an emcee calling out our names as winners and no one there to accept our awards, we huffed and puffed and ran. It was a long freakin' distance.

Drenched in sweat, we staggered into the theater and plopped in our seats just as the first award was being announced. It was quickly clear that we were up against some formidable competition. Some nearby filmmakers had made a Super 8 mm parody of the kid's show *Sesame Street,* which featured singing, dancing, and puppetry. As the night went on and this *Sesame Street* kept racking up more wins, Craig and I were genuinely worried. Did we travel four hundred miles by jet, all the way to Northern California, and then run eight miles for nothing? Then, as the host was preparing to announce the grand prize winner, I noticed it. Behind us, up in the window of the projection booth, I could see the projectionist threading up the 16 mm projector. I elbowed Craig and whispered, "Looks like somebody who shot their film on sixteen is taking the prize." Both of us were positively beaming with big goofy grins on our faces. All of the films in the competition were shot on Super 8 mm, even their beloved *Sesame Street,* except for our movie! Were they saving the best for last? The host coolly sauntered back to the stage. "And now the Grand Prize Winner of this year's festival is . . ." He opened the envelope. ". . . from Long Beach, California . . ." For Craig and me, time came to a stop as we realized we had this one in the bag, and then the host continued, "*The Egg* by animator Kathy Miller." The audience burst into applause and the projectionist rolled Kathy's 16 mm award-winning cartoon.

To save money, Craig and I walked all the way back to the motel. It was about midnight and a cold Bay Area wind was howling around us as we trudged the eight miles in silence, lugging Kathy's grand prize trophy. We didn't feel our legs. We didn't feel the cold. The trophy got heavier and heavier. As we crossed a bridge I was tempted to chuck the damn thing down into the water. Instead, we just continued walking, grumbling and cursing at our piss-poor luck all the way. Suddenly, I stopped in my tracks. There's something about raw and utter disappointment that can sometimes galvanize a young person to action, trigger a fire in the belly. A raw notion, something we had once idly talked about, somehow popped into my brain and I just blurted it out. At that moment it made singular, total sense—it would certainly change my life and career path forever.

"We'll show 'em." "Yeah?" Craig responded. "Yeah. We'll make a feature film before we're twenty years old." Craig thought it over for a moment and then, without a beat, responded simply and profoundly. "Fuckin' A."

HEY, I CAN DO IT BETTER THAN THAT!

Craig and I immediately started trying to figure out a plan for how we could make this proposed feature movie. We knew we would need a story, or even better, a screenplay. We were so clueless, we spent fifteen dollars and actually purchased an advertisement in *Daily Variety,* one of the Hollywood trade papers. It was a "screenplay wanted" ad. The response to this ad was our first indoctrination as to how flooded this town is in unproduced screenplays. There's an old saying in Hollywood: "everyone and their brother has a screenplay under their arm." It's true. We must have received hundreds of them. And wow, were they bad! Of course, at that stage in our development as filmmakers, I'm not sure if we were even capable of discerning a good script from a bad one. We found one script mildly interesting, an escape story. Only instead of jail or a prison camp, this story was about an old man who felt abandoned and escaped from the old folks' home he had been committed to. (Later in life I was able to explore this theme in much more detail in my film *Bubba Ho-tep.*) This led to our first Hollywood meeting and, of all places, it was actually right on the Paramount Studios lot.

The cowriter of the screenplay in question invited us to meet her at her office at Paramount Studios where we could discuss it. One day after school, Craig and I drove the thirty miles up to Hollywood for our big meeting on the studio lot. We were bubbling with excitement as we drove through the studio gates and were dazzled as we saw all the excitement and activity around the huge movie studio soundstages. We peeked inside and saw massive sets, extras in costumes, and movie cameras mounted on cranes. Here we were, seventeen-year-olds, striding across a real Hollywood movie studio lot to a meeting in the Paramount executive office building. This moviemaking was just too easy!

When we arrived at her office we were greeted by a very attractive woman, about a decade older than we were, all of twenty-seven. She looked like she could be an actress. She introduced herself as the writer and quickly suggested we exit the executive offices and have our chat over by the studio commissary. As we walked across the lot to the commissary it suddenly dawned on me that our screenwriter was not a studio executive, but rather a *secretary* for a studio executive. Evidently her boss didn't like her exploring her writing career on company time. I eyed Craig—he had figured it out too. Bummer! The writer was nice, but then she hit us with the second big surprise: she and her partner wanted a minimum of ten thousand dollars, up front, for their screenplay. Our big Hollywood meeting came to an abrupt end when I countered that we didn't have any money and that we were seeking a writer to defer any payment for a screenplay until the film was finished and profits came in.

On the long drive back to Long Beach, Craig and I examined our options. A bunch of scripts had come in and they were all terrible except for one that was just okay, but its asking price was ten thousand bucks. I think this was our introduction to that great Hollywood recruiting tool, that moment when you see really bad creative work and a little voice goes off in your head and says, "Hey, I can do it better than that!"

When we got home, we literally threw all the submitted scripts in the trash and set to work to write our own feature screenplay. I certainly didn't have a clue where to begin. We were seventeen years old, what the hell would we write, and how would one even write a screenplay? Back then there were no books, classes, or web pages available with self-help knowledge on screenplay writing. We were completely on our own.

A lot of credit must go to Craig Mitchell. He had the drive, writing talent, and a sheer fearlessness to just do it. It started with us spitballing story ideas, and the next day Craig would arrive at my parents' house with actual pages of scene drafts. It was truly inspiring!

The screenplay we were working on was about something we knew, life in a typical high school, and something we didn't, which was a family melodrama about a young teen living in a run-down apartment with an alcoholic father and a younger brother. I know why we selected the high school part—we were both living it and had a lot of insight and frustration with that entire American high school experience.

We were keenly influenced by Peter Bogdanovich and Larry McMurtry's *The Last Picture Show* and a lot of that sentiment seeped into our story. Once we settled on the story of a capable young man forced by circumstance and responsibility to become father, mother, and brother to his young sibling, it was easy to imagine ourselves in this character's shoes. Our protagonist, Jim Nolan, trapped in a world of loneliness and despair, was going to be an unlikely hero. Later, our future distributor would coin a tagline that truly summed up the story of our film: "IT'S ABOUT GROWING UP, WITHOUT GIVING UP."

Craig's older brother, Keith Mitchell, was a talented drummer and musician who years later would become an original member of alternative rock band Mazzy Star. Keith was pretty savvy about music and introduced us to cutting-edge musical acts at the time, and without his knowledge, we would "borrow" his records and repeatedly listen to very diverse artists, from John Prine to Roxy Music. Prine became a huge influence, especially since he passed through Long Beach several times, playing in a coffeehouse next door at Cal State Long Beach; we would always attend his shows. In particular, Prine's song "Six O'Clock News," from his first album, was a huge influence on the tone of our film script. To this day I am still a huge fan.

The writing process would take some time. We both successfully graduated from Woodrow Wilson High and did a lot of work on our screenplay that summer. The draft lottery for the Vietnam War came to an end that year, but even if it had not, we both rolled high numbers and were exempt. Then, in the autumn, I was off all of thirty-five miles away to UCLA. I was close enough to be able to commute home on weekends to meet with Craig and brainstorm our epic production.

The best thing about my year at UCLA happened on the very first day I walked in the door of my dormitory. I met Paul Pepperman, who, through serendipity, had been assigned as my new college roommate and who would go on to become my future collaborator and confidante in my early feature film exploits. Paul was a lifelong film lover and prospective prelaw student with a bright mind and a sharp, ironic sense of humor. We became fast friends and spent most nights in the Westwood film district watching movies together. We shared a mutual admiration for the outrageous indie filmmakers of the day and eagerly lined up to see new films from artists as disparate as Alejandro Jodorowsky, Robert Altman, and Robert Downey Sr. (Yes, the *Iron Man* star's father was a brilliant indie filmmaker!)

I immediately tried to enroll in the esteemed UCLA Film School but was repeatedly told that I would need to be a third-year student before application was possible. Consequently I became a political science major but filled out all my electives with film study and criticism courses. On the UCLA campus stood a state-of-the-art motion picture theater, Melnitz Hall, and I watched movies there almost every day. At night, due to the proximity of Hollywood, the major studios would frequently preview their new movies on campus. I have wonderful memories of watching early screenings of great movies like *Minnie and Moskowitz* and *Paper Moon* with influential directors such as John Cassavetes and Peter Bogdanovich in attendance. My grades weren't the best but wow, did I see a lot of films!

"A BUNCH OF THIS"

We figured we needed somewhere around twenty-five thousand dollars to jump-start our first feature film. It quickly became apparent that, at our age, there was no way we would be able to raise this level of funding. I think between us, Craig and I had about eight hundred dollars in savings. So I went to my father, who worked in the financial industry, and asked him for some advice.

My dad had originally started his own investment firm as a side project while serving as a captain in the US Air Force. A graduate of the United States Military Academy at West Point, he resigned from the Air Force after a decade of service and, with no savings, immediately started his own investment company and built it into a very successful operation in our hometown of Long Beach. My dad had spent three years stationed in Tripoli, Libya, at Wheelus Air Base, where he was quickly promoted up the ranks to the position of base contracting officer. That's where I was born. And that's where my dad learned the art of deal-making and negotiation directly from the hard-nosed Libyan merchants and contractors during his tenure there. In Tripoli he was responsible for contracting all the goods and services required by this massive American outpost the size of a small city.

Upon return to the States after being stationed overseas in Libya, my father was ultimately assigned to the Air Force missile systems division, working out of El Segundo, California. This was during the height of the Cold War and there was a major military effort going on there to counter the Soviet threat with intercontinental ballistic missiles. Literally thousands of engineers were working at Aerospace, TRW, and other large companies in the vicinity designing these rockets. And all of these engineers needed financial advice and retirement plans. So there was my dad, during the day negotiating huge multimillion-dollar contracts for rocket engines and at night providing investment and insurance services for all these rocket scientists. All I knew about this as a boy was that my dad was *always* working. As he crossed the ten-year mark in the military, this side job had grown so large that he decided to resign from the military and open his own investment office, taking his initials from his name, Donald A. Coscarelli, and creating DAC Investments, Inc.

In talking with him about finding funding for a feature film, my father made us aware that it would be a complicated process. A lot of regulatory requirements for private placements of investments required lengthy contracts and rigorous protocols. This was not going to be easy.

Right around this time my father was solicited by a salesman who was looking for investors for a feature movie project. My dad figured we all might be able to learn something, so he scheduled a meeting with this would-be producer.

A couple of weeks later this "producer" traveled down to meet with us at my father's office in Long Beach with his lead actor-partner in tow. The actor was a fairly recognizable face who had appeared in dozens of episodic television series, usually playing a smarmy bad guy who gets done in by the fadeout. These two Hollywood operators had a slick presentation with a hard sell. They ignored Craig and me ("the kids") and zeroed in on my dad; he was their true mark. The storyline for their planned movie seemed pretty dumb to us: it followed a trite narrative about a corrupt cop. They wanted my dad to give them fifty thousand dollars for a 20 percent ownership in the prospective film. It was amusing to think about how these two Hollywood Players made the long drive down from Los Angeles to my dad's little investment office intent on fleecing these hicks from Long Beach out of some money for their production. Little did they know that every word of theirs was being closely scrutinized by the three of us, because we were intent on doing the exact same thing they were. Even at our young age it was apparent these guys were hustlers and basically clueless about how to make a good movie. The storyline had no real point and they didn't even have a director. In fact the actor at one point professed that, since he knew the script so well, he might just have to direct the movie himself.

The actor did make a point of leaving us with one pearl of Hollywood wisdom from his vast experiences in the film world. At one point he bitterly made reference to all of the bullshit he had suffered in Hollywood. He proclaimed, "Hollywood? It's just a bunch of this," and he then made a crude masturbatory jerking hand gesture. For decades after, his declaration became a running joke for me, especially during awards season when everyone in Hollywood falls all over themselves giving out their shiny awards. When I'm watching those dramatic acceptance speeches I'll laugh and think about that actor and how there was a certain truth to his sentiment.

After our big investor meeting, my dad cornered us in his office. "So how much do you kids need to produce this movie of yours?" I threw out our prospective budget number of twenty-five thousand dollars, although I really didn't have a clue how much money it would truly cost. He replied, "You know, I had a good year in the market and this movie business looks like fun. And if I was going to invest with anybody, I'd certainly trust my son and his good friend over those two clowns. I'm gonna talk to your mother." It suddenly became clear that we just might have a shot at making a movie.

MY TRUE COLLEGE YEARS

As my first year of college came to an end, the decision to leave UCLA was an easy one. I'd been in school for fourteen years straight and it was time to move on with my life. Plus, thanks to the confidence of my parents and their willingness to risk a chunk of their hard-earned savings on my yet-to-be-proven talent, Craig and I were going to make our feature film. I didn't know it then, but this next four years would be the most difficult, frightening, and exhilarating period of my life, one in which I would learn a hell of a lot more about people, life, business, and filmmaking than I ever would have as an undergraduate at UCLA.

As Craig and I began preproduction on our very first feature film, the first thing we needed was to find a cast. So began one of the most arduous processes of the entire film. We knew we couldn't hire union actors because we had no money to pay for them, so we started hunting everywhere, trying to find unknown but natural actors to play our leads. We scheduled casting sessions anywhere we possibly could. We would go to the local colleges and high schools and hold open calls. We would run ads in the newspapers and movie trade journals. For days and weeks on end we would sit through tediously long open casting calls, interviewing anyone who cared to walk in.

Our first big find was a young, unknown actor who grew up on Catalina

THE WISDOM OF IGNORANCE

As casting continued our first crew hire was my UCLA roommate Paul. Now entering his second year at college, Paul volunteered to help for free whenever he could to assist us in getting the production organized. Craig and I were working like crazy trying to figure out how to actually make a feature film. We put some ads up and started interviewing tech crew who had worked on low-budget movies. We stumbled onto some other low-budget filmmakers including a director named Paul Leder (*I Dismember Mama*) who introduced us to some of his favorite crew members. I remember sitting in a meeting with Leder in which he valiantly tried to dissuade us from filming our script. Mr. Leder believed that the only way to succeed in the low-budget game was to make more exploitive films that had sex and violence, sizzle that would sell. It was his fervent belief that we should be making a teen sex comedy or a horror film instead of our simple drama. This was some sage advice from a veteran, which Craig and I, of course, promptly ignored as we were committed to our script and making a story that was honest and genuine. It wasn't until a bit later in my career that some of this low-budget director's advice rang true for me.

Today, indie filmmakers have it easy in that the digital cameras and technology to make a feature film are readily available. Back then, shooting in 35 mm was a major dividing line between amateur and professional. Having access to 35 mm film stock, cameras, and crew to operate them was a very significant entry barrier to the indie filmmaker. We were lucky to quickly assemble what we thought was a competent low-budget camera, lighting, and sound crew who had a certain level of experience, mostly on exploitation films and even some pornography of the era. Pornography was big in the seventies, and the nearby San Fernando Valley was a hotbed of porn production and a good place to hire tech talent and rent camera equipment on the cheap.

We put together a full paid crew and then surrounded those hired hands with a supporting crew of unpaid friends and other film student volunteers. We brought in two great film students from UCLA, Bob Del Valle and Phil Neel, who had a lot of tech savvy. My next door neighbor Janis Gabbert enlisted as our script supervisor and was an immense help in organizing the production. Also, a good friend of Paul's from high school, Richard Christian Matheson, joined up to work in the sound department as assistant to our hired sound man. (Richard would later go on to a very successful writing and screenwriting career himself—his 1987 film *Three O' Clock High* being a personal favorite of mine.) One of our loyal high school friends, Jim Catti, rounded out the volunteer team along with E. G. "Manny" Culman, Steven Thrift, and Jim Hagopian.

The day of September 23, 1972, production began on our epic. Craig and I were both still eighteen years old, and this would be both a blessing and a curse. Simply put, the older hired crew members had no respect for us. Absolutely zero! From that first day, we would line up a shot and as the lighting commenced, all we would hear was grumbling from the crew about us and also about our inexperienced unpaid student friends. Yes, we were inexperienced and yes, we frequently did not know what the heck we were doing. But our intentions were good and we were so eager to learn and experiment and to make a good film.

Craig and I had never really worked with actors. To say we were clumsy was an understatement. Angus really suffered at first from our inexperience. We scheduled a rehearsal of the major dramatic scene in the film, what we referred to as the "father confrontation scene." With good intentions,

Gregory Harrison had invited along his acting coach, Wayne, to assist. As the rehearsal unfolded there were difficulties with the scene and the frustrations of everyone mounted. At one point Gregory had the youthful temerity to tell Angus how he should play a line. Angus was a more classically trained actor and having another actor giving him direction simply pushed him over the edge. Angus stopped in his tracks, turned, and affixed this intimidating glare at all of us (he would use this to great advantage later as the evil Tall Man in *Phantasm*) and growled, "Do I take direction from you (he looked at Gregory), you (he looked at Wayne), you (he looked at Craig), or you?" His powerful visage landed on me and I just stuttered out a lame response that Craig and I were the directors and we alone would give him direction in the future. But this too was a problem: frequently Craig and I would give the actors conflicting directions, and again, Angus was the most frequent recipient of this. About halfway through shooting we finally figured out that we must speak with one voice and only one of us would give direction at a time.

It was extremely disheartening that our paid crew started to take advantage of our inexperience. When the camera assistant would call for a film magazine to be reloaded, production would shut down for a full half hour or longer, while this guy laboriously removed the empty magazine, checked out the camera movement, and then loaded up a full one. This was a hidden signal to the rest of the crew to take a nice long break at the expense of their naïve student directors. Later, on subsequent movies, both Paul and I became completely proficient at swapping out 35 mm Arri film magazines and could do it competently in less than sixty seconds.

On the second day of shooting, one of our student friends was going on the lunch run and the gaffer casually asked if they could have some beers for lunch. In retrospect it was sheer lunacy to accede to that request, but not knowing any better, I approved it and we brought back four six-packs of Coors beer for the grip and lighting crew. When we started up after lunch we couldn't find them. They had disappeared! Paul scouted around the apartment property, then came and got me and brought me down under the rear staircase, saying, "You've gotta see this." There among the trash cans was our entire electric crew, all drunk on their asses, unable to walk, let alone come back to work. Beer was never provided again.

Another problem was that our so-called professional crew had a hard time taking direction from two eighteen-year-olds. Any time we were uncertain, or made a mistake, the cameraman or even the paid script supervisor would ridicule us, and our creative choices, right in front of the rest of the crew. Looking back I can only guess there must have been some frustration on the part of these crew members toward Craig and me, that we were directing a feature film at such a young age and that they had to work for us.

THE SATURDAY NIGHT MASSACRE

I t was Saturday, the last day of our first production week, and we were still stuck shooting in our rented tenement apartment in the creepy part of downtown Long Beach. As we staggered toward the end of our first week of shooting, our production was a mess. Paul did a rough estimate of what we had accomplished and came to a staggering and unbelievable conclusion. We were finishing up our fifth day of shooting and we were now five days behind schedule! Obviously some drastic changes needed to be made, but we had no clue what they were. We had hired a low-budget crew of older people (twenties and thirties!) who mostly came from very cheap exploitation films and pornographic movies. They were unfriendly, moved slowly, and enjoyed ridiculing us and our student interns. Then there were the forced delays with the film magazine changes. The full half-hour breaks for this nonsense were killing us. It was even worse at night. A bunch of them were bunking downstairs at my parents' house and they were pretty disruptive, drinking and fucking.

During lunch, Paul, Craig, Janis, and I huddled and examined our options. We decided there was no way we could continue with this crew without either bankrupting my dad or ending up with an unfinished movie. But how could we make a movie without a crew? We had made a bunch of student films, but could we figure out how to use the 35 mm film cameras, the lights, and the sound equipment?

We came to a decision. We had no choice. The only way to finish this movie was to do it ourselves. During that lunch, Paul started polling our student friends, asking if they had learned enough to do the jobs of the crew members they were apprenticing under. The answer came back quickly, and it was the same with everybody. We had all been making student films and everybody agreed the technology on this feature film was no different, the cameras and film were just larger. Whether you are shooting on 35 mm or Super 8 mm, film is film—you just need to light it right and keep it in focus. All were confident that we could take over. A plan was now in place, a coup was being plotted. Hopefully, bloodless!

As day dragged into night and our plan was solidifying, we had to face up to firing this paid crew. None of us had ever fired anybody. Plus, we were eighteen years old and they were all a lot older. These people certainly deserved to be fired, but how would we do it? Well, we accidentally stumbled into an easy way. As we were about to finish a take you could hear the camera run out of film. "Runout!" called Larry the camera assistant. "Thirty minutes!" The crew started to break and I couldn't believe we were going to have to suffer through this waste of time again—especially since our camera rental house had informed us that it should take at most five minutes to change a film magazine. I couldn't contain myself. "It's going to take you thirty minutes to change one mag, that's ridiculous!" I didn't understand then that film crews are a lot like cops—they stick together. Our "director of photography," a twenty-seven-year-old named Parker, was always looking for a chance to slap down his "kid" directors. Parker got in my face and let me know they were sick of taking our orders, that our student interns were idiots, and that we didn't know what we were doing. Paul and Craig backed me up. "Your crew's not that great," said Craig. Paul then piped up, "And your crew is slow. That mag change should take five minutes!" None of them knew how to take this turn of events. We had never really spoken up or talked back to them before. We waited for a response. After a long moment, the director of photography let out a long, "Well, shit," then turned on his heel, "I am outta here," and headed for the door. Larry the camera assistant chimed in, "I'm with you, Parker." And pretty quickly the rest of the paid crew, the gaffer, grips, and sound, followed them out the door. There was a moment of silence in the apartment and suddenly it was like that great scene in *The Wizard of Oz*. Ding dong the witch was dead!

We also started shooting with a lot of hand-held camera. It was one of our student filmmaking techniques that our previous crew had no use for. Now, Craig and I would trade off shooting extended sequences, following our characters, in which the hand-held movement of the camera added an immediacy and dynamic to each scene.

For a first film our screenplay was far too ambitious. It required us to re-create a nighttime high school football game, which required almost forty uniformed players and a lighted field. Some scenes required hundreds of teen extras and access to high school campuses. Looking back on it, I would never attempt such things today on such a lean budget.

I am willing to bet that most of the "experienced" crew who walked out on that memorable Saturday night expected a follow-up call from us, begging them to come back and help us finish our movie. Well, suffice to say, they never heard from us again. I learned a valuable lesson about staying close to my roots and making movies with a small, dedicated team of creative collaborators. I also learned that instead of firing someone, it is a hell of a lot easier for all concerned if you can find a nice way that encourages them to quit.

A KIND CRITIC

A s filming dragged on and the budget increased, my father had good reason to be worried. (Note to aspiring filmmakers: Never live in the same house as your investor!) The pressure on all of us was immense. However, my dad calmed his nerves in a creative and clever way. He phoned the *Los Angeles Times* newspaper offices and asked to speak to the head film critic. Back in the day, Charles Champlin answered his own phone. And when my dad called, he just happened to pick up. My father went right into his story, about how his son and a friend were making an indie movie, they were only eighteen, and how could he possibly hope to get his investment back without losing it. The good-natured Chuck let my dad ramble on about our film and at the end of the story he told my father to get back in touch when the "boys" had something to show. A few months later us boys were ready and we headed up to Hollywood to screen our epic for Mr. Champlin.

This screening was the first time we had shown our as yet untitled film to anyone. Our movie was cut in the same format as was used all the way back to the days of the silents—in one-thousand-foot reels that ran approximately ten minutes each. (A hundred years ago, before feature-length was standard, shorter films were distributed as "one-reelers" or two-reelers.") Since the film was still in a rough cut, our sound was assembled in what was called a double-system format. In addition to each reel of positive print picture, there was a corresponding sound reel of 35 mm magnetic stripe film.

It was an extremely unwieldy format, especially since the pieces of film and sound were spliced together with tape. Woe be to a filmmaker unlucky enough to have one of these tape splices break during a screening—then any hope of synchronization would be in the projectionist's hands, which is not the place a filmmaker wants anything to be.

Champlin arrived at the CFI screening room, said his hellos, and I sat beside him. The lights went down and the movie began. After about ten minutes, POP! The screen went blank. The room lights came up and I could hear the projectionist cursing loudly back in the booth. One of our tape splices had broken! Craig sprinted back to see what was happening and it was up to me to entertain Mr. Champlin during the delay. An extremely awkward conversation ensued as I promised that it would just be a couple of minutes until the screening resumed. Five long minutes later Craig returned and the screening began again. This time we made it about fifteen more minutes and then, POP!, and the screen went blank again. The room lights came up and I could hear the projectionist swearing again, even more loudly. Craig raced back again to the booth. During the screening for Charles Champlin, the film broke four times. But the good news was that Chuck stuck with it and watched the entire film with us.

After the screening, in the hallway outside, Champlin did not seem overly impressed with the film. He got out of there quickly (who could blame him?) with a simple, "Let me think it over and I'll call you next week."

I took the weekend off and headed up to the Sierra Nevada Mountains with Paul and we backpacked with friends up to Twin Lakes in the Sequoia National Park. Once we made it up the mountain it was a relaxing trip after the hectic week prepping for the Champlin screening. That Sunday, as we hiked back down to the trailhead parking lot, on the park ranger bulletin board Paul spotted a note pinned to it. It read, "DON COSCARELLI—CALL HOME!" I raced to a nearby pay phone and my dad picked up. "Where were you??? I've been looking for you everywhere!" Realizing my dad had actually badgered a park ranger into putting that note up, I asked what the heck was going on. "Champlin called. He had lunch with the president of Universal Pictures and told him about the movie. The studio boss wants to screen the film at his house this weekend!"

The full story was that Champlin had been invited to lunch by Sid Shein-

berg and Lew Wasserman, the two head honchos of Universal. At that time
these were two of the most powerful men in the movie industry. Chuck told
them all about the screening and about these two eighteen-year-old kids who
had shot an entire feature film independently down in Long Beach. Champlin told them that he believed the movie still needed some work, but he
felt the core storyline was compelling and the acting very strong. Sid sparked
to Chuck's story and asked him to set up a screening.

That Friday, Craig and I lugged our film cases out to my mom's car and
we drove up to Universal Studios and dropped them off in the shipping
and receiving department addressed to Sid Sheinberg, President, Universal
Pictures. The night before we had checked and rechecked all the tape splices.
It was going to be a long weekend!

On Monday morning Mr. Champlin called and gave my father a phone
number and said that Sid wanted to speak with one of the boys. I was genuinely terrified of calling this man. Sid Sheinberg ran a major movie studio
and I lived with my parents. What would I say? My father was always pretty
good with sage counsel at times like these. "Just call the guy up and listen
to what he has to say. Remember, he's just like everybody else in this world,
he puts his pants on one leg after the other." Even though I really wanted
to climb into my bed, get under the covers, and hide, I walked into the den,
closed the door, took a deep breath, and dialed.

"Sid Sheinberg's office." "Uh, yes, my name is Don Coscarelli and I was
told by Mr. Champlin that Mr. Sheinberg wanted to speak with me." His
secretary didn't know what the hell I was talking about and asked imperi-
ously, "Please tell me what this is in regard to." I hemmed and hawed and
finally just told her to tell him that Don Coscarelli was on the line. She
clicked off and I didn't know if she had hung up or if I was supposed to
wait or what. After about a full minute of dead air, the phone clicked and
Sid Sheinberg was on the line. "I saw the movie you boys made. And I liked
it. I think you have something there. What I'd like to propose is that we, at
the studio here, could help you finish your film and then put it out into
theaters." I told him I thought that would be fantastic. "Why don't you come
up to the studio and we can talk about it." I eagerly agreed and told him
that I'd have my dad call him and discuss the business side of things.

Over the next couple of days my dad started negotiating a distribution deal directly with Sid. They came to a basic agreement on terms, which included Universal paying us a distribution advance of two hundred and fifty thousand dollars. Our little low-budget film, shot with friends and students in Long Beach, California, was now guaranteed to make a profit.

AN OFFICE ON THE UNIVERSAL LOT

The big meeting was set and Craig and I loaded into my parents' car and drove with them the thirty-five miles up to Universal Studios. The studio lot was so large that it had its own zip code and is officially listed on the maps as Universal City, California. Dominating the lot on Lankershim Boulevard was the sixteen-story executive office building of Universal Studios, notoriously known around Hollywood as "the Black Tower." We rode the elevator up to the fifteenth floor and were ushered in to meet Mr. Sheinberg.

Sid had a large office with a spectacular view of the San Fernando Valley. Courtesy of the boss's wife, Edie Wasserman, it was decorated everywhere with antique furniture much like the rest of the building. Sheinberg was much taller than I expected and younger, just thirty-seven, but Sid certainly had the commanding presence of a studio president. He talked a lot in the meeting and Craig and I pretty much listened. It was quickly apparent that he genuinely liked our movie and its young stars. However, Sid had serious concerns about the last act of the film.

Right around this time we learned that it's pretty much common knowledge in the literary world that first-time authors frequently try to make their first works more important than they inherently are by choosing to either kill their protagonist at the end or have them go insane. Sometimes this can work and become a stunning artistic statement, such as in Dennis Hopper's powerful finale in *Easy Rider*. Unfortunately, I think that is what

Craig and I were shooting for when we fell right into this trap and chose the latter path. We made a choice to have our hero, Jim, go crazy and delusional from grief at the fadeout. In our defense, we had written ourselves into a corner and made a fatal plot mistake at the inception, which was pretty much impossible to rectify. We had killed off the charming young kid who costarred in our film! And there's no worse box-office poison in Hollywood than having children die.

The simple plotline of our film was that Jim Nolan, a likeable and earnest young high school football player, was forced to be father, mother, and brother to his eleven-year-old sibling Kelly. Their father, a down-on-his-luck salesman, was frequently absent due to his battles with alcoholism. They all lived in a run-down tenement on the wrong side of town. Jim supports this family by working long hours at a local fast-food restaurant after school. He leads a double life as a popular kid in high school during the day and then as breadwinner and caretaker to his brother at night. The father takes his frustrations out on Jim's younger brother and is frequently physically abusive. At the end of the second act he takes it too far and young Kelly is killed. And Jim subsequently goes crazy. And that was the part of the film that Sheinberg and others had problems with.

Sid's plan was that Craig and I should start working right there on the studio lot with one of his creative executives and a top film editor to try to solve this story flaw. This sounded like a terrific plan and we left the Black Tower very excited to be working with Sid Sheinberg and Universal Pictures! A few days later we received notice that Mr. Sheinberg had assigned Universal Studios executive Peter Saphier to run point on the finishing of our film and to be our direct liaison with the studio.

A week later we had our first meeting with Peter in his office halfway up the Black Tower. Peter was a great guy, charming and funny with a wicked streak of gallows humor. Being a production executive at Universal was a notoriously tough job. Competition for advancement was cutthroat and there was a saying around the lot that Universal executives "had to walk with their backs to the wall." (So a competing exec wouldn't shove a knife in their back.) They were all overworked and pretty much lived in fear of Sid and Lew Wasserman's ire. Peter was in his midthirties, enthusiastic about movies, and both Craig and I immediately took to him because he had this self-deprecating sense of humor about himself and his particular predicament as a Universal Studios junior executive. The first thing Peter said was, "You guys need to meet Spielberg. He's been working on the lot here for a couple years now. I'm sure he'll be curious to meet the new kids on the block."

Steven Spielberg had been Sid Sheinberg's first major director discovery. I don't know if we'll ever know the true story of how that came about, but legend has it that Spielberg wanted to make Hollywood movies and as a young man in the late sixties started sneaking onto the Universal lot. I guess at some point the jig was up, Spielberg was caught, and then Sid heard about it and wanted to meet this kid. At that point Spielberg began directing episodic television for Universal and the rest is history. Craig and I were huge fans of Spielberg's TV film *Duel,* which was based on the short story by the brilliant author Richard Matheson, who also happened to be the father of our former sound man. We followed up on Peter's offer of an introduction, but were told Spielberg was now on location in Texas.

Within a few days Peter arranged for us to visit the Universal editorial department to start work there. At the time we arrived on the lot, Universal was the largest producer of episodic television for the major networks, responsible for eight hours a week of prime-time shows. Consequently, we found ourselves working in an immense editorial factory with literally dozens of postproduction crews laboring round the clock to create product to feed this hungry beast.

The Universal editorial department was run by William Hornbeck, who was an Academy Award–winning editor in his own right. Bill had started editing during the silent era at Mack Sennett Studios, cutting the famous Keystone Cops two-reelers. Prior to becoming an executive at Universal, Bill had personally edited many great films, including *It's a Wonderful Life, Shane,* and *Giant.* Bill had been reviewing lists of his editors and had decided that the best choice for us was editor J. Terry Williams. Terry was another great guy who was an Oscar nominee for his editing work on Norman Jewison's *The Russians Are Coming, the Russians Are Coming!* Terry could be gruff, but he also had a dry sense of humor and even though he wouldn't cop to it, I think he really was inspired by the challenge of working with these two teenagers on their rough cut and trying to solve its inherent problems.

Concurrently, Peter had managed to get us assigned our very own office, right on the studio lot. It was a funky old freestanding two-room office bungalow that composer Henry Mancini had just vacated. It was situated at the end of the main drag with all the vintage star dressing room offices. Right across the small street was a large dressing room complex for actress Lucille Ball. We never did see Ms. Ball during our entire tenure there; in fact we speculated it might all be for show. Every half hour a Universal Studios Tour tram would ride by and the tour guide would call out, "And right there on your left is the dressing room of one of our greatest stars, Miss Lucille Ball!" Craig and I would frequently be the only people standing there. We would smile and wave, the tourists would wave back, but they didn't know who the hell we were.

When the Universal deal closed I went with my parents to sign the contract up in a conference room in the Black Tower. The attorneys produced the documents and the signing ceremony was over quickly. The remarkable part was that I walked out of the Black Tower that day clutching a check in my hand made out in the nice fat sum of one quarter of a million dollars. Not only would my parents get their money back and Craig and I some cash, we would be able to pay the deferments that most of our cast and all of our crew had been working under. Yippee!

FILMING ON AND OFF THE UNIVERSAL LOT

As the postproduction on our movie continued, we realized that we needed to film some additional sequences so that the new cut would make sense. We took Peter to lunch to discuss and as we crossed the lot on the way to the commissary, there on one of the loading docks was the star of a new Universal picture. This actor had been given the name of Bruce and he was a twenty-five-foot-long mechanical rubber shark for Universal's new movie, *Jaws*. As we stared at this prosthetic beast, Peter said, "You guys should still meet Spielberg. I know he'd want to meet you." (Later we were told he was now on location in Martha's Vineyard on the East Coast.)

After our pitch, Peter used his political skills to wrangle us some budget to shoot the desired scenes. It always helps to have an advocate working for you in a studio environment. Peter made an impassioned plea to Mr. Sheinberg and we had our cash. Since we were working on the Universal lot, the pickup shoot was envisioned with a full union crew; the amount budgeted of $80,000 would buy us just three days of shooting. Something was just plain wrong about us shooting for seventy-some days on our little indie picture down in Long Beach and then for similar money only getting three days on the Universal lot. But what the hell, we didn't care and it wasn't our money! Craig and I would be directing a full union crew on the Universal Studios lot and I had just turned twenty.

The filming went well, the crew was competent and helpful, but every once in a while our indie roots would cause us to cross a line and we'd actually get yelled at. On a traditional movie, crew members would never dare have the audacity to yell at the director. The director is treated like a king on the set and the only one who might raise their voice could be a difficult actor or a powerful producer. But crew, never!

One night we were shooting on location in an alley in the port district of San Pedro and I noticed some rusted-out old trash cans and I darted over and dragged them into frame to add some texture to the scene. "Hey, you can't do that!" Suddenly these burly art department guys were in my face and giving me a dressing down about how only set decorators were allowed to touch the scenery. I, of course, demurred and slunk back to my position behind camera. But it would get even better.

Later in the shoot one of our actresses was having a hard time getting the scene right. Craig and I had developed a shorthand way of working so we could get extra takes by blaming it on a tech issue to take pressure off the actors. "We need another one. Glitch in the focus!" That way we could do ten or twelve takes and the actor could relax, figuring it wasn't their fault. We learned early that we would always get a better performance from a relaxed actor.

We were filming a scene on the Universal lot with a new actress and she just didn't have a handle on the reading. We had already done five takes; she was getting jumpy and we were running out of time. So I called out, "Camera missed it! Nice take but one more for camera." The actress breathed a sigh of relief but then the union camera operator let out a yelp and hurtled off the camera dolly and charged me. "That move was perfect! Where the hell do you get off popping your mouth off in front of the crew that my work is bad!!!" I couldn't do anything right with this crew.

As the last day of Universal pickup shots came to an end, it was apparent that we would not complete two major new sequences that were important and necessary to finish the story. Back on the lot Craig and I hatched a plan. Why couldn't we just shoot the missing scenes down in Long Beach with our indie crew? We conspired with Peter over lunch in the Universal commissary and pleaded with him to get us four thousand dollars to cover the film and camera rental costs. In exchange we would return with the finished sequences for just a fraction of what a Universal crew day would cost. Peter resisted at first, concerned that things just were not done that way at Universal and the studio heads and the craft unions would definitely not approve. It was a hard argument for Peter to win, though, as we were relentless in our youthful exuberance and just browbeat him until he finally conceded that it might be possible to advance some "expense reimbursement." Even though Peter predicted trouble, and demanded utmost secrecy of us, he went to bat for us and managed to get the check cut for our production money.

That weekend we got the gang back together at my parents' house and spent two nights shooting scenes around Jim's old car. It all went down perfectly until that next Monday when I made a fatal, greedy error. Our Universal assistant editor heard us talking about the shoot and volunteered to hand-deliver our film over to the camera department and get it processed and printed, at no charge to us. I should have realized then that this would lead to trouble but the tantalizing prospect of getting free lab work did me in. I handed over the negative and within hours the shit had hit the proverbial fan.

Never in my wildest dreams could I have imagined that this small mistake would have the most powerful man in Hollywood in a lather and our good friend Peter called on the studio boss's carpet begging forgiveness. Lew Wasserman was a titan of the film industry and stories abound about his ruthless rise to power and total domination of first the agency business and then the television and movie businesses. He was an old-school mogul much like the Harry Cohns and Louis B. Mayers of old. Wasserman set an exacting standard and woe to the junior executive who crossed him. Evidently when his fiery temper took hold, legend had it that grown men would cower as he berated them, spittle flying from his mouth as he cursed them.

That day Peter received a summons to the fifteenth floor of the Universal executive building. Mr. Wasserman wanted to see him. I can only imagine what was going through Peter's mind on the long ride up the elevator to the top of Universal's feared Black Tower. He was probably seeing his Universal career evaporating in front of his eyes. When he arrived in

Wasserman's grand, antique-filled office, Peter could immediately tell that Lew was not happy. A union head had phoned Lew and, irate, he challenged the studio boss as to why Universal could possibly be doing nonunion filming. Wasserman demanded an immediate answer from Peter. Were they doing nonunion filming? Did Peter, in fact, attempt to subvert the union labor contract that had been so laboriously negotiated to keep the labor peace? And of course, Peter did the only thing he could do. He blamed it on us. "Those kids! I can't control them! They went out and did it on their own!" This excuse did catch the studio boss by surprise. As the distracted Lew Wasserman ruminated on how these two teenage filmmakers might destabilize Universal's carefully structured labor relations, like many Universal executives before him, Peter quickly made himself scarce and backed out of Wasserman's office.

Peter immediately informed us of our transgressions and I'm not sure we had much sympathy for him. Coming from our sixties and seventies upbringings I guess we always saw Universal and the Black Tower as the proverbial Man, as in "working for the Man," that mythical, oppressive figure that always needed to be talked back to and rebelled against. Boy, were we naïve.

Later in postproduction when Sid and his marketing team affixed the title of *Story of a Teenager* to our film, we saw it as another example of the Man, out of touch and uncool, influencing our film in a bad way. I had the temerity to write a memo of protest to Sid on behalf of Craig and myself. At that time, Sid Sheinberg ran Universal Studios with an iron fist and answered only to Mr. Wasserman, who might have been an even tougher hombre than he was. This memo of mine basically stated that we hated the title and demanded that he change it. Sid immediately responded by interoffice memo and quickly put us in our places. His written slap-down, dripping with sarcasm, basically said that if we were so smart and knew so much about everything, that we should be happy to refund Universal all the money they had expended and then go out and distribute the film ourselves the way we wanted.

As we read Sid's memo, Craig and I looked at each other in shock. The money Universal had advanced to us was all gone! My father had been re-imbursed, all the cast and crew had been paid their deferments, and Craig had leased a new Porsche and I had bought a used Corvette. This was the first of many wake-up calls to come about how much the power of money dominates the filmmaking process. The person, or studio, with the financial power runs the show. Period. The end. Those few moments of terror really taught us something about how fortunate we were to have a major studio backing us, and a major studio boss giving us pretty much whatever we wanted to finish our movie. If Sid wanted to call the film *Story of a Teen-ager,* then that was his call. What did we know anyway? We never could come up with a title we liked before we came to Universal. Sid's title was as good a title as any. We immediately wrote a dutifully apologetic memo back to Sid, thanking him for his support and stating that we were more than happy to move forward with *Story of a Teenager* as our title.

THE GREAT FRED MYROW

(with an appearance by Jim Morrison)

One of the most important decisions to be made as we entered postproduction was who would be our composer. Craig and I both wanted something intrinsically different musically for our film, but as the Universal music department started scheduling meetings with composers, we could see that the studio really didn't "get" us or our style. Leave it to Peter to come to our rescue! Try as he might to be a good company man, from time to time Peter would come up with some insanely off-the-wall creative ideas. He told us about a family friend, a young composer who just might fit the bill to score *Story of a Teenager*. His name was Fred Myrow and he had a stellar background in classical music. Fred had recently moved into movie work, scoring just a few movies so far including *Leo the Last* for the wonderful director John Boorman, *Scarecrow* starring Al Pacino and Gene Hackman, and most importantly, *Soylent Green* starring Charlton Heston. These were meaningful credits to us. Boorman was one of the great directors working, *Scarecrow* was a beautifully crafted American slice-of-life road drama, and *Soylent Green* is people!!! Peter quickly got Fred over to the Universal lot to meet us.

Fred Myrow may be one of the most enthusiastic, creative, and amazing people I had ever met. Full of energy and inspiration, Fred would become a lifelong mentor to me and, later, contribute to the success of some of my best films. Fred was born with music in his genes. His father, Josef Myrow, was an Academy Award–nominated songwriter and film composer, writing such greats as "You Make Me Feel So Young," and his grandfather, Irving Mills, was a major music publisher and longtime manager of Duke Ellington. Barely out of his teens, Fred was composer in residence under Leonard Bernstein at the New York Philharmonic and the recipient of several Fulbright awards, Rockefeller grants, and even a Guggenheim Fellowship.

Fred watched the cut of our movie and was visibly moved and also excited by the choices we had made in our temporary music tracks. He quickly analyzed our tastes, surprising us with an analysis that we liked atonal sounds and also more conventional choral voices. Fred volunteered to join up with us on what he called this "great adventure of a movie" and promised to create us a soundtrack that would be the best possible mash-up of styles, as diverse as both Shoenberg and the Beach Boys.

The music department at Universal at that time was a very powerful and conservative component of the studio. They always had a very strong presence in the record industry and film music. At Universal Studios a longtime executive, Harry Garfield, ran the film music department. Mr. Garfield absolutely did not like our choice of composer, probably because Fred had never worked in-house on any Universal TV series. The feeling was mutual as Fred was convinced that Garfield and his underlings were constantly trying to undermine him. This would create ongoing drama for us while we worked on postproduction at the studio.

FINDING AMERICA

One of the things I loved about Fred Myrow was his willingness to challenge the traditional operating systems in search of creative truth. Fred taught us so much about music and how it worked with film, but he also opened our eyes to many other aspects of creativity. He was always full of excitement and enthusiasm for creative endeavors and introduced us to a lot of his friends and collaborators who were doing really innovative things. We met Fred's inventive musical collaborator, Marc Fleischer (son of director Richard Fleischer and grandson of animation pioneer Max Fleischer), who was assisting him with our score. He also brought us to meet with Francesco Lupica, who at that time was experimenting with an instrument he had created called the Cosmic Beam Experience. Imagine a huge electric guitar made from a steel girder strung with piano wire. This thing was immense, some twenty feet long, and the sounds Francesco and Fred got out of it were literally mind-bending.

At the same time Fred was also tight with many of the vocalists from the Roxy Theater musical hit then playing on Sunset Boulevard called *The Rocky Horror Show*. Fred got us backstage to meet the cast including Tim Curry, Meat Loaf, and Richard O'Brien, and this was well before they shot the classic movie version of it. Fred was a superb raconteur and had so many stories about people he had met or worked with that it was almost too hard for us to believe all of them. The funny thing about Fred was whether he overexaggerated his stories or not, they always seemed aimed at teaching us something or opening our minds to creative possibilities.

One story he kept returning to that Craig and I were pretty skeptical of was Fred's collaboration with the great rock star Jim Morrison of the Doors. His story was just incredible to hear because the Doors were such a seminal rock and roll band that had an immense influence on me in my formative years. According to Fred he had met Jim Morrison in the late sixties working on a short film with him, and in 1970 they started collaborating on a musical. Fred told us that Jim was always over at Fred's house, working late into the night on this musical. Then, one night Jim told Fred he had to fly off to Paris to meet his girlfriend Pamela, but promised that they would get back to work on the musical when he returned to the States. The sad truth is that Jim Morrison did go to Paris and died there tragically at age twenty-seven, never again to return to America. Obviously, Craig and I had a hard time believing this story, especially as it would be impossible to verify. We just chalked it up as a tall tale from Fred's typical overexuberance about all things creative.

Through Universal we had incredible access to all kinds of resources. One of the most remarkable was that Craig and I were given an open account in the name of Universal at a nearby Studio City record store. This was back in the days of vinyl. We were allowed to go in the place and select as many records as we wanted, for "soundtrack research," and all we needed to do was to present the cashier with our film's Universal accounting number and that was it. One of the reasons this was a somewhat legitimate expense is that early on we decided a song from a pop or rock artist would be a fantastic underscore for the opening credits of our film. Another great perk is that we were free to book screening rooms and watch any movie in the Universal vault on 35 mm, again for "research." Pretty sweet!

In the beginning, the Universal music department was extremely helpful and put us in touch with several great talents. First up was Elliot Roberts, a well-known music manager. Elliot came over to the studio and watched our rough cut with the idea that maybe his client, singer-songwriter Joni

Mitchell, might be interested in contributing a song. Elliot decided it wouldn't be right for her, but said he would keep thinking about music options for us. A few weeks later Elliot was back at Universal with client Graham Nash of supergroup Crosby, Stills, Nash & Young. It was exciting to meet Graham in person; CSN&Y was an extraordinary band and he was kind and generous with his praise, but our movie just wasn't his cup of tea either.

Then, out of the blue, we heard that one of the Universal A&R executives, Artie Mogull, was having drinks in Las Vegas and ran into Elliot Roberts. Elliot said that it had finally come to him that a client he was involved with might be perfect to do the song. And we were asked if we knew of a band called America. Of course we knew America. A vocal group comprising three talented guitarists who had met as ex-pats in London when their fathers were stationed over there, yet they had an organic, roots-based, American folk rock sound. They had debuted with a gigantic hit record titled "A Horse with No Name." America would be perfect! They were coming through LA soon and a screening date was set.

Craig and I were with Fred at the Universal screening room waiting for America to arrive. Their road manager, a chap named Bill Siddons, walked in first. He saw Fred and suddenly the two of them were locked in a tight bro-hug. Fred was so excited. "Guys, this is Bill. He was Jim's road manager for the Doors." Craig's and my jaws dropped, literally. It wasn't just a tall tale, Fred had been telling the truth! Bill was a friendly and nice guy and he and Fred proceeded to catch up on lost time.

Bill related how it had been his job to purchase the tombstone for Jim Morrison in the Père Lachaise Cemetery in Paris after his death. As Bill told it, as road manager the details and costs for everything fell to him. This was the first time he had ever had to make funeral arrangements for one of his artists and he took it very seriously. After Morrison's funeral he had returned to the States but was always curious if the cemetery had installed the proper grave marker that he had ordered and paid for. So on the recent European tour with America, Bill insisted on visiting the grave in person and was stunned by what he saw. He described all the surrounding graves, defaced by fan graffiti, fans scrawling the word "JIM" everywhere. He consulted with

the cemetery officials but none of them had a suitable solution for this problem. As they continued to talk Craig and I chuckled and promised never to
doubt anything Fred told us ever again.

The band members—Dewey Bunnell, Gerry Beckley, and Dan Peek—
arrived. They were friendly and down-to-earth and seemed enthusiastic
about working with us on the film. Dan Peek seemed especially moved by
our film and promised to give it some serious thought. We were ecstatic that
finally artists of substance had responded to our film. But the next day Harry
Garfield came back into the picture, and after a brief conversation with
America's management team, the deal was suddenly off. He told us that the
price quoted, fifteen thousand dollars, was far too much money. Craig and
I considered going to our traditional ace-in-the-hole "nuclear option," which
was to casually mention to the target Universal executive that "maybe we
should talk to Sid about this." But Harry was a tough guy, had survived at
Universal for a very long time, and we ultimately decided that tactic might
not work so well with him.

We had learned early on that whether cultivated by higher management
or not, a culture of fear ruled at Universal and most everyone treaded very
carefully around Sid Sheinberg and Lew Wasserman. It started with our best
exec pal Peter, who, whenever we had an unsupervised visit with Sid, would
pepper us with questions: "Did my name come up? Did Sid say anything
about me?" I think the fact that we had this open line of communication to
Sid really freaked out everyone at Universal that we worked with. Traditionally, everything moved up the chain of command and only the very top
executives had direct contact with the President and Chairman. Yet here
were these two young wild cards, who could talk directly to Sid Sheinberg.
In fact, we did just that. Whenever we had a new story idea for the movie, we
would go talk to Sid about it. Craig and I would just elevator up the Black
Tower to the fifteenth floor and, unannounced, walk up to his secretary
and ask if Sid was in. Frequently he would be sitting alone in his office on
the phone negotiating with somebody and he would wave us right in.
Thinking about it now I believe Craig and I were probably a pleasant and
creative distraction from Sid's high-pressure job. We were too naïve to be
afraid of him and were completely happy to collaborate creatively with him.

If Sid had a good idea, we would incorporate it into the movie, and if we didn't like it, we were unafraid to tell him so. Unlike most of the people working at Universal we did not fear Sid Sheinberg . . . we liked him!

As the weeks went on, we heard nothing more from the Universal music department about America and a title song. Craig and I resigned ourselves to the fact that this song would now become Fred's responsibility. We didn't know it at the time but Fred was planning a killer score with a killer group of studio musicians. The first day of the recording sessions I met some of these acclaimed artists, which included core members of what were later to become known as the Wrecking Crew. The Wrecking Crew was a small group of immensely talented studio musicians who played on some of the greatest popular music recordings in the fifties and sixties. They were an infamous crew of studio backing players who started as the house band for producer Phil Spector and went on to collaborate on hits with talent as great as Sinatra, Elvis, and the Beach Boys. Not only would we have the great Hal Blaine on drums but Fred also managed to lure the legendary Carol Kaye on bass guitar.

We loved how Fred's score turned out but still pined for a song to open the film with. It had been almost half a year since the screening for America, with complete radio silence about the topic out of the Universal music department. I decided to take things into my own hands and tracked down America's new managers at Hartmann & Goodman. The manager in charge, Harlan Goodman, gave me some stunning news. He told me that Dan Peek had liked our film so much that after the screening he had gone home and written a title song. His bandmate Gerry Beckley had contributed a chorus and they had already recorded the song at the Record Plant up in Sausalito. The song had been produced by George Martin—yes, *that George Martin,* the guy who produced all those classic Beatles records! Their label, Warner Bros. Records, was releasing the new album, entitled *Hearts,* the following month. And yes, they had reached out to Universal several times and had never heard anything back!

Damn that Universal music department! Craig and I huddled immediately and decided it was time to unleash the nuclear option. I took a deep breath and rang up Sid. When he came on the line I expressed our exasperation with the music department and passionately made the case for how much this song would add to our film. Sid contemplated for a few moments while I waited for the worst. Then he told me the words I wanted to hear: "I'll take care of this for you guys." A few days later America's title song, "The Story of a Teenager," was mixed into our soundtrack.

END OF A PARTNERSHIP

When Craig and I arrived at Universal, Sid Sheinberg kindly offered us seven-year contracts to write and direct for the studio. At first we could not believe these kinds of contracts still existed, vestiges of the old studio system of the thirties and forties. The way these contracts worked was that the studio would guarantee you a fee for a year's work and at the end of the year they would have the option to renew, and they could do so for seven straight years.

I dismissed this offer out of hand. I'm not exactly sure why but one of the reasons was that I absolutely did not want to direct episodic TV, as I considered the quality level of many of the shows being made by Universal to be pretty darn low. I also did not like the idea of being exclusive to one studio—I wanted to make my own films. It was very kind of Mr. Sheinberg to offer us these contracts at a time when the only evidence in existence that we had any ability to direct or write was our one, raw, and unfinished film. In distant hindsight it might have been a smart move to take that seven-year contract, immediately start working in the studio system, and abandon this crazy life of the indie filmmaker.

Even though we had no clue how our first film was going to perform in the marketplace, Craig and I were each thinking about what our next project might be. We were fortunate to have several meetings with some talent agents scheduled for us by the Universal executives. Some of them showed interest, but the general response from most of them was that we were awfully young and as a directing team no one could tell if, when separated, we had any individual talent.

Ultimately neither of us ever signed with an agent. Looking back on it, this was probably a huge mistake. The early success engorged my youthful confidence and led me to believe I could make it in this movie business by relying only on myself, family, and close friends. This turned out to be true, but my career was subsequently limited in ways that I would later regret.

The intense pressure cooker of making our first feature film took a toll on my relationship with Craig. Both of us had strong creative opinions and sometimes we would have serious disagreements. Once we started working together at Universal it got worse. One of the complicating factors was that while the Hollywood attorneys we hired had made an excellent distribution deal for us with Universal, they made one serious mistake. In one of the side letters to Universal, a junior attorney from our law firm had agreed that Craig and I would furnish our services in the completion of the film at the studio for no charge. Essentially Craig and I accidentally became indentured servants and worked on our film at Universal for well over a year for no pay, except during those days we were filming. We did a lot of hard work writing, directing, and supervising during this period, plus we had to commute the seventy miles round-trip each day from Long Beach to Universal City. Craig and I had a rueful saying that one of us would always utter every morning as we got in the car: "Another day, another no-dollar."

It became readily apparent that neither of us had much interest in working together as codirectors again. Craig had a number of screenplays in process and I was much more interested in directing my own films and working with pal Paul Pepperman as my producer. Craig and I had been making movies together since the eighth grade and we both decided it was time to change things up.

BOMBS AWAY

From the get-go, none of the higher-ups at Universal had much incentive to passionately market our movie. There was no question it would be a tough sell: *Story of a Teenager* was essentially a somber character study with a dark ending. Many of the executives at Universal treated the film as a trifle. We actually once overheard it referred to by a marketing executive as "Sid Sheinberg's folly." In some respects our film was considered radioactive, because the head of the studio was invested in the film and no executive below him wanted to make a mistake with it and garner any blame. Consequently, once it was finished, the film was pretty much ignored as the distribution department floundered around trying to figure out a release strategy.

The marketing department finally decided it would be a great idea to "sneak preview" our film and see just how audiences would respond to it. The strange part was, they decided to sneak the film right in our backyard at a mall cinema just on the edge of eastern Long Beach. I don't know what they expected to learn, but they had turn-away crowds that night as all our friends and supporters turned up in droves, so many in fact that they had to immediately book a second screening on the spot for later that evening. Unfortunately, Sid didn't make it down to the preview that night, and I always regretted that he never saw our film with an audience. He had done so much for us and our film that I wish he could have experienced for himself how well it played that night. I think it would have made him very happy.

The audience loved *Story of a Teenager*. Craig and I were beaming for days afterward.

The excellent audience response at the sneak preview jogged the marketing department into action. They decided it would now be prudent to test market our film in a couple of cities prior to a national release. Theaters were booked in Denver and Minneapolis, and Craig and I were flown to both cities to be the face of the publicity.

This was my first lesson in one of the major perks of being a film director. You get to see the world on the distributor's dime! Today, I read stories about film talent complaining of all the publicity requirements involved in their jobs. I guess there are a lot of spoiled folks in this business. How could one complain about visiting major cities, staying in the finest hotels, being chauffeured around in limousines, and dining in the finest restaurants? On top of that they give you a cash per diem and much of the time they fly you first class. And the only requirement is spending a few hours a day talking about yourself and your work, and usually over as much free alcohol as one can imbibe. Over the course of my career I've visited major capitals on almost every continent. For me it has been one of the great blessings of my career in film.

The response to the press screenings in Denver and Minneapolis were excellent. Feature writers seemed genuinely fascinated by our story about teens making an indie movie and then completing it at Universal. Craig and I limoed from interview to interview and found it easy to tell the tale of how we made our film. However, we started to get the sense from the local Universal branch offices that there was not much faith in *Story of a Teenager* doing any business when it opened the following week. As our trip came to a close in Minneapolis, Craig and I were walking through downtown and saw a huge line of people stretched all the way around the block. As we rounded the corner we saw that this was the huge turnout for the new Universal blockbuster, *Jaws*. Well, Universal was guaranteed at least one major box office hit that summer.

EVICTED!

The results came in from the test market dates in Minneapolis and Denver. While we had some decent weekend crowds, there were very little ticket sales during the week. Also, there was that highly successful shark picture in the marketplace, which was gobbling up every other movie's grosses. No one in distribution and marketing wanted to make a move with our picture before the test market numbers came in, and now that the results were not exactly overwhelming, nobody even wanted to discuss the picture. Besides, they obviously had other fish to fry with their major hit movie, which was going to make Universal some serious bank. I tried to call up the various marketing execs and inquire about what they were planning for our film and was told that they were still assessing how the studio would proceed.

With the film now completed, and technically in release, Universal suddenly realized that they did not need us wasting their valuable office space. It was politely but firmly suggested by studio services that we shut the door on the way out. Craig and I were all of twenty years old, and we had lost our own little office on the Universal lot. During our tenure we had some great times there and enjoyed the terrific perks that came along with that office—including priority tickets to the nearby Universal Amphitheater for great seats at high-demand concerts, at face-value prices. We would invite all our high school and college friends up to Universal for parties in our office prior to these concerts. No one else on the lot did this kind of thing;

no one there was as young as we were, and they probably would be afraid of getting fired. (Of course Craig and I could not be fired since we weren't getting paid.) The studio guards were always cool about it and would give us a wink and ignore us as they made their rounds. It was a genuinely terrific time, one I will never forget. But all things must pass. My "college years" were over and it was time for me to leave the studio system and get back to making indie movies my own way. Truth be told, I would never have an office on a major studio lot ever again. Oh, and I never did meet Steven Spielberg . . . but he did throw a nice reference to one of my movies in his film *Ready Player One*. See if you can spot it.

MAKING ANOTHER INDIE—*KENNY & COMPANY*

A round my father's small investment company in Long Beach, there was a lot of buzz about his success in the Hollywood movie business. Many of his Long Beach clients had heard about the Universal deal, some had seen *Story of a Teenager,* and many asked about joining up with him on his next movie venture. When I heard about this I started ruminating on subject matter for a modestly budgeted new film.

While at UCLA, Paul and I would frequently reminisce about our respective childhoods, which was a bit of a joke since we were only about eight years removed from being kids ourselves at that time. We shared a dorm room in Westwood and we would regale each other about hilarious and ridiculous experiences we each had in our youth. These trips down memory lane would always end up with us howling in laughter at some of these crazy childhood escapades. It sparked an idea: perhaps I could make a realistic movie depicting everyday life through the eyes of a twelve-year-old boy that could be both funny as hell and also true-to-life poignant. I had a memorable childhood of my own and had fond memories, much like the fictional Tom Sawyer, of running with a pack of neighborhood kids and getting into all sorts of strange, hilarious, and unforgettable situations. Also, by that time I had been introduced to a number of terrific international films; one that particularly impressed me was François Truffaut's *The 400 Blows.* Truffaut's classic film was a modest and realistic view of life in postwar France through the eyes of an innocent yet savvy boy of twelve. Sure, it starred one of the greatest child actors ever in young Jean-Pierre Léaud, but might it not be possible for me to find a kid as soulful as him and tell a boy's story that was present-day and focused a little more on the humor and joy of childhood?

Kenny & Company was the first entire screenplay that I wrote by myself. I had no formal training in how to write. What I did have is a brilliant and talented mother, Kate Coscarelli, who was a terrific writer in her own right and a few years later would go on to a successful career herself as a best-selling novelist. As a boy, when I would have difficulty writing my school reports, my mom would try to help, but frequently she would get frustrated with me and just take over and write them herself. I'm fond of telling this story, but it's absolutely true—I learned to write while watching my mother write my school reports.

As Hunter S. Thompson is reputed to have said, "Writing is backbreaking work." He's not wrong about that; of course the strain is not physical but mental. For me it's the capricious nature of creativity. How one day I'll achieve an immense amount of innovative work in ten minutes and the next I will struggle for ten hours and get nothing. Frequently one will hear a common mantra about writing: "Write what you know." With *Kenny,* I had that in spades. I set my story in the same kind of suburban neighborhood I had grown up in and populated it with avatars representing many of the personalities I had grown up with as a boy.

My protagonist Kenny essentially represented me as a witness of, and participant in, that strange, funny, frightening, and exhilarating process of growing into adolescence. The character of Kenny's best friend Doug, a fearless and whip-smart kid who was not afraid to challenge authority, was based on several kids I had known and looked up to as a child. I personally never had the nerve to talk back to an adult, but watching some of my friends do so was a totally invigorating and awe-inspiring experience. Then there was Sherman, the little kid from across the street who would follow our heroes everywhere. Sherman knew he might take some hard knocks while rolling with Kenny and Doug, but he would also be exposed to some valuable life lessons and exciting thrills and maybe even gain entrée into that coveted club that all little kids aspire to: becoming one of "the big kids."

I also firmly believed that Halloween night was one of the most sacred holidays for children, and might be even more valued than Christmas.

Halloween, at least when I was growing up, was the one night of the year which promised total freedom for a kid. Around dark you would put on that costume you had been obsessing over for months and slip out into the dark of night, alone with your pack of friends, no parents around anywhere. There was a genuine promise of adventure, loot, laughs, and even some terror. You were completely on your own. Anything was possible. I loved Halloween.

The basic storyline as I laid it out followed these three boys and would take place over the four days leading up to Halloween night. Sure, there would be a neighborhood bully to battle and a love interest for Kenny, but my true goal was to convey what everyday life was like for a normal boy of twelve as he was growing up. For kids, adults and their actions are often simply incomprehensible. I wanted to show that. Much like *Story of a Teenager,* I intended to tell a simple story based on character. I was still under the influence of those great seventies filmmakers like Bogdanovich, Bob Rafelson, Robert Mulligan, and Paul Mazursky. For *Kenny,* character and comedy would be key.

Once the first draft of my screenplay was finished, Paul moved into my parents' house down in Long Beach and we began to prepare. We figured that if we really scrimped, we could probably do the movie for about the same budget as *Story of a Teenager.* This would allow me great creative freedom, but it would again require enlisting a small crew of friends and students and mostly nonprofessional actors. Unfortunately, again we would have no money for a professional crew, so in addition to directing, I would be forced to photograph and edit the film, and Paul would be required to do almost everything else, from assistant director to assistant camera to assistant editing!

CASTING THE KIDS

For the casting of *Kenny & Company* we went back to the open auditions process that had worked so well on *Story of a Teenager.* Now it was just Paul and me, stuck for hours and hours on end, in various locations around Southern California auditioning child actors. Our first big success was when über-kids'-agent Toni Kelman sent one of her new signings over to audition. Much like that magical day a few years previously at the Century Plaza Hotel when I met Angus Scrimm for the first time, this interview would have a profound impact on my career and horror movies in general.

When young Michael Baldwin entered the casting office he had a quiet confidence that belied his young age. Something about this eleven-year-old gave the distinct impression that he was completely secure, serene, and real. He was really unlike any other child actor I would ever meet. Paul and I spoke with him for a few minutes about the new skateboards of the day, with their "Chicago trucks" and "Cadillac wheels." It was not like we were conversing with a kid, but rather a peer. Michael came in to read for the role of Kenny's best friend, Doug, that archetypal best friend who has no fear of adults and always has your back. What I found most remarkable about Michael was that he brought life to this character with an astonishingly subtle and nuanced reading. Plus, Michael came from a fabulously artistic family headed by his dad, Gerard Baldwin, who was an Emmy-winning animator and director of classic cartoons including *Mr. Magoo, Rocky and Bullwinkle,* and *George of the Jungle.* This kid, from a young age, had been doing professional voices for animation. As Michael left the meeting I was floating on air. We had a genuine actor in Michael Baldwin, not just some kid actor, to center our entire movie around.

When Jeff Roth came in to read for Sherman, the little kid who tags along with Kenny and Mike, he had us in stitches from the start. Jeff was nine years old, adorable and yet just clumsy enough to fit right into the part. When I gave him some direction to enter the room so we could videotape his interview, he promptly tripped over the camera cable and sent our thousand-dollar video camera crashing to the floor. His sheepish look to us when he realized what he had done was priceless. The camera was fine. And Jeff got the role.

We had completely struck out in our search for our title character. We looked at literally hundreds if not thousands of kids. All we needed was an everyday kid—a normal American boy, a Tom Sawyer for the modern era. Paul and I fanned out, searching everywhere, looking for kids.

It all happened at the elementary school carnival. Paul spotted him over by the Goldfish/Ping Pong Ball Toss stand. Blond, sparkling blue eyes, twelve years old, just a great-looking kid. Paul came back to the house so excited he could hardly get the words out. "He's the perfect Kenny!" Paul said. Dan McCann had never acted in anything. Period. He was just a normal, nice, everyday kid from Long Beach. We invited him over to my parents' house to read for the part and for a nonactor, he did darn well. Dan's skills were raw, but he listened to direction, tried to make adjustments based on those directions, and had an easygoing way about himself that was very appealing. In my mind I could immediately see him as a pal to Michael and Jeff.

Paul called Dan up later that night to give him the good news and the kid was nonplussed. "Sounds fun. But you'll have to talk to my dad." Dan's stepfather, Jack Colton, had been an actor and dancer himself in several movie musicals in the 1950s, including *The Band Wagon, Stars and Stripes Forever,* and *The West Point Story.* (Amazingly, my father also appeared in *The West Point Story* in an uncredited role. My dad was an actual West Point cadet who just happened to be standing right beside James Cagney during a critical dialog scene on the parade grounds.) Jack was a no-nonsense guy and he wanted to know the details of our production. As Paul went through this process with not only Jack but also the parents of Michael and Jeff, it became clear that what we needed was for these parents to sign their kids over to us for the entire summer. I guess Paul and I must have presented ourselves as trustworthy, earnest, and honest, because they did just that. And we gave their kids a terrific summer they would never forget.

CAMP KENNY

My parents' home in Bixby Hill became the designated production studio for *Kenny & Company.* The kitchen became the commissary, the downstairs rooms became the sets of Kenny's house, and their garage was cleaned out and transformed into our soundstage, where we built several elaborate sets. A backyard pool became the hangout for the kids—when they weren't filming they were swimming. It was the perfect place to make a movie. Although not so great for my mom and dad, and to this day I don't know how they put up with it.

During the production of *Story of a Teenager,* I learned that having too large of a crew could slow things down whereas a smaller crew, student film-style, can be much more creatively engaged when everyone is actively working across *all* departments and making genuine creative contributions. Everybody does everything! The sound man might be drafted to help with a large-scale lighting rig, the script supervisor into set building, and a grip might be doing on-screen stunts. We put together a tiny but impressive crew from friends and students in the Long Beach area: brothers Darrell and Dennis Kitchell to do lighting and logistics; eighteen-year-old Laura Stam, just graduated from high school, to handle continuity; best friends Steve Elders and Steve McKenzie to do camera and grip; award-winning student filmmaker Corey Leedom for production and dog-handling; Don Booth and Willie Bell on sound; Mike Rose on grip; and George Singer on everything else, including skateboard stunts. Best of all, my sister Anne came on board and designed and sewed the amazing Halloween costumes for the boys, including a hilarious full-body penguin suit for Sherman. Working with Anne, we made a creative decision that little kid Sherman would wear swim fins on his feet instead of shoes, which looked hilarious, but made life a living hell for young Jeff Roth during his running scenes.

My mom was back to work again on *Kenny,* covering multiple job descriptions including production design, makeup, and, of course, cooking all the food. She brought along her good friend Shirley Nisbet to help with props and wardrobe; Shirley just happened to be the owner of a huge Long Beach retail institution, Dooley's Hardware, which generously provided costumes and gear at cost.

It was a surreal experience to re-create many moments from my own childhood in the exact locations I lived them. The nearby Los Alamitos school district provided us two of their school campuses to film at, including the elementary school I attended as a boy. Most people have fantasies about reliving their youth, but I actually got to do it. In retrospect it was one of my favorite experiences as a filmmaker.

After shooting I holed up at my parents' house to edit the film. When it came time for music I reached out to Fred Myrow, who was extremely enthusiastic about helping out with a score. The problem was how to create the music without any budget for a recording studio or musicians. Enter Reggie Bannister. My favorite actor, who was also an accomplished guitarist and musician, quickly crafted an indie recording plan for us. Reg introduced us to a brilliant nineteen-year-old music producer named Paul Ratajczak, who happened to live nearby in North Long Beach. Paul had hand-built a recording studio in his girlfriend's garage. He gave us the tour and showed us his prize sixteen-track mixing console, purchased from a major recording studio in Hollywood, where it had been used on dozens of famous records including a bunch by Frank Sinatra. Fred gave the studio a resounding thumbs-up, and Paul and Reg worked their contacts and pulled together a house band from local musicians who would perform Fred's compositions.

THE JIM-MOBILE

After a lot of complaining about the title and the test marketing, Sid Sheinberg and Universal Pictures graciously agreed to let us retitle my first film and offered to try one more go theatrically with it. After a seemingly endless and agonizing search, we jettisoned the title *Story of a Teenager* and finally all settled on a new title in *Jim The World's Greatest*. The title was not perfect but we hoped it might be good enough to give us another shot.

While editing *Kenny,* Universal made plans to book *Jim The World's Greatest* into the Avco Center Cinema in my old college district of Westwood. We decided to wholeheartedly support the release with as much street-level marketing as we could possibly muster. This was my first experience with the kind of grassroots marketing required in selling an indie film, even though ours had the backing of a major studio. Paul and I created the flagship for this initiative with what we called the "Jim-mobile." We hijacked the *Kenny* production van, strapped a three-foot-tall gold crown on top, and branded the sides with the title of the film.

We spent the weeks leading up to the opening driving all around Los Angeles to parades, movie lines, and concerts, handing out flyers and generally creating ridiculous publicity havoc. At a civic parade in the nearby city of Carson, as the Jim-mobile passed the reviewing stand, the grand-marshal, actor Fred Williamson, took one look at us and burst into uncontrollable laughter. At a movie line in Westwood, *Kenny* script supervisor Laura Stam was tossing *Jim* buttons out to the crowd and accidentally hit an elderly woman in the head. Within moments an ambulance-chasing attorney signed the victim up and we had our first Jim-mobile personal injury lawsuit to contend with. It was a helluva lot of excitement and fun, but in the end it wasn't enough and *Jim's* short-lived second shot at box office gold ended with a whimper. *Jim The World's Greatest* was banished to the film vault, never to be seen again.

In the meantime, I had finished postproduction on *Kenny & Company* and we started the process of shopping for a distributor. Universal had no interest in this one, but their competitor over in west Los Angeles, 20th Century Fox, did. Studio head Alan Ladd Jr. and his team watched the film and decided it would make for a good end-of-summer release. In hindsight, I think the Fox marketing team completely missed what *Kenny & Company* was about. They saw it as a movie about being twelve years old and decided to seize on one small component of the film, skateboards, and market it directly to children. Yet I still believe the movie is really about *not* being twelve years old anymore, and should have been aimed more at an audience of adults with fond reminiscences about their childhood. In any case, their key tagline, "HAVE A HAPPY DAY, *KENNY & COMPANY* ARE COMING YOUR WAY," certainly didn't do us any favors.

Just like with Universal, Fox determined that *Kenny* should be test marketed prior to a nationwide release. The film opened in Orlando and did sold-out business at the daytime matinees. Fox's marketing to kids worked perfectly during the day, but the evening screenings were almost empty. Their decision to aim the marketing to kids ultimately was a disaster.

Kenny & Company never played in the major markets of New York, Los Angeles, and Chicago, and much like *Jim The World's Greatest*, it was as if neither film ever existed. Although the joy of re-creating fictional versions of the worlds I grew up in as both a boy and a teen were fantastic experiences, I had now made two feature films and very few people had seen either of them. Having the opportunity to make these two films my way, with friends both old and new, was a genuine gift that I did not take lightly. But now I was faced with two choices: give up filmmaking, or make a movie that could not be overlooked. Not being a quitter, I chose the latter.

Fox, meanwhile, quietly vaulted *Kenny & Company* and concentrated their efforts on another "small" picture of theirs that would be opening in the spring. It was that science fiction one—you know, that one directed by George Lucas.

A TURN TO HORROR

believe it was inevitable. As a child I was drawn to horror films. There were three very obvious and concrete reasons that helped rewire my eleven-year-old brain into an obsession with horror.

- A Saturday night horror movie show on my local television station entitled *Chiller,* which I would watch religiously.
- Less than ten miles from my childhood home stood the cheesy and infamous Hollywood Wax Museum with "living" statues of every classic monster from Frankenstein to the Mummy.
- Somehow, pre-Internet I managed to find and secure a subscription to Forrest J. Ackerman's seminal monthly horror magazine, *Famous Monsters of Filmland.*

On Saturday nights my babysitters were given explicit instructions by my parents that under no circumstances was I to be allowed to watch "that horror show" on TV. I learned quickly that my teenage babysitters had much more important things on their minds than policing my TV habits. They loved the telephone and talking to their girlfriends and boyfriends, so we reached an easy détente. They were under no requirement to entertain or even supervise me and could talk on the phone to their heart's delight. In exchange, I was at liberty to watch *Chiller* as much as I wanted. *Chiller* played some extremely freaky movies that terrified and fascinated me at the same time. Films like *The Hypnotic Eye,* in which a deranged hypnotist used mind control to force a series of women to disfigure themselves in scalding hot water, or *Caltiki: The Immortal Monster,* where the spirit of a vengeful Mayan goddess is awakened and mayhem ensues, or the terrific *Enemy from Space* (aka *Quatermass II*), in which Brian Donlevy discovers that diminutive aliens have infested an industrial facility with the goal of infiltration of the British government and total domination of world society. Films like these played every Saturday night along with genre staples such as *Godzilla* and the entire catalog of the Universal Classics including *Frankenstein, Dracula,* and *The Mummy,* and they all had a profound impact on me.

My first visit to the Hollywood Wax Museum in Buena Park, California, was a real eye-opener. This musty old museum of wax figures was filled with large dioramas re-creating scenes from classic Hollywood movies. There was Judy Garland and Shirley Temple and Laurel and Hardy. But around the corner, down a dark corridor, I nervously stumbled upon the horror section and found life-size wax re-creations of Boris Karloff as Frankenstein's monster, Bela Lugosi as Dracula, and Lon Chaney Jr. as the Wolf Man. These horror icons, who thrilled and terrified me on the screen, now loomed right there before my very eyes. Better still, the museum gift shop sold color postcards of each diorama and I was able to collect images of my favorite monsters to pin to my wall and gaze at every night before bed. Once I started collecting them, my elementary school friends did too, and they became a coveted currency of trade on the playground. Sheer horror heaven!

Famous Monsters of Filmland was delivered every month to my door. Each issue featured a graphic and glorious depiction of a movie monster, from classics like *Frankenstein* and *The Phantom of the Opera* to movies from the fifties such as *The Creature from the Black Lagoon* and then-current horror stars like Vincent Price. The magazine contained display features with all the classic and current horror movies, many of which never played in my hometown. I have no memory now of how I came to find *Famous Monsters of Filmland,* let alone order a subscription, as this was not a widely circulated publication. But somehow I did, and then many years later was surprised to learn that every contemporary horror filmmaker I admired also tracked down and subscribed to *Famous Monsters of Filmland* in their youth. It was like an infection, preying on young minds susceptible to horror!

Neither of my first two films set the box office on fire. Making my two indie movies, which turned out pretty darn well under the circumstances, was extremely hard work. For them not to be seen by anyone was absolutely and utterly soul-crushing. When casting about for a new project I firmly resolved to make a movie that would be commercial and could not be denied. I remembered that someone once told me it was common knowledge that horror films always made money. For me it was a moment of crystal clarity. I loved horror films + horror films make money = I will make a horror film. Simple arithmetic.

In the first public screening of *Kenny & Company* something astonishing happened. In my film, on Halloween night, our three young heroes enter a haunted house located in a suburban garage and a neighbor in a very freaky monster mask leaps out. While attending this screening, I witnessed the entire audience gasp and jump. For a young filmmaker this was one powerful response. I determined then and there that I needed to make a horror film that was truly scary and one that would make audiences jump. The more times the better.

Though neither Universal nor Fox had made much money on my previous films, my investors on both films had done very well from the studio advances. On top of that, my father and I had both made some money too and could reinvest that back into a new project. No studio was beating down my door to finance my films, but there seemed like there might be a financial path to funding an indie horror film on a lean budget of just under three hundred thousand dollars. But, what kind of horror film would I make?

The fear of death and dying came early to me. I was just seven years old, lying in my bed one night, unable to sleep. Like a sledgehammer out of the dark, it suddenly hit me. I would not live forever, no matter what. One day this body of mine—this head, these hands, these feet—would be dead. It's pretty sad to remember, but I think this may have been the first actual panic attack I ever experienced. From that point on I had a pretty healthy fear of death. Humans are the only sentient species on this planet who know they will die and yet have developed an extremely powerful defense mechanism against this knowledge: Denial. Total denial. And like the rest of my species I had developed an extreme version of this. *It won't happen to me. I'll never step in front of that bus. Every plane I fly on will be mechanically sound. I will not die . . . for now. Later, maybe, but I won't worry about it now.*

Like most everyone else I had developed a sincere trepidation of the symbols of death—graveyards, mausoleums, funerals. And it struck me that setting a film in this world would be the perfect place to create fear.

In my hometown of Long Beach there also happened to exist an immense three-story marble mausoleum now known as Forest Lawn–Long Beach. Back then its name was Sunnyside and this place was immense and creepy. The sound of your own footsteps would echo down the marble halls to great effect. I started thinking about Sunnyside as a location for a horror story. The more I thought about it, the more I realized that a movie that was set in mausoleums, cemeteries, mortuaries, and embalming rooms could be creepy, strange, and scary.

Coincidentally, Reggie Bannister came over one day and told me he had just read a Ray Bradbury novel entitled *Something Wicked This Way Comes* and suggested it as the basis for a new movie. What excited Reg was that the Bradbury book featured a story about two boys investigating a strange dark carnival which arrives in their small town. Reg believed that *Kenny & Company* actors Michael Baldwin and Dan McCann would be perfect to play the leading roles of Will Halloway and Jim Nightshade. I quickly read the book, and loved it. Reg was right. *Something Wicked This Way Comes* was an elegant and melancholy fantasy of youth with themes of belief, fear, and aging.

My producing partner Paul and I decided we would attempt to track down Ray Bradbury and secure the movie rights from him, for no upfront money of course. Somehow Paul tracked down Ray Bradbury's office phone number and address. This was back in the day when very few people had answering machines so when we would dial his number, the phone would just ring and ring with no answer. We decided we would visit Ray Bradbury in person—just drop in and talk to him.

As we exited the elevator in the Los Angeles office building, Bradbury's door was immediately apparent. It was the one with a doormat out front with the words GO AWAY emblazoned on it. Taped to the door was an impassioned letter from Mr. Bradbury stating he was a working writer and did not have time for interruptions. Both stern and pleading at the same time, it begged the reader to leave him alone and posted the name and address of his agent for business inquiries. After reading the blunt warnings neither Paul nor I had the nerve to knock on that door. We copied down the agent information and left.

Ray Bradbury's agent was all too excited to share the good news with us. "You guys called a week too late. I just closed a deal with Disney for them to make a movie of *Something Wicked This Way Comes*." After this wild-goose chase I determined it was time to get serious and write my own horror film.

One of the movies I loved and would eagerly watch on *Chiller* again and again was director William Cameron Menzies's terrifying 1954 film *Invaders from Mars*. An element from this film was a great inspiration to me, and a theme I thought I might be able to incorporate into my new film. In *Invaders from Mars,* one night a young boy witnesses a Martian spaceship land in the field behind his house. Strange things start to happen in his town and to his neighbors but no one will believe him when he tells them about the spaceship. Yet this kid *knows*. Why could I not have a young boy as the protagonist in my new film and have him see strange things up at the local graveyard—and no one would believe him, not even his beloved and trusted older brother? It would be up to this courageous and smart young kid to investigate and discover the source of the mystery. And who to play this boy? Michael Baldwin, of course.

With this concept in mind I journeyed up to Big Bear Lake in the nearby San Bernardino Mountains to be able to write without distraction. Paul came up to the cabin to brainstorm for the first couple of days, but then he left and I was alone. I pretty quickly cobbled together a simple scenario of a boy living under the care of his older brother, both of them orphaned since their parents had died. I spent time developing their personas because I was convinced that if I expected audiences to respond to the thrills and chills, they would first need to be fully invested in realistic and believable characters. A mortuary, mausoleum, and graveyard would be the key settings of this tale. With no telephone and no TV, just pen and paper, I had no choice but to write.

Isolation plays strange tricks with the mind, especially when one is writing a horror film. I would purposely force myself to wander around the woods surrounding the cabin after dark. I had a flashlight in my pocket but I would keep it there, off. When the moon was down, it was pitch dark and the devil himself could be standing beside me and I would not know it. It was scary to stand blind and vulnerable in the dark, and I would force myself to think about my young protagonist, Mike, and what he would be feeling as he moved through the graveyard and explored the forbidding mausoleum.

I now needed to develop the overlord, a villain for the story who would inhabit and rule this domain of death. This bad guy would need to be one tough customer. As I continued to develop this character, I decided it would be smart to try to figure out who might play this potent bad guy, just like I had done with Michael Baldwin. And then I remembered the actor who had intimidated me on my first film, that very tall man who could shut me up with just a glare. Our villain would be played by Angus Scrimm.

In every film, the heroes need a sidekick, an unassuming loyal friend who will be there in the third act to support them with badly needed strength and courage at a critical moment. I decided to play against this typically macho trope, with our character instead being a free-spirited, guitar-slinging ice cream vendor. And my choice for this postmodern sidekick would be the inimitable veteran of my previous two films, Reggie Bannister. This turned out to be one of the best creative decisions I ever made in the making of *Phantasm*.

While I was up in the mountains Paul bumped into Angus in Hollywood at a screening. Paul decided to let him know what I was working on. As Angus tells it, Paul mentioned that I was working on a new film, a horror film, and that I was writing a pivotal role for him as an alien. "An alien . . ." Angus repeated as his mind raced with the possibilities of playing an immigrant from another country, working his way up by his bootstraps to success in America. Paul stopped Angus in his tracks. "Not from another country, Angus. From another world."

BALLS TO THE WALL

The screenplay I came home from the mountains with and then later refined could be condensed into this short synopsis: "The residents of a small Oregon town have begun dying under mysterious circumstances. Following the death of his parents and then a friend, thirteen-year-old Mike finds himself compelled to investigate. After discovering that the town's mortician (a sinister and malevolent character Mike nicknames 'the Tall Man') is responsible for murdering and reanimating the dead, Mike seeks help from his older brother, Jody, and best friend and ice cream man Reggie. Working together, these three friends must lure out and confront the Tall Man, all the while avoiding his rabid minions and his flying chrome killing device, the deadly silver sphere."

When I was fifteen years old I experienced what turned out for me to be a profound dream. This odd nightmare found me trapped inside a maze of immense, never-ending corridors, unable to find my way out. High in the corner of one of the corridors there was a CLUNK and a WHOOSH, and a chrome sphere, about five inches in diameter, appeared and zoomed toward me. I ran. And ran. And as this strange orb hurtled toward me, it suddenly evaporated. I slowed to a walk, then again heard the CLUNK and WHOOSH and spotted another chrome orb jetting toward me. I was terrified. Again I ran. As the ball neared, I could feel it touching the back of my neck, and I suddenly awoke to find myself safe in my bed.

Have you ever had a dream stick with you for months or years after you experienced it? I frequently forget my dreams immediately upon waking, but this one I remembered. A few years later, as I was writing the screenplay that was to become *Phantasm,* I found myself remembering this odd dream from my past. I immediately decided to use this nightmare to create a signature weapon for the sinister undertaker character I was creating. What if, on his exploration of the Tall Man's mausoleum, my intrepid young hero Mike was confronted by one of these orbs? As it barreled toward him he would turn and flee, but what if, unlike me, as it neared, Mike dived to the floor and it screamed right over his head, just missing him? Good stuff, yes? But where would it go from there?

For a while I considered having the ball latch on to someone, and then we would see a wicked-sharp hypodermic needle extrude and, spider-like, inject the victim with some poison. Then I decided to make it more dynamic. What if instead of a needle, a drill bit came out instead, drilled into the cranium, and then pumped out the poor sap's blood! Now that was an idea a young horror filmmaker could sink his teeth into. While still in high school Sam Peckinpah's *The Wild Bunch* exposed me to blood flow as an art form. Peckinpah worked in pints. I decided to work in gallons. As preproduction progressed on *Phantasm,* this "ball" idea would become an obsession, an ongoing research-and-development project for the entire crew as we struggled to figure out work-arounds to several major problems. How would the ball fly? How would the ball drill into an actor's head without killing him? And how would we pump out blood, a lot of blood, and make it look realistic?

I distinctly remember at the time telling Paul and other crew members that this would be the signature effect of the film and we should be prepared to allocate whatever resources we had to this one gag at the exclusion of any other. There would be nothing more important in the film than getting the ball scene right.

One of our capable crew members, Marc Schwartz, was tasked with finding a solution to the flying question. Marc did a lot of work with very thin piano wire. The idea was to stretch it the length of the mausoleum hallway and then use small eyelets to attach the sphere to the wire. We tried to push it along the wire or tug it along with a string, but all these tests looked just terrible. At one point we even attached a model rocket engine to the ball, but it was far too unstable.

We didn't have much luck with the question of drilling the actor's head until Janis, our script supervisor from *Jim The World's Greatest,* introduced us to an effects wiz named Willard Green. Will was a gentle, grandfatherly mechanic who owned a movie effects shop on Vine Street in Hollywood called Turntable Rentals and Sales. Will was an expert practical effects fabricator, but his bread and butter was building huge rotating turntables used by auto companies for their commercials and trade shows.

Paul and I went down to his shop and I explained my idea for this killer sphere sequence. Will was immediately intrigued and came back to us a few days later with a detailed bid and some sketches. Will offered to build us a rig that would contain extruding blades, a spinning drill, and include a blood tube with syringe. He suggested creating vacuum-metalized plastic hemispheres, which could snap onto the front of the rig. Using this plan we could shoot the sphere straight on, or profile, just by swapping out different hemispheres. Even better, Will had figured out the blood-pumping rig. He would provide us with a separate hemisphere that attached to a hose, and he demonstrated how the actor could run the blood hose up through his sleeve. By holding the hemisphere just so, he could hide the blood hose, which would run down his pant leg to a pump and a bucket of stage blood. He even offered to loan us a pump to spout the blood.

We immediately made the deal with Will, thrilled with so much potential for progress on the sphere scene. Will was not much of a horror fan. However, the more he worked with us, the more he found himself getting caught up in our enthusiasm and bloodlust for this weird scene. Will took it even further when he offered to provide us with some shredded foam rubber that we could mix into the stage blood, to give the effect of brain matter pumping out of the sphere.

A couple weeks later we were back at Turntable Rentals and Sales and Will gave us a demo of the finished sphere rig. It mounted handily on a C-stand (the old crew saying "Gaffer tape and C-stands hold up the industry" is so true), with gleaming chrome blades, which would snap out when a lever was thrown. There was a similar setup with a chrome-plated drill bit. As we took delivery, Will handed us an invoice that read:

Design and construct Spherical Space Weapon special effects system as per
instructions from Paul Pepperman & Don Coscarelli. Consisting of sphere,
activating mechanisms, protective head guards, bleeding effect, guide
harness. Loan of drill motor, speed control, pump. Total price $1,163.00

For that sum total of eleven hundred and sixty-three bucks, Will had
succeeded in figuring out a big chunk of how our sphere scene would work.
Now we just needed to figure out a way to make that damn ball fly!

We entered into leases on two properties in which to shoot *Phantasm*. The
set for the brothers' house would be a two-story home set in a run-down
suburb near Van Nuys airport. The house was fairly spacious and had a number of bedrooms where our crew, including me, could live during production. Since nobody was being paid up front, including a place to live at no
cost was a welcome bonus. This was a smart lease: the house also served as
our production office and central headquarters for the production.

We next leased a small new warehouse in an industrial district of
Chatsworth. This was where we would build our mausoleum and other necessary sets. Just six years after meeting director Douglas Trumbull in his
Canoga Park warehouse, I was following in his footsteps and shooting in
my own warehouse just a few miles away.

I enlisted Mark Scott Annerl, my best friend from high school, to design
our mausoleum set. Though Mark's day job was as a top landscape designer
at Mark Scott Associates in tony Newport Beach, California, he had some
fun laying out the plans for the main location for our horror movie. I explained how I hoped the set would seem much more expansive than the small
warehouse we had to work in. Mark came up with a clever design in which
we could change statuary so that the hall could show different looks. He
also designed a hallway intersection, which he referred to as the "Octunda,"
in which characters could exit down one of eight nonexistent halls and then
reenter at the other end, thus doubling or tripling the size of the set.

Marc Schwartz volunteered to head the mausoleum construction, as he
had some building experience. He, Kurt Tiegs, and Stephen Miller went to
work building our mausoleum despite the fact that none of them had any

previous set-building experience. Consequently they built that set as solid as a house. Our only complaint was that every few days we would receive a call from them asking us to bring them more wood.

The warehouse we leased in Chatsworth was brand-new construction, and what was so exciting for me was that the slab cement floor was completely flat. This was a godsend: it would allow smooth tracking shots as the characters moved through the mausoleum. I wanted *Phantasm* to be filmed in a more fluid style than my previous films, and rolling our camera dolly over a smooth, level surface without having to build track would allow me to achieve that easily.

To create the traditional mausoleum look of marble, they tried painting the plywood surface but it never looked realistic. Enter my mother, who had a simple suggestion: to cover the walls with marble contact paper. We ended up purchasing over a hundred rolls of the stuff, but once it was applied correctly, it gave the set an amazingly realistic look.

Even though she received the following credits in pseudonym form— wardrobe by Shirl Quinlain, production designer S. Tyer, and makeup by Shirley Mae—my mother, Kate Coscarelli, never really got the credit under her own name that she deserved on *Phantasm*. She did everything: designed and sewed the dwarf-creature robes, costumed all the actors, and designed and applied their makeup, including creating the look of Angus as the Tall Man. She borrowed one of my father's black suits and took it to a local tailor and had it fitted and narrowed to enhance his tall, thin appearance. My mom requisitioned a pair of my father's black boots and had them outfitted with elevator lifts to make the man tall. She also constructed and fabricated the alien insect creature that torments the characters of our two brothers, Mike and Jody, and, to top it off, she even cooked for the cast and crew. My mother was the true unsung hero of *Phantasm*.

Other loyal *Phantasm* crew members enlisted for the duration and made significant creative contributions to *Phantasm,* including: Dena Roth, Jacalyn Welan, Adele Lustig (who was also responsible for fixing me up on a first date with my future wife!), Michael Gross, Wendy Kaplan, Steve Chandler, John Zumpano, Colin Spencer, Doug Cragoe, Mori Biener, James Becker, and Bruce Chudacoff. I could not have made *Phantasm* without them.

To save money our resourceful production manager, Bob Del Valle, cold-called various vendors trying to get equipment and props donated to our production. His first success was with Fender Guitars when they donated the Stratocaster and Twin Reverb amplifier that Bill Thornbury ultimately would play on-screen. Next, Bob convinced Hodaka Motorcycles to contribute a brand-new Road Toad dirt bike for young Mike to ride in the film. But best of all, since the screenplay made casual reference to the beer several times, Bob was able to talk Moctezuma Brewery into delivering fifty cases of Dos Equis amber beer to our production house. We featured this great beer throughout the film, but most of all, our entire crew drank a lot of it. Many mornings it was beer for breakfast!

On my previous films we shot mostly on weekends. With *Phantasm,* I really made an effort to shoot it conventionally. However, when shooting began we managed to go only six days before we were so logistically out-of-control that our low-budget production ground to a stop. To get the production value I wanted, and to solve the various puzzles of all the special effects, we needed time. So again, we only shot on weekends, and then Monday through Thursday Paul, Bob, and I could regroup to scout locations, develop special effects, and solve the myriad other problems for upcoming shoot days.

With two films under my belt and now another in progress, I was developing my own growing company of repertory actors, which contributed a slew of great acting talent to *Phantasm.* We had Michael Baldwin back from *Kenny & Company,* Angus Scrimm from *Jim The World's Greatest,* and Reggie Bannister from both.

There were two new, major cast additions. For the role of Jody, Bill Thornbury was submitted to us by an agent, and I was immediately charmed by his friendly and affable nature. Bill was an accomplished musician and had just recently taken up acting. My favorite casting technique was to include already-cast actors, so I paired Bill with Michael Baldwin for an audition and the two bonded immediately. It was obvious to all of us that they could effectively portray the brothers that anchor the film.

Kathy (Kat) Lester was nineteen years old. In her first interview, she immediately dazzled Paul and me with her seductive charm. She came to the interview clad in a slinky lavender dress, and little did I know what a significant piece of wardrobe that would become. Again I brought in a previously cast actor, Bill Thornbury, to read their introductory scene, and sparks immediately flew. In the original screenplay her character was simply an underling of the Tall Man, and for her first few scenes there was no intention of anything else. But Kat had a compelling way of grabbing the camera's attention, so rather than let her upstage the Tall Man, I crafted a weirdly novel way to merge them. This small decision really made *Phantasm* unique and challenged the audience. Neither Kat nor Angus learned about this character change until principal photography was complete. To say they were both later surprised would be a huge understatement.

Due to our budget limitations, I had no choice but to be the cinematographer again on *Phantasm*. Both shooting a film and directing it at the same time requires a lot more physical labor and concentration than simply directing alone. It requires designing the lighting setups, checking exposure, and physically figuring out the camera placement and movement. For my most recent films I have left the cinematography to others, and I certainly do miss it. Yet for someone who grew up around cameras, lenses, and film, holding a camera and watching a scene unfold through the viewfinder is what filmmaking is all about. It is so easy to change the angle or to change a lens. You just do it—you don't need to ask anybody. You are front and center in the closest proximity to the actors possible, so you can talk to them intimately or whisper instructions from right behind camera even during the shot.

We were lucky to meet Roberto A. Quezada, who joined up and became a key member of the *Phantasm* team. Roberto had a terrific visual sense and an innate ability to divine photogenic locations. He took over the lighting and made a major impact in the visual style of the film.

When older brother Jody is lured to the graveyard for a sexy midnight tryst with the Lady in Lavender, I wanted their encounter to be both shocking and seductive. The problem was that I had no actors! In their defense Kat Lester and Bill Thornbury were both engaged to be married. Neither was eager to remove any clothing on-screen prior to their weddings. Try as I might I could not convince Kat to bare her breasts and Bill refused to lower his pants under any circumstances. What's an indie filmmaker to do? The only answer was to treat it like a special effects sequence. I needed to break the sequence up into its component parts and just figure out a way to achieve each shot. I was able to get them to film the approach to the wide, flat tombstone where the soiree would take place. They even agreed to lie on top of one another as long as the clothing stayed on. Paul managed to track down a "nude model" in Hollywood who volunteered to film the scene topless for a fee. We then convinced a crew member to stand in for Bill and shot the model, while wearing Kat's lavender dress, tugging his pants down. The continuity of the scene was tricky to edit, but I was able to use cutaways to young Mike, who was watching the encounter from a distance. At the first public screening, when the close-up of the photodouble's breasts pops on the gigantic screen Kat's mom blurted out to her, "You should have used your own breasts. Yours are much better." Kat agreed and to this day wishes she had shot the scene herself. Oh well.

We still had no idea how to levitate that sphere. We had figured out a way to get it to fly around a corner. That was easy. We simply hung the sphere by a piece of fishing line from the top of the mausoleum set and pushed it; like a pendulum, it rounded the corner nicely. As we were working on the scene and discussing the flying sphere conundrum, somebody on the crew asked, "Why don't you just chuck the damn thing?" Could we throw the ball from behind the camera and then reverse the film?

Enter David G. Brown, our art director and a key collaborator in the making of *Phantasm*. Dave was an extremely hardworking and resourceful crew member with a sunny disposition whom we had recruited out of UCLA.

Dave had also done some baseball pitching in high school. Bingo! We set up a test and lined Dave up behind camera with just enough room for a pitcher's windup.

Reverse motion is easy to achieve today using software, but back then we used an old-school technique from the dawn of filmmaking. We mounted our 35 mm Arri IIC camera upside down and filmed in normal forward motion. We then flipped the piece of film from end to end, which created the reverse motion effect. We also shot at a slightly accelerated camera speed to slow the ball down and add some otherworldliness to its motion. When we viewed the tests it was stunning. Everything worked in our favor. Using reverse motion made the ball move slowly at first and then accelerate as it passed by camera. Plus, we found the sweet spot on camera speed at sixty frames per second. We had made the ball fly!

Since Dave Brown's baseball skills worked so well, we put him to good use in the next shot of the sequence, in which Mike dives by camera and the flying sphere whizzes over his head. In this setup, Michael Baldwin would get a running start and leap through frame onto some foam pads on the mausoleum set floor. On cue, Dave would hurl a fastball right above him. This gag went down like clockwork, and when we reviewed the footage in the editing room, it worked like a dream.

In the next major sequence, the mausoleum Caretaker character, played by the very game actor Ken Jones, pops up and grabs Mike, who then bites into the flesh of his arm. As Mike wriggles free, the sphere smashes directly into the Caretaker's forehead. We struggled to figure out a way to have the ball hit Ken without hurting him. We tried a ball on a string and, pendulum-style again, swinging it into his forehead. It smacked him pretty hard and bounced right off, looking fairly ridiculous. Finally we settled on going back to our previous success and shooting the shot in reverse motion.

The idea was to attach the ball to Ken's forehead with tape, then yank it off with fishing line and film it in reverse. We affixed the ball to his head with tape and started filming. The tape was not working and the sphere kept drooping prior to the shot. The tape was also tearing Ken's skin raw, forcing my mom, who was doing makeup, to keep adding more and more powder to cover the welt. Finally we jettisoned the tape and went with a small loop of fishing line, tied around Ken's head. We did a take this way and it worked perfectly.

After finishing up the impact scene we had some fun torturing young Michael Baldwin with the bloody bite scene. To free himself from the Caretaker's grasp, I had envisioned Mike biting down hard on Ken's arm, causing blood to flow. The way we decided to do this was to fill Mike's mouth with stage blood and have him struggle with Ken and then chomp down and release the blood. The problem for Michael was that he would have to hold several ounces of the foul-tasting stage blood in his mouth for a good minute as we rolled camera and then ran through the beginning of the scene. The kid was a trooper and made it look extremely realistic. If you watch the sequence today, you can see which shot it is as Mike's lips are tightly sealed shut until he bites. He got it in just two takes and I don't think he ever enjoyed a tooth-brushing like he did after that scene.

The major scene left to complete in the sequence was the drilling, draining, and killing scenes. For the drilling, we sat Ken in a tall director's chair and placed Will Green's sphere rig directly in front of him. We then placed a small marble wall panel in front of the camera to hide it in the sphere reflection. A small hole was cut in the panel for the camera lens to shoot through. The fun part about this scene, if you pause and still-frame the movie at this point, is that if you look closely into the reflection in the sphere you can see exactly how we did it.

My mom wanted to protect Ken's forehead from the spinning drill bit so she worked her makeup magic and glued a small piece of plastic to Ken's forehead right at the point of impact for the drill. She then covered it with a thick skin-replacement makeup. She also covered the sphere blades with the same material, along with some stage blood, to create the effect of them impaled in his forehead. We were now ready to shoot.

Paul would operate the drill. His orders were to push it out to reveal the blade, start it spinning, and then push it forward into Ken's head. Dave Brown was selected to work the blood syringe, and I watched the scene behind camera through the viewfinder. We did several rehearsals so Ken knew when the drill would come out, when it would start spinning, and when it would cut into his "skin." This was the money shot of the film and a hush came over the crew as the camera rolled.

I called for action. Ken gasped as the drill came out of the sphere and grabbed the ball. I gave a hand signal to Paul, who started the bit spinning and moved it into contact with Ken's "skin." Ken screamed and I signaled for Dave to squeeze out the blood, which would shoot down the drill bit. Dave pushed on the blood syringe and . . . nothing! The blood tube had clogged! Meanwhile the drill bit was cutting into the makeup and the artificial skin was tearing away from Ken's forehead. I frantically gestured to Dave, then yelled, "Blood!!!" Dave rammed the syringe with all his strength and finally, SPLAT, the clog broke free and blood spattered all over Ken's forehead.

Watching the scene in the editing room the next day, we were all stunned. This so-called mistake ended up making the scene *great*. As the drill cut into the makeup it genuinely looked like a drill tearing into real flesh, and the sudden, explosive splat of blood, and Ken's surprised reaction, made it look like the drill had realistically punched through the hapless Caretaker's skull and directly into his brainpan.

Ah, the serendipitous delights of horror filmmaking!!!

MOPAR MANIA

In the parking lot across the street from Woodrow Wilson High was where I first saw it. A sassy-grass green, 1970 AAR Plymouth 'Cuda. Black fiberglass hood, 340 six-pack engine, white interior, and badass pistol-grip four-speed shifter on the floor. Brand spankin' new. This was the Detroit muscle car of my dreams. It made a powerful impression on my sixteen-year-old self that metastasized into a full-blown lifelong obsession. The long sleek hood, the short rear deck, and the rumble of the naturally aspirated, multi-carbureted engine thrilled me. I was an American boy and muscle cars of that era were the epitome of power and cool. (Global warming had not been discovered yet.)

The kid that owned it, who was a full grade younger than me, would hop into his slick ride after school, gun the engine, and burn rubber all the way out of the school lot. I would be left gaping alongside best high school pal Mark Scott Annerl, the smell of monoxide mixed with rubber like the proverbial "napalm in the morning." Mark would frequently retort, "How does a little shit like that deserve to drive a car so fine?"

When searching about for a car for the brothers to drive in *Phantasm,* I spotted an ad for a 1971 'Cuda for sale and quickly grabbed it. I decided to customize the car in the style of the street machines of the period. The rear wheel wells were flared; we added mag wheels, and painted the car gloss black with a beautiful gold pin-striping by actor Bill Thornbury's brother.

At first, it was not an easy relationship. In the seventies, the Detroit assembly lines were not known for their "fit and finish," and it was rumored that workers on the assembly line were notorious for a lot of weed-smoking on the job. The *Phantasm* car definitely had issues. That 'Cuda broke down a lot, creating nothing but headaches during production. In fact, one of the most important questions every morning of the *Phantasm* shoot was whether we could get the damn car started.

I learned about another, more coveted iteration of this Mopar muscle car, which was referred to as the "Hemicuda." This ground-pounder featured the legendary Chrysler 426 cubic-inch Hemi, a beast of an engine with hemispherical combustion chambers. This was a drag-strip engine shoe-horned into a street car that was extremely rare and desired. On *Phantasm III*, I worked with expert restorer Greg Buhlinger to upgrade a 1970 Grand Coupe convertible into a correct triple-black convertible Hemicuda, which appeared in both that film and *Phantasm Oblivion*.

It was especially gratifying to witness over the years that much like the *Bullitt* Mustang and the *Vanishing Point* Challenger, the *Phantasm* 'Cuda has become an auto legend itself. Michael Baldwin and I were delighted to appear on an episode of the popular Velocity channel show *Graveyard Carz,* in which we supervised as host Mark Worman completed work on a beautiful *Phantasm* tribute 'Cuda. Back in the day, a lot of 'Cuda owners painted their rides black in honor of the *Phantasm* car and even today it's thrilling and humbling to occasionally see one roaring down the highway.

BIG IN JAPAN!

During preproduction on the *Phantasm* shoot, I received my first taste of the world of international film sales. Here's how it worked: An intrepid producer raises a small amount of money to make their film. Then, instead of selling all rights worldwide to one big company, they split the rights and license domestic rights to a North American distributor and then license territory-by-territory to each international country. The goal is to avoid "cross-collateralization," in which one big distributor charges failures in one territory against success in others. That way, if you have a hit in, say, Japan, you keep all of that incoming yen and don't have it charged off against a failure elsewhere. And if your film was good, every five to ten years you could relicense the rights again.

My father received an unsolicited phone call from a Japanese theatrical distributor who expressed interest in *Kenny & Company* for distribution in Japan. We had held on to international rights, and someone at 20th Century Fox had told the Japanese about our film, so we set up an afternoon screening at the Aidikoff Screening Room on Sunset Boulevard. In the early evening I received a phone call from my dad to relate the response. "They like the movie. They're still here and (his voice dropped to a whisper) they just offered fifty thousand dollars for Japanese distribution rights. What do I do?" There was a long pause as both of us hung on the phone line, each considering the potential windfall. We had earned the full cost of the film back already and then some from the Fox sale. At a loss for words, I finally blurted out, "Ask for double and see what they say." He quickly responded, "Oh, yeah. Right. I'll call you back." My father was the one who had taught me a lot about negotiation over the years. He always told me that you never immediately accept an opening offer. Doing so either conveyed lack of value in the product or desperation by the seller. It's funny that in this case I was parroting his own teachings back to him.

Toho-Towa was a distribution arm of the legendary Japanese film studio Toho Co., Ltd. They imported films to their country and were very interested in bringing *Kenny & Company* to Japan. My father quickly closed a deal with their president, Mr. Shirasu, for an advance of seventy-five thousand dollars against a very fair cut of their earnings. This was terrific news.

A few months later, after the contract was signed, I had my first in-person meeting with the head of acquisitions of Towa, Mr. Tomioka. During the meeting, he told us that they believed that Japanese audiences would find *Kenny & Company* fascinating, especially its depiction of childhood in America. They had decided to give our film a brand-new name for the Japanese release, *Boys Boys,* and informed us that their executive team had watched the film and decided it was worthy of a major theatrical release all across Japan. He then proceeded to tell us that they would like me to come to Japan for the opening of the film and to bring the three boys who starred in *Kenny & Company* along with me. Warning alarms went off in my head. "What about their parents?" "I am sorry but we do not have the budget for any additional travelers." "Wait, you want me, at twenty-four years old, to chaperone three wild kids across a foreign continent?" "Yes."

I called up each of the parents of the boys and told them of Towa's request. To my utter astonishment not one parent had a concern; all were excited for their kids to join in on an all-expense-paid tour of Japan. They freely provided me with signed waiver forms and the overwhelming responsibility for any kind of life-or-death decision concerning their medical care was now solely in my young hands.

With the three boys—Dan McCann, Michael Baldwin, and Jeff Roth— in tow, I boarded a Japan Airlines 747 bound for Tokyo. Our arrival at the old Haneda Airport on Tokyo Bay was simply an out-of-body experience for which we were completely unprepared for. As soon as we cleared customs it was as if the Beatles had landed in Tokyo, and Dan, Mike, Jeff, and I were the Fab Four. The Towa marketing team had been working in overdrive to turn *Kenny & Company* into a huge media sensation. We didn't know it yet, but for months the boys had been featured all over the Japanese press, in magazines and newspapers, heralding the coming of the three young stars from America with their fantastic new film. As we stepped out of the gate we were immediately swarmed by a huge pack of screaming twelve-year-old Japanese girls all intent on grabbing, hugging, and kissing the boys. I looked over and saw a look of total panic in the eyes of Michael, who was the tough one of the bunch. "Let's get the heck out of here!" he yelled. We all ran. And, of course, the Towa marketing team had news crews and reporters there to document the boys' escape from this fangirl mayhem.

We all tumbled into a waiting limousine as the frenzied girls clawed at the windows. Jeff made the mistake of rolling down a window to sign an autograph and his hand was snatched by several girls. We desperately grabbed his arm and managed to yank his hand back in and the limo rolled away. Welcome to Tokyo!

What followed was a whirlwind tour of Tokyo, Osaka, Nagoya, and Miyazaki to promote our movie. We all did a bunch of television interviews. Michael Baldwin had been promoted by Towa as the greatest skateboarder in America, yet when we filmed the skateboard sequences in *Kenny & Company* we utilized an expert skateboarding stunt double for him. The truth was that Michael could barely even stand on a skateboard. The TV shows would always ask for him to skateboard into the studio and do some tricks. Since this was impossible, it forced us to work up some clever improvisations. Michael would glide onto the stage on his skateboard, which was the one trick he could do, and then our irrepressible "Sherman" would barrel into the studio on his skateboard from the other direction and wipe out comically in front of Mike. The studio audience always loved it. Jeff was a good sport about it, he enjoyed getting the laughs. Plus, Towa had partnered with a Japanese jeans manufacturer to create a line of special *Kenny & Company* "skateboard pants" with padding in the knees and hips, which would protect Jeff during these pratfalls.

One of the major promotions the marketing team had planned was to fly us down to the southern tip of Japan to the resort city of Miyazaki to meet the greatest home run hitter in baseball history. Sadaharu Oh of the Yomiuri Giants was a baseball legend. With a career record of 868 home runs, his stats far surpassed American legends Babe Ruth and Hank Aaron. Although there is a general consensus that Japanese ballparks are somewhat easier to hit home runs in, and the pitching better in the American major leagues, nonetheless Oh's record is an astounding feat that has not been matched to this day.

Mr. Oh was retired from playing and was now coaching at the Giants spring training facility. Our intrepid Towa marketing team convinced Oh to meet with the boys, give them some batting tips, and maybe get a nice publicity photo op.

As we arrived at the Yomiuri Giants clubhouse, one of the Towa publicity guys handed me a box of a dozen brand-new Mizuno baseballs. He told me to tell one of the boys to ask Mr. Oh to sign them. "Sure," I said, and as I walked in I figured if anybody could get these balls signed, Michael Baldwin could. His response was, "No prob," as he tucked the box under his arm and we went into the clubhouse. Mr. Oh, a man of both Chinese and Japanese ancestry, was waiting for us. He was warm and friendly and invited us to join him out on the practice field. Mr. Oh proceeded to demonstrate his famous "flamingo" batting stance, in which he would lift his knee to his waist as he waited for the pitch. Not only did this stance coil his body so he could unleash his powerful swing, but, much like a cobra, it also mesmerized and distracted the pitcher's concentration. Each of the kids tried it and the news photographers got some great shots. As Mr. Oh led us to the exit, Michael, in his most innocent voice, asked, "Mr. Oh, would you mind signing these for us?" Oh nodded and very generously signed each one with both English and kanji signatures. We said goodbye, bowed, shook hands, and headed out of the practice facility. Little did I know that a major international incident was about to explode.

As we arrived at the car one of the Towa guys grabbed for the case of baseballs. "I'll take that, please." Michael yanked the box out of reach and retorted, "Sorry guys, these balls are ours." It was as if Michael was suddenly channeling his smart-aleck, no bullshit character from *Kenny & Company*. All the Towa marketing guys suddenly stiffened, then became very agitated and started yelling among one another in Japanese. The most senior PR guy stepped forward. "Mr. Coscarelli, we need that box of balls. Please return it to us." I looked to Michael, who defiantly responded, "Hell no. We're the ones that got 'em signed, we're keeping 'em!" The other kids surrounded him in solidarity. I tried to defuse the situation and gently asked Michael, "Do you think if we each kept a signed ball then maybe we could let them have some? They are the ones who furnished the balls." Michael thought this over and then magnanimously turned to the PR guys. "We each get a ball and Don gets one too. You can have the rest of 'em."

It was a grim ride back to the hotel, with no communication between the Japanese and the Americans. Later I learned that the head honchos at the Towa head office back in Tokyo each wanted a signed Sadaharu Oh baseball and the junior PR execs had been tasked with getting them. These nervous executives had used the kids to carry out their plan because they lived in fear of their bosses. It seemed a few suits were going to get stiffed.

The trip culminated in the major Japanese premiere of *Kenny & Company* in Tokyo. Prior to the screening we were brought to the Towa corporate offices. Up on the rooftop of the building, the sun was setting over Tokyo as a kickoff party for *Kenny & Company* was in full swing. The centerpiece of the event was thirteen teenage American girls, recruited from ex-pat families living in Tokyo, all outfitted in special *Kenny & Company* cheerleader outfits. Our "Team Kenny" cheerleaders each carried a gold-and-blue shield emblazoned with a letter from the film's title. The girls began a choreographed routine chanting the letters K-E-N-N-Y in an energetic and gymnastic American cheerleading style. A big contingent of Japanese press was there and they eagerly snapped photos and videos.

That night our limousine pulled up in the back of the theater for our premiere screening. We were escorted backstage to introduce our film. For the event I had been told to wear a suit and tie and was informed that the Towa brass had invited me to a special dinner at an expensive and exclusive restaurant in the Ginza district after the introduction. The boys were specifically not invited.

We were brought down a corridor and out onstage behind the curtain. They told us that in a few moments it would open and we were to each make brief remarks to the audience and then depart. We could hear sounds of the audience on the other side of the curtain. An announcer suddenly called out on the PA system in Japanese something roughly translated as, "And now, from America, the director and stars of *Boys Boys*!!!" The curtain slowly drew open and to our utter shock and surprise, there in front of us was one of the absolutely largest movie audiences I had ever seen in my life. This two-thousand-seat theater was packed with cheering Japanese! Through the interpreter, the boys made some sweet and funny remarks to the crowd, and I finished with a welcome and thank-you for coming out to see our movie. As we were hustled back out the corridor I had a sudden moment of realization and stopped dead in my tracks. "I'm staying to watch the movie." The head PR guy protested, "That's not possible. You have dinner with bosses." Damned if I would miss the one opportunity in my life to watch my movie with a crowd of two thousand Japanese! I just barged toward the theater entrance and they had no choice but to get me seated right in the middle of the crowd. It was fascinating to note that the audience seemed to get all of the film's humor despite the cultural and language differences. It wasn't perfect, though: one of the most sensitive lines in the film, in which our hero Kenny is told that his family dog must be euthanized, received one of the largest laughs of the night. (I'm still trying to figure that one out.) Of course, every fifteen minutes the PR guy would return and interrupt, "Bosses waiting. Must go now." For this one moment of the trip, my courtesy went out the window, and I just waved him off. "Not now!"

Kenny & Company was released to great success in Japan and was a box office home run for Towa. Michael Baldwin ended up being embraced by his young Japanese fans as a major movie star. Literally bags of fan mail would arrive from Japan addressed to him. Why did Japanese fans, mostly girls, gravitate to him? Of course for the obvious reasons—he was a great young actor, cute and charming. But I always felt it went a bit deeper than that. His character was loyal and true, but also not afraid to stand up to adults. In Japan, with its deep cultural history of respect for elders and authority, I think Michael's performance showed these kids something completely new and empowering. In any case, upon return to Tokyo a few years later for a film festival screening of *Jim The World's Greatest,* I had the pleasure of noticing a ranking of Japanese movie stars in a fan magazine. And there was Michael's picture, over three years later, still listed in the top five stars, just behind Sylvester Stallone and Bruce Lee.

Meanwhile in the US, 20th Century Fox did nothing more with *Kenny & Company* and it disappeared into their film vaults. It would be two full decades before Mark Ward, a longtime friend and wiz executive at the now defunct Anchor Bay Entertainment, was combing through the lists of 20th Century Fox catalog titles and came across *Kenny & Company* listed there. He was able to sublicense the title from Fox and single-handedly resurrected *Kenny,* releasing it to great acclaim for the first time on DVD in the States. Thanks, Mark!

PHANTASM'S FIRST SCREENING

Back from the whirlwind trip to Japan, it was time to dive back into *Phantasm*. With the movie shoot now complete, and with the leases on both our Van Nuys location house and Chatsworth warehouse expiring, we vacated both and moved editing over to Hollywood to the Goldwyn Studios lot. Samuel Goldwyn himself was long gone by the time we arrived, and his lot was then home to mostly independent companies and television producers.

The key reason for the move was that I had squirreled away enough money in the budget so we could do our sound mix at the famous Goldwyn Studios sound facility, which, at the time, was considered the premiere audio mixing facility in Hollywood. I was determined that *Phantasm* would have a state-of-the-art sound mix. Having been burned back in my student filmmaking days with bad sound, I learned from that experience how important good professional sound is, especially when making films on a budget. Audiences equate good sound with good movies, and it's the easiest way (although not inexpensive) to elevate a low-budget film.

Since Paul and I both happened to be homeless at the time, we would occasionally trade off sleeping in the editing room, which was previously an actor dressing room and had a comfortable couch and shower. Nights on the lot were an interesting experience. Actor Buddy Ebsen (*The Beverly Hillbillies*), who was shooting a TV series on the lot, lived nearby in his dressing trailer downstairs, and the sounds of him playing acoustic guitar and singing would waft in through the window. Down the hall, actor-producer Jack Webb (*Dragnet*) would frequently wander the halls after his late-night card games, feeling no pain and carrying on in song.

I had been hunched over my Moviola editing machine, working in our Goldwyn editing room for close to a year. It can be easy to get lost in your cut, to lose objectivity, watching the same sequences over and over again. While it is sometimes dangerous, I have always welcomed the challenge of screening an early cut for a crowd. When you are watching your work with an audience, frequently your attitude toward those sacred-cow scenes, that you as director have fallen in love with, can change in an instant. Before, alone, the film seems to play just fine—but with a crowd the flaws are magnified, dramatically. When you suddenly realize the audience is bored and restless, it's difficult to stifle yourself from shrieking out, "I'm going to cut that scene! Pretend it's not there!" I have run edited versions alone prior to screenings and pronounced them perfect and ready to screen, and after an audience screening am right back in that same editing room, ready to hack and slash out big sections I previously was enamored with.

We decided it was time to screen our very first cut of *Phantasm*. But we were going to do something different. My brother-in-law at the time was a psychologist working on several research projects. I asked him about designing a questionnaire we could submit to audience members, which might provide serious insight into the quality of our film. We were way ahead of our time: just a few years later, all the studios were investing heavily in research screenings. My brother-in-law was more than happy to oblige and created a four-page list of questions that managed to target which scenes the audience liked and didn't like. Paul secured us the use of one of the larger screening rooms on the Paramount lot. Now we just needed people.

We decided to pay the audience five bucks each to watch our rough cut. Since *Phantasm* was in such a raw state with no music, sound effects, or optical effects, we needed to give them an incentive to stay and give comments. It started with friends and then quickly branched out across the city as we solicited anybody we could find. The night of the screening we had a full house of over a hundred people. My mother was drafted as a "neutral host" of the research screening so that Paul and I could watch the reactions of the subjects. She got up and welcomed everyone and told them they each would receive their five-dollar bill on the way out the door, *after* they handed in their finished questionnaire.

I had told the actors to stay away because I did not want their presence at the screening influencing the audience response. But across the theater I saw what appeared to be an older gentleman, with a cane and a hat, making his way to his seat. It was Angus Scrimm, in disguise as an elderly man! Was he speaking in a cockney accent??? Later I learned that Angus found himself compelled to be there for the first screening and figured that if he came in disguise as an old Englishman, nobody would know he was there. It worked.

The screening began and *Phantasm* really started off with a bang. The moment when Angus made his first on-screen appearance as the Tall Man was simply stunning. His hand clamped down on Bill Thornbury and his line, "The funeral is about to begin, Sir!," caused the audience to howl in fright and levitate out of their seats. Paul and I were ecstatic! From there on, though, the audience reaction rapidly devolved. The cut was rough and not having any visual effects really messed up the narrative. When we would reach an unfinished effects scene, the projector would stop, and my mother would step forward and explain what was to come. "In this scene, young Mike opens an antique store cabinet and finds a photo inside of the Tall Man. It comes to life and the Tall Man turns and looks at him. Please roll the projector." And the screening would continue. These breaks destroyed any momentum the film might have, despite providing the necessary plot points so the audience could comprehend what they were watching. After the questionnaires were handed in and the audience filed out I moved outside to gauge the audience reaction as they exited. One interchange told me everything I needed to know as one viewer said to another, "That was terrible." "Yes. Horrible." It was back to the editing room for me.

The feedback from the screening, though painful, was also extremely helpful. I learned that the cut was too long and that some sections were completely incomprehensible. I also learned that the audience generally loved the cast. The cards told us that Mike, Reggie, and Jody were terrific heroes and that the Tall Man and his alter ego the Lady in Lavender were impressive and powerful villains. Determined to fix the problem areas, I went back to my Moviola.

My original screenplay contained a vast array of sequences that established the world of the two brothers, Mike and Jody. From the screening I learned that once the sphere began to fly, the film kicked into high gear and we needed to streamline the character development to get to that action more quickly. Many sequences detailing the brothers' lives were left on the cutting room floor, including the brothers eating a turkey dinner, the older brother Jody's flirtations with his girlfriend and her sister, and several scenes with their elderly aunt who lived nearby. If all the many outtakes were replaced, *Phantasm* probably would have run three full hours.

Removing all this exposition was a gamble, but I made a calculated decision that I would trust in the audience to figure out many of the open questions. I had recently seen Italian master Dario Argento's fabulous *Suspiria* and it was all about mood, style, and atmosphere. There was not much in the way of explanation and critics and horror audiences loved it.

This sentiment also translated to the conclusion of the film, in which I finally decided not to wrap it up in a nice package and explain everything, instead just ending with a shocking, brutal impact. I made a risky choice that *Phantasm* would be, at its core, a mystery; it would be the audience's responsibility to figure it out.

Around this time I made contact with Fred Myrow to discuss a score for *Phantasm*. This time around, Fred decided to enlist a friend of his to collaborate with him. Malcolm Seagrave, like Fred, was also a classically trained composer with a background in chamber music, who loved rock music. I shared with them the two records that I had recently been obsessed with. One was *Heaven and Hell* by the progressive electronica maestro Vangelis. The other was Pink Floyd's *Dark Side of the Moon*. I told them about my love for an instrument called a Mellotron, which could be heard in many progressive rock records of the day. They liked this idea and eagerly promised to work a Mellotron into the score. I was especially enamored with the choral voices selection on the Mellotron, which created a moving but freaky choir sound. Perfect for *Phantasm*!

Fred and Malcolm went to work. A few weeks later Paul and I received an excited call from Fred asking us to come over immediately to his house

off Wilshire and La Cienega where they had been working. When we arrived the two men were literally bouncing off the walls with excitement. They
sat down at the piano and began performing a duet for us of their elegant
and eerie *Phantasm* theme, beginning with that epic eight-note figure. This
composition would become one of the defining elements of not only *Phantasm* but its four sequels to come. Today, it is considered one of the classic
horror movie themes, so you can imagine what it was like to hear it performed live for the very first time. I was stunned and elated at the power
and mood of their unique composition.

Fred and Malcolm's plan was to rent a bevy of cutting-edge synthesiz-
ers, including the Mellotron, and take them into Paul Ratajczak's little studio in Long Beach. Using those instruments and many other unconventional
ones, including Indian tablas, Fred, Malcolm, and Paul worked for several
weeks, along with David Johnson and guitarist Bill Cone. The result: an
accomplished and insidious score that perfectly complemented *Phantasm*.

PHANTASM'S LONELY JOURNEY

I n screenwriter William Goldman's highly regarded book *Adventures in the Screen Trade,* he posits the theory that when it comes to the movie business "nobody knows anything." I personally know that statement to be a fact. And I can prove it.

Keep in mind that we now know, as of this writing, that my little horror film, if considered simply as a commodity, would ultimately generate tens of millions of dollars in revenues to all the various theatrical and home video distributors worldwide who ended up distributing it. (And boy, do I wish I had received all that money, but unfortunately, success in Hollywood is frequently defined as making a lot of money for other people.)

So Paul, my father, and I started calling around to distributors in order to set up screenings for them. All of the major studios watched *Phantasm.* Not one studio had any interest in distributing. Not one! What I had not yet learned was that "no" was always the safest answer for a Hollywood executive. The movie business is inherently risky, and if one "knows nothing" they are better off taking as few risks as possible. Messed up, huh?

With our rough-cut print in the double 35 mm system, twenty reels would need to get lugged from the car trunk, usually up a narrow flight of stairs to the upstairs projection booth at each studio. Paul and I would trade off doing the lugging. Paul always liked to loiter around while the screenings were in process and see if he could gauge any interest from the attending studio executives. One time he found himself accidentally trapped in an elevator with a bunch of execs who had just watched the film and were mercilessly ripping it apart.

Paul was also there in the Warner Bros. projection booth when one of their executive big shots was watching *Phantasm*. At the halfway mark— just moments before the most memorable scene in the movie, in which the sphere drills into the Caretaker's forehead—suddenly the lights went up and the intercom squawked on with the exec telling the projectionist to wrap it up. He had seen enough. Galvanized to action, Paul dashed down the hall and cornered the exec before he could get into the elevator. Paul pleaded with him to please just watch the very next scene. The exec grunted an OK, went back in, sat back down, and watched the now famous scene of the victim getting drilled and killed. Then the big shot popped back up and exited. "Not for us" is the only comment he tossed over his shoulder as he exited into the elevator.

We even had a meeting with the head of the ultimate exploitation film distributor, American International Pictures, cigar-smoking Samuel Arkoff. Sam and his team liked the movie, but ultimately decided it was too risky for them.

I was getting nervous. We had one tiny company who up until that point mainly distributed movies on the college circuit and otherwise nothing else. It was called New Line Cinema and its president, an entrepreneurial gent named Bob Shaye, really liked and wanted *Phantasm*. He had some good marketing ideas, but we were holding out for a distributor with some national presence. Enter Avco Embassy Pictures.

Avco Embassy Pictures had been formed in the sixties when the Avco Financial group bought producer Joseph E. Levine's Embassy Pictures. Their high-water mark had been their release of *The Graduate,* directed by Mike Nichols and starring Dustin Hoffman. Levine was now long gone and Avco Embassy had fallen on hard times. A new regime had been installed in the person of an eager executive named Bob Rehme. We screened *Phantasm* for Bob and some of his key executives. They definitely had interest but were on the fence about making an offer. Later I learned that they would have been happy to offer us a money advance but they had no money! During this period Avco Embassy was struggling for its very survival.

Rather than wait around, we made a very big decision to roll the dice and book a sneak preview of *Phantasm* in a real theater with a real audience and invite distributors to witness how it played. This kind of screening is a real gamble when one does not have distribution yet. You never know on a given night how a film might perform in front of a regular audience. What if they hated the movie and booed? Would prospective distributors stand up and walk out?

Leonard Shapiro, a friendly and helpful executive at Avco Embassy, connected us with the Pacific Theatres chain, and we booked a Saturday night sneak preview screening at the huge Hollywood Pacific Theatre right on Hollywood Boulevard, the same theater in which I had first seen *2001: A Space Odyssey* a decade previously. Hell, if it was good enough for Kubrick, it was good enough for me!

The Hollywood Pacific was one of the grand old movie palaces, built in 1927 and seating almost a thousand people. This would be the very first paid public screening of *Phantasm*. On the day of the screening we ran an expensive display ad in the *Los Angeles Times* featuring a remarkable illustration by artist Jim Warren of the Tall Man's head bursting open with fingers crawling out.

As the big night rolled around I was terrified. After all this hard work, how would the movie play, and what might be the response from the distributors? There was a big crowd and with a large Coke in hand, I slunk down in my seat and waited for the movie to begin. As the film started the first thing I noticed was a crazy sexual tension in the audience as the graveyard sequence with the Lady in Lavender played out. This was an extremely strange experience for me. I had caused audiences to laugh and jump in their seats before, but this was the first time I had directed a sequence that sexually stimulated an audience. Except for actress Kat Lester's moans of pleasure, you could hear a pin drop. I looked around and noticed the men mostly, with their attention riveted to the screen as the Lady in Lavender mounted and ravished her doomed prey. I realized that the movie was playing well when we cut from the quiet mausoleum interior to the Morningside Mausoleum exterior with Mike blasting by camera on his dirt bike. The engine roar caused a jolt in the audience. This was good! Best of all was the next sequence, when older brother Jody encounters the mysterious Tall Man for the first time and Angus clamps his hand down with a thud. "The funeral is about to begin, Sir!" The audience shot out of their seats with a gasp. I gave Paul a subtle high five. I could relax now; this screening was going to play just fine. But then something completely unpredictable happened.

A wildly drunk woman seated way down in the front of the theater on the right side suddenly started to howl with laughter. And she wouldn't stop. Anything that occurred on-screen would trigger her to howl with a weird choking laughter! I was mortified. Distributors were in the audience trying to decide the fate of our film. What could I do? Have the ushers drag her out of the theater and risk causing a disruptive scene in front of the distributors? So I had no choice but to sit there and endure it. Every time the Tall Man showed up on-screen—she was cackling. When the kid was working under the car and the dwarf-creatures were skittering around his garage—she was howling. About an hour into the screening, after the ball drilled into our Caretaker's head, she finally shut up. I don't know if that scene shocked her into submission, or if she just passed out cold in her seat from whatever influence she was under. I never did find out who she was or what her trip was, but I was convinced that this degenerate had destroyed my screening. As the credits rolled and the audience exited the theater, I was quite surprised that no one mentioned the antics of that lunatic.

Our sneak preview was a certifiable success. Everybody loved the movie, including the distributors in attendance. Unfortunately, in typical fashion, none of the major studios showed up. Of the indie distributors who attended, not one upped their offer, not even Avco Embassy, which was the largest of the bunch (and they were still not offering any upfront money, just a backend percentage). This was so disappointing. Both my first two films had major studios willing to give us an advance for far more than each film's budget, but with *Phantasm,* a seemingly much more commercial prospect, nothing.

Bob Shaye and his upstart New Line Cinema did make a significant money offer and made a strong case that he could turn our film into a box office hit. We ultimately decided to sign with Avco Embassy. They had similar enthusiasm, but they also had a network of regional branch offices across the country to service the distribution of the film, which we really thought would make a difference. A few years later Bob, with director Wes

Craven, created his own horror franchise with *A Nightmare on Elm Street,* which employed a dream logic similar to *Phantasm.* The success of that film elevated New Line Cinema into a major player in Hollywood.

This time around we held back international rights on *Phantasm* and hired an international sales agent, in Mark Damon of Producers Sales Organization, to actively assist us with territorial sales. Mark was one of the pioneers in the international sales business and was a dedicated and enthusiastic salesman for our film. My father and I learned a lot from watching Mark maneuver through the international markets and play the various territorial distributors off one another to negotiate strong up-front advances and solid backend deals for our film. On later films we would use this knowledge to do the selling ourselves. The fact that *Phantasm* was not dialog heavy, had unique action sequences, and focused on accessible themes of loss and death helped make it extremely successful worldwide.

BARNSTORMING AMERICA WITH THE TALL MAN

W hat Avco Embassy Pictures lacked in financial resources they made up for with sheer enthusiasm and marketing savvy. It was a thrill to watch James Spitz, Avco's distribution chief, as he rallied his sales troops after a marketing screening of *Phantasm*. "Gentlemen, the name of this movie is not *Phantasm*. It is MONEY!" All his regional reps burst into cheers!

Then Avco Embassy received some devastating news. The Motion Picture Association of America Classification and Ratings Administration had reviewed *Phantasm* and slammed us with an X rating for violence due to the blood level in the sphere sequence. An X rating would have destroyed the film's commercial value. The sphere sequence defined *Phantasm* in the minds of audiences, and if it was eviscerated, the movie would not have had the impact it did.

At first, I refused to make any cuts. The person at Avco Embassy who was in charge of dealing with the MPAA was Jon Davison (who later produced great movies like *Robocop* and *Starship Troopers*). We worked with Jon and it seemed to us that cutting the blood sequences shorter actually made the effect more violent. Finally we gave up and tried the old editor's trick of making our print look worked on by scuffing it up and making a lot of splice marks without deleting *any* actual blood shots. The rating board saw right through that trick and the X rating was confirmed. Luckily a sharp and savvy executive named Walter Keenan over at Avco Embassy personally made a final plea to the MPAA and succeeded in getting us the R rating. I also heard a story later that, supposedly, Walter went to the meeting armed with an expensive bottle of Scotch whisky, which helped grease the wheels for us. I never did get confirmation on whether that tale was actually true or not, but I have subsequently found that a nice bottle of Scotch can solve a lot of problems.

Rory Guy

February 16, 1979

Dear Don,

If "Phantasm" achieves the distribution we hope for, one of the fascinating prospects is that — inevitably, the way things fall out statistically — a sizable portion of the young among your worldwide audience will be seeing a horror film for the first time.

Thus, your "Phantasm" will forever be the archetype of horror that they carry with them for the rest of their lives — the original by which they measure every subsequent exposure to the horror genre, as "Dracula" and "Frankenstein" were to my generation.

The Tall Man will be their Karloff and Lugosi, all their nameless nightmares of Dreaded Evil at last embodied, etched in the amber of their consciousnesses for as long as they each shall live. I'm glad he's Angus Scrimm and not me.

Unsettlingly, for the old and infirm who will in all likelihood turn up here and there in your audiences around the world, the eerie concept of Death dramatized by "Phantasm" may be their final such representation in films before they totter off to their own Last Resting Places. Let us hope they have the preconditioned convictions with which to dismiss "Phantasm" as uneasy fiction.

Yours in the most morbidly gleeful anticipation,

Mr. Don Coscarelli Jr.   *Angus*

I MEANT TO SIGN THIS "RORY." ODD HOW OBDURATELY HE PUSHES HIMSELF IN ON MY LIFE LATELY. EVEN MY AGENTS HAVE STARTED TO CALL ME "ANGUS."

Angus was an avid letter writer. I received hundreds from him. This one from a month prior to release is a treasure of mine. I love Angus's excitement about *Phantasm*'s impending release, his inimitable humor, and his prescience.
(Courtesy of Don Coscarelli)

Avco Embassy booked *Phantasm* to premiere in Southern California. In advance of the opening they did something remarkable to build word of mouth. For the entire month prior to opening, every Saturday night they planned to hold a midnight sneak screening of the film in the Westwood district, near UCLA.

On the night of the first sneak preview, my girlfriend (and future wife) Shelley passed by the theater about two hours before showtime and called in with a report. Paul picked up the phone and listened, then yelled, "Shelley, you're fucking lying to me!" Shelley was calling in from Westwood to report that there was already a huge line of people around the block waiting for *Phantasm*.

Avco Embassy was all about promotion and showmanship, as these tactics paid dividends and were also inexpensive. They started with a "hearse stuffing contest" in front of the Westwood theater in which a UCLA fraternity and sorority were drafted to see how many bodies they could pack into the *Phantasm* hearse. A bevy of news crews and photographers showed up to learn that the final tally was twenty-seven sweaty college students.

At these sneak previews the plan was to also have a surprise appearance by Angus Scrimm in full Tall Man costume as the film ended. These appearances were patently ridiculous, but the audiences just ate them up and they generated a lot of buzz. As the film's credits came to an end a bright spotlight would suddenly flash on and the theater curtain was yanked back to reveal Angus looming in the wings. He would growl his trademark line, "Booooooy!" Then he would point to the back of the theater and suddenly a basketball-size sphere, wrapped in aluminum foil, would whiz down over the audience's head on a string. It always got a huge roar from the crowd.

One time the above technique got way out of control. Angus and I were in Brisbane, Australia, and the Aussies were gung-ho to create a huge marketing spectacle in every theater we appeared at. They gave Angus a large butcher knife to brandish (I think they were still under the influence of the recent *Halloween* release) and had a special effects technician standing by with a huge fog machine. As the screening came to an end, they cued the tech and he started pumping out fog . . . a lot of it. As the fog rolled down from under the curtain someone in the audience screamed out, "Fire!" The entire audience bolted out of their seats. Quick-thinking Angus leaped out from behind the screen, still wielding the butcher knife. "It's just me," he deadpanned. The audience stopped in their tracks and just stared, then burst into a huge laugh of relief and all ran down to the front and swarmed around Angus.

The head of marketing at Avco Embassy, Herman Kass, had little money for television ads, so he replaced that with relentless publicity tours. Angus Scrimm and I were drafted to represent the picture and were sent on a nationwide tour to every corner of the Lower 48. Back in those days this was easy to do as Avco, to save costs, distributed regionally. Therefore Angus and I could barnstorm through the Southwest in advance of the opening and then be dispatched to the Northeast for those openings three or four weeks later. It was a crazy experience. Our typical day would start at dawn for the local morning TV shows. I would appear as the young filmmaker and beside me would be my horror star Angus Scrimm in full Tall Man makeup, including his black suit and elevator boots. It was great fun, as I was the straight man who would set up the story and film clips and then Angus would sneer into camera and then hit them with his punch lines in character that always got a laugh. "I have a freezer full of Corpsesicles. May I offer you one?" Then it would be off to the radio stations to do their drive-time shows, followed up by lunch with a local film critic.

The response from critics was generally positive, but every once in a while our publicist would warn us that the local film critic we were meeting did not like our movie. Angus was the one who taught me that we should not be dismayed by such news but should use the opportunity to convince the recalcitrant critic that our movie was actually pretty good. So this would become our challenge. We would never be confrontational; we would always be self-effacing and genial.

It would start with the food and drinks. Avco Embassy pretty much gave us an unlimited budget to wine and dine critics. Angus really knew his liquor, and if the critic was so inclined Angus would order wines and whiskeys and we all would quickly be feeling no pain. Then it was my job to portray the earnest young filmmaker who was just doing his damnedest to make a movie that was different and worthwhile (which was the truth). Then Angus, since he had been a film critic himself, could talk with some experience about the difficulties of writing relevant film criticism. We would wrap it up with some serious conversation about filmic influences. Angus had been a film fan for decades and could lead us into the history of horror film, and we could discuss in depth revered horror filmmakers such as Fritz Lang, James Whale, and Val Lewton. As the meeting drew to a close, we would bid the critic a fond farewell and most often, within minutes, our publicist would come back with a response something like, "He told me that the more he thought about it, the more he liked your movie."

As our American publicity came to an end, Angus and I were invited on a three-week tour down under by Graham Burke and Greg Coote of our Australian distributor, Village Roadshow. *Phantasm* needed to be retitled in Australia due to a recent soft-core porn release there called *Fantasm*. Not wanting any confusion, our distributor retitled it as *The Never Dead,* which in retrospect was actually a pretty darn good title. It was a memorable time in a great country meeting lots of wonderful Australian horror fans and being shepherded around by our ace Aussie publicist, Harvey Shore. We traveled all over the country and generated a lot of interest, which included several national television appearances.

One afternoon in Sydney a friendly journalist casually asked if we were familiar with the work of Peter Weir, the Australian director of films such as *Picnic at Hanging Rock* and *The Last Wave*. Angus and I responded with enthusiasm as Weir's films had been very popular in the States, and we were both huge fans. Surprisingly, the journalist rang Peter Weir up and within minutes we found ourselves at the director's house. With typical Australian hospitality Peter treated us to an afternoon of drinks and snacks, and I'm fairly certain he had no clue as to who we were because *The Never Dead* had not yet been released in Australia. However, Angus and I relished this surprise opportunity to meet and question this affable and brilliant filmmaker about some of his very artistic and yet inscrutable films.

Upon return to the States, the very last interview I was assigned in support

of *Phantasm* was in New York City at Rockefeller Center for an appearance
on NBC's then late-night show, *The Tomorrow Show*. I guess it must have
been a slow news day but somehow, of all people, George Romero, the director of the legendary *Night of the Living Dead,* and I had been booked to
spend an hour with host Tom Snyder and promote our respective horror
films. George was publicizing his new sequel *Dawn of the Dead.* In the NBC
green room I was seriously nervous, having never appeared on a major American network before. Also, the Avco Embassy publicist mentioned to be
careful, that Snyder might go after us about excessive gore and violence in
movies. George arrived and immediately put me at ease. He counseled that
there were two of us and only one Tom Snyder, so we could tag-team him.
From that point on it was fun for me. The set was so dark you couldn't even
see the cameras and George was so relaxed the entire tenor changed. In his
inimitable progressive fashion, George was happy to deflect the tougher
questions into political discourse with Tom and that made it a breeze for
me. After the show George and I walked out together onto Fifth Avenue
and exchanged contact info and promised to stay in touch. I received a big
Romero bear hug and then was on my way.

Phantasm ended up being a critical and box office success, not only in the
States but around the world. The summer of 1979 had been called "Hollywood's Scary Summer" by *Newsweek* magazine, and it was very satisfying
to see the box office charts in *Variety* listing Ridley Scott's *Alien* as number
one and *Phantasm* as number two. I had learned a lot about marketing from
the scrappy independent distributor Avco Embassy, lessons that would serve
me well on my future indie endeavors. After several long years and a lot of
hard work, I was finally finished with *Phantasm,* or so I thought.

TAMING THE BEASTMASTER

"One of the most popular movies on cable television of all time."
—*Los Angeles Times*

"Do you know what HBO stands for? *Hey,* Beastmaster*'s On!*"
—Billy Crystal, *Saturday Night Live*

can't sleep on planes. I was on a return flight from Sydney, Australia, to Los Angeles. Fourteen-some hours of mind-numbing tedium, perfect to contemplate my future. The opening of *Phantasm* had gone great, it was a certifiable hit in the great Down Under. In fact, *Phantasm* was now a world-wide box office phenomenon and, amazingly, a critical success to boot. Heady times for a struggling twenty-five-year-old indie filmmaker! What to do next? I immediately ruled out a sequel to *Phantasm*. The film had a very distinct ending with the demise of the hero. How could there possibly be a sequel? (Little did I know that I would ultimately write and direct three sequels and produce a fourth.) No, it was time for something new. And with the financial success of *Phantasm* it should be something big.

For a number of years an idea had been knocking around in my head. In sixth grade there was a bookmobile library, basically a big van full of books that would pull up to my elementary school. I read every science fiction novel in their collection, including books by Robert Heinlein, Andre Norton, and Isaac Asimov. Norton had written one book that had a title that stuck with me over the years. *The Beast Master* was written in 1959 and Andre Norton was a popular young-adult author of the time. *The Beast Master* told a somewhat wonky tale about a Navajo hero named Hosteen Storm with a telepathic link to a team of genetically altered animals. This "Beast

Master" and his crew are shipped out on a spaceship to an alien planet in another galaxy to herd livestock. Meanwhile, Earth is destroyed by an evil alien race. The intergalactic scale of this book was obviously a bit large for me, but could there be a way to tell this story on an earthbound budget? What about moving the setting from outer space to someplace more earthly? Perhaps the prehistory of the Bronze Age? Loincloths are certainly a lot cheaper than spacesuits.

On that flight home, the saga of the Beastmaster began as I furiously started jotting down the first outline on paper. Little did I know that this would be the beginning of an epic adventure for me that would be both thrilling and ridiculous, terrifying and heartbreaking, and that there would be wonderful and disastrous consequences for my filmmaking career.

WELCOME TO THE JUNGLE

B ack in Los Angeles, I got right to work, teaming up with the very capable Paul Pepperman to cowrite the screenplay for *The Beastmaster*. Paul had never written a screenplay before, but on my first three films he had served in almost every other capacity. His knowledge of movies and movie history was vast, plus he understood what I was shooting for storywise and started pitching great plot ideas immediately. It was going to be a great collaboration.

I think our basic mantra in writing this story was to meld the heroism and honor of a Japanese samurai film with the fun and sentimentality of a Disney animal movie. As a kid I was a huge fan of what were pejoratively referred to as "sword and sandal" movies. The muscular actor Steve Reeves starred in many of my favorites, including *Hercules, Hercules Unchained,* and *Goliath and the Barbarians*. The plots were always the same—one powerfully built lone warrior rallies the repressed people to overthrow the bad guys. *The Beastmaster* would tell the tale of this lone warrior, his entire home village slaughtered by marauding barbarians. On his trail of revenge, he would discover an innate ability to communicate with animals and create a clever and robust fighting force consisting of himself, a black panther, a brown eagle, and two cunning ferrets. Storming pyramids, battling hordes, and saving damsels in distress would ensue. On paper it was perfect.

One would think that after directing a horror film with such worldwide critical and box office success, I would have been inundated with offers from

Hollywood to finance my next film. Unfortunately, this was far from the case. I'm still not certain if it was the slow regional rollout of *Phantasm* or the fact that the distribution was handled by an indie distributor like Avco Embassy, but its success did not seem to resonate much with the Hollywood powers-that-be. I received a few oddball horror offers to direct films like *Death Ship* and *The Beast Within,* but nothing mainstream from a studio. I guess it was a different time. There was no Sundance Film Festival yet, and the major agencies were remnants of the old guard; nobody was chasing independent directors the way it's done now. I never imagined that finding the funding for *The Beastmaster* would be so difficult, but it certainly was. An entire year would ensue of seeking funding and waiting for studios and investors to decide the fate of this film.

One of the first places we solicited was the Walt Disney Studios. A forward-thinking executive over there had contacted me with the intent of bringing in different types of filmmakers than the company traditionally worked with. It sounded like a solid plan: *The Beastmaster* was probably the tamest, most family-friendly project I had ever worked on. The executive was able to set up a meeting for Paul and me with the man who had inherited control of the studio when Walt Disney had died. The president of the studio was now Walt's son-in-law, Ron Miller. It was our first time on the Disney lot and wow, was that ever fun! We headed up Snow White Boulevard, hooked a left on Minnie Avenue, a right on Dopey Drive, and we arrived at the Animation Building where the executive offices were. We were escorted into Mr. Miller's spacious office and introduced.

Tall and athletic, Ron Miller had starred at USC on the football team, married Walt's daughter Diane, then played a season with the Los Angeles Rams before joining Disney. As Paul and I made our pitch to Miller and his brain trust, we could quickly tell that it was falling on deaf ears. This caused us to push harder and we genuinely sold our hearts out. Unfortunately we were wasting our time pitching to this crippled regime, which was just two years away from being ousted by Walt's other side of the family and strong new management. Disney was still making G-rated films at this time—the entire company was reputed to be suffering from hardening of the arteries and a general lack of direction and creativity. At that point, the prospect of Disney Studios financing a film that had any swordplay or barbarian hordes was remote, despite the animal content. Ron told us so directly. We submitted the screenplay anyway and received an official pass a few days later. This was again another case proving that nobody knows anything. Walt's son-in-law couldn't visualize it, but *The Beastmaster* would go on to solid financial success and spawn two sequels and a television series.

We approached a contact at MGM. They read the script but their response was not what we were expecting. They described *The Beastmaster* as "an interesting piece of juvenilia, but not for us." The rejections were getting me worried.

We even tried going back to our old stomping grounds at Avco Embassy Pictures. In the intervening two years, the success of *Phantasm* had not only brought Avco back to financial health but had also introduced them to an entirely new business model. Avco Embassy was now known as the "House of Horror." After *Phantasm* showed the way, Avco Embassy distributed a slate of modestly budgeted genre films to great success, including John Carpenter's *The Fog* and *Escape From New York,* as well as *Prom Night, Scanners,* and *The Howling.* Figuring the perfect place for us would be back with the gents we teamed up with on our last movie, Paul and I scheduled a meeting with Bob Rehme, who had so capably masterminded the successful distribution of *Phantasm.*

We gave Bob the pitch and told him we would be willing to make our epic on a very lean budget. In the meeting we were stunned to learn that Rehme and his Avco Embassy team had decided to give the *Beastmaster* project the thumbs-down. All he would offer was that if we could raise the funding to make the film independently, Avco would be happy to distribute the film for us, but they would not be able to invest any money in the production. This response was extremely disappointing. I felt we had taken a genuine risk in putting our faith in a failing company with some likeable and enterprising executives by licensing *Phantasm* to them for no up-front money. That risk paid off handsomely for both of us, and in the process *Phantasm* saved their company. Now that Avco Embassy was back in the black, they were funding movies for a lot of other filmmakers but, for some unknown reason, they would not return the courtesy to me. I refused to let this series of rejections diminish my faith in the project. I firmly believed I could make a great film of *The Beastmaster,* I just needed to find a way to get some money.

Paul and I went back to the drawing board and started rethinking *The Beastmaster.* Could we make it on a lower budget as an indie film? Coincidentally, an international distributor who had been very successful distributing *Phantasm* in France and Germany approached us. He wanted to know what my next project was. Paul set up a meeting for us with this man at his estate up in Bel Air, an opulent section of Los Angeles adjoining Beverly Hills. I didn't know it then, but this meeting would lead to *The Beastmaster* getting made—and at the same time almost destroy my career.

CLICK, CLACK, CLICK, CLACK. The first thing I noticed about our future financier of *The Beastmaster* was the annoying clatter of the worry beads he was fingering in his hands at all times. Whenever we met with him, he would be running these damn wooden beads through a string on his finger and making that irritating noise. His mansion was on the north side of Sunset Boulevard with a sweeping view of the Bel Air Country Club. He was of Lebanese descent and had married an heiress to a German beverage fortune. He was loaded. As we were ushered into his gaudy living room to discuss the project, the first thing I noticed, other than the sound of his beads, was an odd sculpture that depicted a small telescope peering up into a statue's naked human ass. To this day I'm still pondering the meaning of it.

Our moneyman introduced himself by telling us of his path into the movie business as a director much like myself, describing himself as one of the greatest television commercial directors in Lebanon. Paul and I started referring to him as the Commercial Director (CD). He also told us that he had made a lot of money distributing *Phantasm* in Europe. The CD said he liked our screenplay and believed he could secure funding for it from overseas. Then he brought up the title of a movie that would bedevil *The Beastmaster* until this very day.

"I hear that Italian producer Dino De Laurentiis is moving into production on *Conan the Barbarian,* starring Arnold Schwarzenegger. The timing is perfect for your film." From a financial perspective this man was right. There was only one *Conan* movie, and in every international territory there would be other distributors who wanted to get into the resurgence of the sword and sandal business. Once we agreed to financial terms he smartly attended the inaugural edition of the American Film Market in Los Angeles in order to license out international distribution on a territory-by-territory basis. He had an excellent market there and sold out the world distribution rights to *The Beastmaster,* gaining significant financial commitments.

I need to pause this narrative right here and explain some facts about something I believe I have been unfairly accused of. Due to the unfortunate coincidence of *The Beastmaster* being released *three months* after *Conan the Barbarian, The Beastmaster* was immediately, and forever, branded as a "*Conan* rip-off" by ignorant reviewers and imitative commentators. How could one ever write, direct, film, edit, and release a film in three months? It's not physically possible.

As I write this today I am placing my right hand on a copy of the Bible and I hereby swear to you dear readers: I have never in my life read a book or comic book written by Conan author Robert E. Howard, including *Conan the Barbarian,* nor have I ever read any of the literary adaptations of his work. I never read the John Milius and Oliver Stone script for *Conan the Barbarian.* I didn't see Milius's *Conan the Barbarian* movie until July of the year it was released, which was well *after The Beastmaster* was completely finished. I did see a few of Frank Frazetta's epic Conan paintings, but frankly I was more influenced by his non-Conan paintings, of which there are many brilliant examples. Both *Beastmaster* and *Conan* of course follow the traditional "hero's journey," or monomyth, as espoused by mythologist Joseph Campbell, as do many popular films (including *Star Wars*). There are many significant differences from *Conan,* including the Beastmaster's unique ability of communicating with other species and the allied concept of reliance on a fighting team composed of animals. In addition, our hero is not a hulking, monosyllabic thug but an earnest young man, quite inquisitive and loquacious, who is trying to make sense out of his life and to do the right thing. All right, I am certain Wm. Shakespeare is now calling to me from his grave telling me that *I doth protest too much.* But when you endure the agony I did to finish a movie on the epic scale of *The Beastmaster,* with less than a quarter of the budget of *Conan the Barbarian,* and then to have it casually and constantly dismissed as a *Conan* rip-off, it really hurts. *The Beastmaster* may be a movie with serious flaws, I will cop to that, but it is not a fucking *Conan* rip-off!

I am very sorry for this rant. Let's continue and I'll try not to interrupt again . . .

From the outset, Paul and I could sense that we might have made an error in entrusting the funding of our film to the Commercial Director. The creative interference started immediately in casting. I asked that we make an offer to the great German actor Klaus Kinski to play Maax, the villain of our movie. We heard back that Kinski's price was five thousand dollars more than our budget for his role. I asked that we raise our offer and promised I would find a way to offset his cost somewhere else in the budget. My request was denied.

The next hint that there might be problems was more troubling. It came to be known as the black eye incident. The CD had hired an assistant named Jeff as "president of production" for his company. It was Jeff's job to supervise Paul and me, and also the other film their company had in production. That film was a very low-budget affair about a kid who could summon demons and cast spells using his desktop computer. Evidently there were problems in the shooting of that movie and Jeff was sent to the set to meet with the director. Jeff came back the next day to the office with a big black shiner on one of his eyes. He told us the director had punched him. Jeff was a friendly guy and was probably just relaying an unwelcome message to the director from his boss, who, I guess, was more than happy to let Jeff be the punching bag. Evidently the contents of that message were so inflammatory they caused the director to erupt like a volcano and punch the messenger. Was I going to be getting messages like that too?

When we made *The Beastmaster,* digital visual effects were not possible due to the very limited processing power of the computers at that time. Consequently, all that animal action implied in the title would have to be done the old-fashioned way, with trained animals. But could we get the featured animals to perform the action as the screenplay described? Paul and I started interviewing animal trainers and learned a surprising fact. These animals we wanted to feature could not really be taught any tricks. They would go to where the food was. That was it. And if they weren't hungry, then shooting would be over for the day.

We wanted to be mindful of animal safety and selected a talented and well-respected animal trainer by the name of Steve Martin, who had a company called Working Wildlife. Steve conceded that it would be a big challenge to get his black panther to do all the action required, but felt with enough lead time and a few trims to the script it probably could be accomplished. We gave Steve the go-ahead and he started lining up the animals. About this time our moneyman intervened again. He had been at dinner with a film producer he knew who recommended a friend of his who was an animal trainer. We tried to explain to the CD that we already had secured the services of an excellent trainer and wanted to stick with him. Again, we were ignored; Steve Martin was unceremoniously sacked and the new trainer was hired in his place. The new trainer insisted that we replace the panther with a tiger as he told us they were easier to train. He informed us that the tiger could be easily dyed black to appear like a panther and that he just happened to have access to four mature tigers. I would have preferred featuring the black panther as originally intended, but I had been removed from the animal decision-making process.

From the outset, *The Beastmaster* was intended as an epic-size film, made on a minimal budget. We quickly determined that we would need to shoot in our backyard of Southern California and that we needed some inexpensive but resourceful collaborators.

At first we tried to make the movie *Phantasm*-style and were lucky to bring our longtime collaborator Roberto Quezada on board as production supervisor. Then we started scouring the local film schools to seek out hungry young talent. One of our first hires was Frank K. Isaac Jr., a recent film school grad from USC who was resourceful, hardworking, and bright. We immediately assigned Frank to supervise our makeup effects crew. Our film required a huge amount of prosthetic effects, and Paul and I had taken a risk on a skilled artist who had no experience supervising an entire film. Deadlines were being missed and the entire project was put in jeopardy. Within a couple of weeks Frank, just out of film school, had to personally fire that entire crew, secure and remove the molds and other work-to-date, and then interview and hire an entire replacement effects team. It was a trial by fire but Frank stood strong. We immediately rewarded him with a battlefield promotion to assistant producer.

Roberto and assistant Daniel Peterson went to work searching for someplace to shoot our Bronze Age production. Right out of the box they hit the jackpot, stumbling upon a ranch on the northwest side of Simi Valley just forty miles from Los Angeles. The property had almost every exterior location we needed—a huge desert bowl surrounded by towering cliffs where we could build the massive pyramid called for in the screenplay, and small microclimates throughout the place with different types of geography and vegetation. Paul struck an incredible deal with the owners of the property, the Union Oil Company. Union agreed to give us access to the entire ten-thousand-acre parcel for almost a year at the meager price of just a thousand dollars a month. Roberto and Dan then went on an extended scout of Arizona and Nevada for more exotic locations, with the idea that the production could travel there for just a couple of days. They found several spectacular locations at the Valley of Fire State Park outside Las Vegas and on the Arizona side of the Colorado River just north of Willow Beach. We now had a smart low-budget plan in place to shoot the bulk of our film interiors in a warehouse in North Hollywood, most of our exteriors in nearby Simi Valley, and a very short road trip for scenics on the Nevada/Arizona border.

The Beastmaster required some serious world-building. In addition to the many interior sets the screenplay also required several massive outdoor constructs including the walled city of Aruk and Dar's home village-on-stilts, Emur. Our production designer, Conrad E. Angone, worked round-the-clock with his team of craftspeople to accomplish this feat. They built a huge city gate with bridge and surrounding tar moat. The centerpiece of the city was an immense pyramid, which Conrad cleverly built around an existing hill on the Union Oil property. I gave Conrad some photos of the great Mayan pyramid at Tikal and told him, "Build us something like this." And he did. It was a simply magnificent set, with one flaw. Much of the action took place on the pyramid steps and to get the grand vertical appearance of the Tikal pyramid, the steps up the front had to be very narrow.

Climbing up the pyramid for the crew was a terrifying experience. Most of us had to crawl on our hands and knees to get to the top. With my size 12 shoes I was no exception. To choreograph a swordfight on those steps would be insanity. The problem was solved when we found an actor to play the Beastmaster who had the athletic agility to run up those steps, swinging a sword all the way.

One of the greatest hires of *The Beastmaster* was our terrific, Academy Award–winning cinematographer, John Alcott. After doing the cinematography on my first three films and essentially learning on the job as I did it myself, I was simply thrilled at the prospect of working with John and learning from him. John was Stanley Kubrick's loyal go-to lighting cameraman. He took over from Geoffrey Unsworth and shot a large chunk of my favorite film, *2001: A Space Odyssey*. He photographed spectacular Kubrick classics like *A Clockwork Orange* and *The Shining*. In 1976 John was honored with an Academy Award for his cinematography on *Barry Lyndon,* arguably one of the most gorgeous films ever shot. When I learned that John had left the employ of Kubrick and was shooting an indie horror flick up in Montreal, I put Paul and Frank on the case. Within days John was signed on and ready to move out to shoot his first film in Hollywood . . . well, in close proximity anyway.

On the surface, John was a quiet man, very laid-back, but inside he had a steel spine and would not brook any inattention or mistakes from his camera crew. There was an "upstairs/downstairs" level of discipline that he expected, and in his quiet way he would train his assistants like a drill sergeant. I noticed it that first day at lunch. During the lunch break, before they were allowed to eat, his camera assistants would scramble to serve John and his camera operator Doug O'Neons their meal on a table in the camera truck. Once I even noticed a camera assistant making like a sommelier and pouring them wine from a bottle into wineglasses. It was all very upper crust.

John was a master of shooting in low light. He loved the shallow depth-of-field this style created, which he used to great effect in his classic *Barry Lyndon*. John brought along a special briefcase to the set, and one day I looked inside to find dozens of small flashlights of varying sizes and wattages. He liked to augment the actor eyelights with these flashlights. Frequently during a shot there would be John, with one of his small flashlights in hand, aiming at the actor's face, providing just a glint of additional light in their eyes. John also taught me about what he called "negative light." He would use black surfaces and place them near to the actor's face to absorb light. For years I had been working with reflected light but had never even thought to try this opposite subtractive technique.

Working with John were the best times I had on *The Beastmaster*. With him it was always about creativity and hard work with a shared artistic goal. Not everyone on this huge crew would be as like-minded as John. There would be serious—and for me, unimaginable—challenges ahead.

WHY I NEVER SIT IN A DIRECTOR'S CHAIR

I can never allow myself to sit in a director's chair on a movie set. Standing is a good thing. There are lots of reasons to stand. For one, when you are shooting a major stunt scene, especially one including colliding cars or explosions, it's smart to stay on your feet. If something goes awry, which occasionally does happen, you can run like hell. When working with the large cats, the lions and tigers, the trainers always remind us that it is a smart idea to stay on your feet. Tigers and panthers love to jump things that are smaller than they are. This rationale behind standing in regard to the big cats actually eludes me. If you have ever witnessed the speed at which a great cat can strike, you will understand that whether you sit, stand, or climb a tree, it's all meaningless. If a tiger wants to get you, it will get you.

An excellent reason to stand is to speed up the day's work. I always park myself right beside the camera so everyone can see that the director is ready to go. He's not in meetings with the producer, looking at his script, or reading his email. He's on his feet at the center of the set, at attention, engaged; he wants to get the damn shot. But none of these are the real reasons why I never sit on a movie set.

The reason I stand is because of something that happened on *The Beastmaster*.

Actors require a lot of attention. But that is the job description of the director. To attend to the actor, to explain the scene and character in a way they can understand, to guide and counsel them through the challenges, assist with selecting wardrobe and props, and generally to help them to create the magic of bringing a character to life. With many actors this can be the best part of making a movie. Most actors are truly creative souls that love nothing more than exploring a new character in detail and preparing themselves for shooting. Doing this kind of work with committed actors is a pure joy.

With *The Beastmaster,* I had cast actor Marc Singer in the lead role of Dar. (I named the character after my best friend from childhood, Dar Horn.) I looked at a lot of talent, and I selected Marc because I had seen him portray Petruchio in an American Conservatory Theater production of *The Taming of the Shrew* on public television. In that role he had an energetic and comedic interpretation of Shakespeare, along with a stunning physique. Marc had a body that would rival even my childhood bodybuilding actor favorite, Steve Reeves. He was perfect for *The Beastmaster.*

Marc had been doing some serious workouts in preparation for the role. That first day he appeared on set for his first scene—muscles glistening in his studded, leather-skirt wardrobe—everything just stopped. You could hear a pin drop. Men, women, children all stared in awe at this god of a man who had muscles where one didn't even know there could be muscles. We had us a Beastmaster all right!

For some unknown reason Marc and I did not quite click. When he was first suggested for the role, I was Marc's biggest booster. Once I met him and saw how talented he was, I championed him relentlessly for the role. Despite some reservations by our producers, I still managed to cast him in our film. As part of his deal, Marc was booked for a couple of weeks of rehearsal prior to the start of production, but for some reason he was reluctant to meet with me. His agent finally did get him in for some meetings but I was worried he was having second thoughts about the role.

Things started to get odd on the very first day of filming. We were filming a sequence in which the Beastmaster was trapped in quicksand. The special effects team had sunken a tub in the ground and filled it with water, with a layer of vermiculite floating on the surface to mimic the quicksand. They even had a heating system so the water would be temperate for the actor. Marc was in the quicksand, we got several great takes of his close-up, and it was time to move on. Marc stopped the crew and insisted on another take. For a moment it felt like my authority as director was being questioned. There was no need for another take. But I let it pass, gave him another take, and that was it.

Things escalated on the second or third day of shooting when Marc interrupted me while I was speaking with our moneyman. He approached us and began complaining to the Commercial Director about how I didn't spend enough time discussing the character with him. I had a sense from early on that my status in keeping my directing job was tenuous at best and ridiculous statements like these from the lead actor were just the sort of thing that could get me canned.

A day or two later, still in the early days of shooting, we were filming the battle sequence involving the destruction of the Beastmaster's home village. I set up a shot requiring Marc to dash through the devastation. I was watching the scene unfold from a tall director's chair just beside the camera operator.

I called for action and on cue Marc ran toward camera. The horses and extras were in perfect position and his performance was right on. It was a great take, except for one thing. The Beastmaster cleared the camera lens, but never stopped running. He hurtled directly at me going full speed and WHAM! He smashed into me and knocked me clean out of my chair. I tumbled backward and hit the ground hard in a cloud of dust with, surprise, the grinning Marc right on top of me. Why would he do this? As I got to my feet, dusted myself off, and checked my skinned elbows, there stood the Beastmaster laughing as I became the butt of his "joke" in front of the crew. He gave an excuse that he was so focused on the scene and "in the moment" that he just didn't see me. Was this guy fucking with me? Or was he trying to undercut my authority, literally? In any case, that's where I developed my aversion to director's chairs.

BEASTMASTER UNCHAINED

Actors generally are in a strange predicament. Before filming, they have no power whatsoever. They are begging for a job. Once they are cast, and once shooting starts, they are basically irreplaceable and have all the power. That is why it is so rare to hear of a film firing a starring actor once they are well into production. It just is not done. Alfred Hitchcock summed it up ruefully: "Disney has the best casting. If he doesn't like an actor, he just tears them up."

Things devolved as production went on. We were filming an elaborate water sequence on Pyramid Lake in which the entire team of actors—and the animals—float down a river on an ornate dragon raft. As was our practice we shot out all the actors first, prior to involving animals. Marc and the lead actress performed a cute, flirty scene, with the other actors looking on from the back of the raft. It all went well and then it was time to bring in the tiger. In retrospect, I probably should have nicely asked the actors if they would mind waiting on the raft while we motored back to shore in the speedboat to grab the big cat. Instead, as we sped off, I called over my shoulder, "We'll be right back with the tiger!" I guess this didn't sit well with my star. It also didn't help that as soon as we departed our assistant director announced lunch was being served. I later heard that Marc flagged down a nearby fisherman and forced him to motor the Beastmaster back to shore.

Paul and I jumped off the speedboat and hustled to the animal training area, intent on getting the big animal on the boat quickly. I remember sensing the earth move and hearing some loud thumping noises behind us, but didn't think much of it. I had no way of knowing that the Beastmaster was angrily charging at us. WHAP! Suddenly I was grabbed from behind and lifted in the air. Stunned, I looked over to see Paul dangling beside me. The Beastmaster had us in his clutches and was shaking us like rag dolls. He was screaming, "Don't you *ever* leave me behind again!" For a moment, Paul and I were stunned as it sunk in that we were being physically manhandled and, even worse, humiliated in front of the very large crew by this angry, muscle-bound actor. It's an extremely rare occurrence for an actor to physically grab a director or producer in Hollywood. When it finally sunk in what was happening to us, Paul and I were livid and tried to retaliate. Normally, a producer and director would never wish ill will on their lead actor, especially one whose scenes had not yet been finished. After months of very difficult shooting we both just snapped. We had to take this guy down.

One problem. He was the Beastmaster and we were not.

It was like swatting at King Kong. For months the Beastmaster had exercised himself into tip-top physical shape. The dude was a physical specimen, while Paul and I descended into a stress-filled nightmare of a long shoot with bad food and no sleep. Our muscles were atrophying while his were growing stronger! Finally he showed us some mercy and literally tossed us to the ground. Paul and I tumbled to an unceremonious heap in the dust, still both cursing up a blue streak at him. The Beastmaster turned and stomped away.

Later, after Paul had called and yelled at Marc's agent and we all had settled down somewhat, there was a knock at the production trailer door. It opened and there was Marc, standing alone in the doorway like a forlorn child. "I need a hug," was all he said. So Paul and I did the only thing we could possibly do under the circumstances to keep the project moving forward. We swallowed our pride, stepped out of the trailer, and in view of the entire crew we received a big bear hug from the Beastmaster.

Despite all of my gripes, I still believe Marc was the right choice for the role. His natural on-screen charm and terrific physical performance were key elements of the film's success. His dedication to learning the intricacy of the swordplay and working with the animals was unwavering. Marc breathed life into a character that ultimately resonated with an entire generation of cable TV–watching kids. He's also the only person I've ever met who could wear a leather skirt and make it look macho.

THE LAST CHARLIE'S ANGEL

was intent on finding an actress for the Beastmaster's love interest who had the physical skills necessary to handle the required stunt work and who could also bring some sort of reality to the enslaved princess role as described in our screenplay. I interviewed a lot of actresses and none seemed right. Time was getting short when one of our assistants suggested we meet an eighteen-year-old aspiring actress he knew who was married to a rocker friend of his. The guy raved about her. I was told she was looking for her first movie role and so, despite her inexperience, we brought her in. She was terrific. I was hooked and wanted her for the role. She was a slim brunette with a surprisingly smoky voice for such a young woman. Her name was Demi Moore.

We quickly scheduled a callback so we could get the Commercial Director's approval. Demi came back and gave another reading for him, which was even better than the first. I looked over to Paul and he shot me an approving nod. Bingo! Then, after some rumination and worry bead clacking, the CD weighed in and made his decision known that we would not cast this young woman. He told us that he had consulted with experts and was told her voice was too deep and low to be picked up by the microphones and recorded. Paul and I just sat there dumbfounded.

Our moneyman wanted to see another actress, one that the major talent agency CAA was pitching to him. A couple days later, Paul and I drove in to his office to meet her. When we arrived we learned that her name was

Tanya Roberts. What? *The* Tanya Roberts from the cheesy television series *Charlie's Angels*? You had to be kidding. None of the Angels were considered great actresses, and Tanya's reviews when she debuted as the newest Charlie's Angel were not the best. However, the CD was not particularly familiar with American TV so our complaints fell on deaf ears. Tanya was surprisingly nice and certainly one of the most amazing beauties any of us had ever seen, but once she walked into the room, the executive producer was instantly smitten and she was cast.

So, no Klaus Kinski and no Demi Moore. As for me, I had no choice but to deal with it.

My backup choice for the evil villain Maax was Rip Torn. Rip was one of the truly great stage and movie actors to come out of Lee Strasberg's Actors Studio in the late 1950s. Before I was making films I had seen his towering performance in his critically acclaimed indie film *Payday*. Rip was notorious for his irascibility and our moneyman had concerns about my ability to handle him at my young age of twenty-seven. What I learned quickly was that Rip didn't need to be "handled." I treated him respectfully and he did the same with me. (There's a good lesson there.) Paul and I became great friends with Rip. After the movie was finished we would meet him out in Malibu for frequent sushi lunches. After *The Beastmaster,* Rip went on to great commercial success, starring in *Men in Black* and receiving an Emmy for his superb comedic work on *The Larry Sanders Show.*

Before we settled on the great John Amos to play the role of the young king's man-at-arms Seth, there was an unknown, aspiring Chicago actor we interviewed for this *Beastmaster* role. I first saw him in a trailer for his upcoming first movie and he looked fantastic. Paul and I got the production to fly Laurence Tureaud out to Los Angeles to audition, but before we did so, I wanted to see him on film. We were alerted to a technical screening of his new movie that was scheduled to screen over at MGM. A friendly postproduction exec asked the director if Paul and I could sit in for the purpose of evaluating the actor and he said okay. Pretty cool because the director was Sylvester Stallone. Paul and I kept a low profile in the back of the screening room as Sly bantered with the editors and gave notes to composer Bill Conti while they watched *Rocky III*. Laurence, under his screen name of Mr. T, gave a ferocious performance in the role of Clubber Lang. Excited by seeing his film work, we paid for Mr. T to travel to Los Angeles for an interview.

Despite the incredibly intimidating presence he created on-screen, Mr. T was reserved and gentle in person. His neck was loaded with his trademark gold chains, but he was a genuinely nice guy. *Rocky III* was his first acting role and he said he was appreciative of Mr. Stallone taking a chance on him. I asked if he was going to do any sightseeing while in Los Angeles, and he said no, he would return to his hotel room and spend some time with his Bible. We asked him to read for the role and he performed the scenes capably, and of course his look was fantastic. Why then did we not cast him?

When we were writing *The Beastmaster* we fell into the same trap every writer seems to when writing screen stories based in prehistory or fantasy. These genres all appear to demand "arch" Shakespearean dialog, preferably delivered with that quasi-British accent. Why? You got me there. You can hear it in all the sword and sorcery films from that time and even more recently in the *Lord of the Rings,* the *Hobbit,* and the *Game of Thrones* franchises. None of them are set in Shakespearean England but they all sound like they should be. So without conscious thought about it, I just bought into this conceit and could not imagine casting an actor in my film who was more comfortable speaking in a Chicago "street" patois. In the audition I tried to guide Mr. T into that style of delivery, but he probably thought my direction was idiotic. In any case, we passed on Mr. T and instead went with a much more seasoned actor in John Amos, who was absolutely terrific in the role.

I can only imagine what Mr. T might have said a few years later about his experience auditioning for *The Beastmaster*—probably something like, "I pity those poor fools who rejected me for *The Beastmaster* so I could join *The A-Team* and become the biggest star on TV!" And he would be right.

THE DAY I QUIT *THE BEASTMASTER*

The Beastmaster ended up being my Waterloo. The night before shooting started, when most financiers would ring up and give you a few words of encouragement, like "I hope your shoot goes well," I too received such a call, with a few extra words tacked on. "I hope your shoot goes well, and if not, I will replace you." Great motivation, eh?

During the first week of shooting, things were pretty rocky. The "brain trust" (and I use that term loosely) came very close to firing cameraman John Alcott due to some focus issues with the anamorphic lenses. Anamorphic lenses are a very traditional motion picture tool that squeeze a wide-screen image onto standard 35 mm film; the anamorphic projection lens then unsqueezes the image onto the screen in the theater. Without my consultation, or John's approval, they decided to scrap the first two days of shooting and switch to a standard lens system. (Later, when they realized their mistake and refused to pay for a reshoot, they optically unsqueezed that footage and actually used it in the finished film. Check out the sequence in which young Dar is threatened by the bear—to this day it still looks visually god-awful.) To second-guess one of the greatest cinematographers in movie history about lens choice was an ill-advised and fatuous move.

A couple of days later word came down that I was officially in the doghouse. Our moneyman intimated that I would probably be fired as director of *The Beastmaster*. This idea that I could be fired seemed ludicrous, but after battling on so many creative fronts during preproduction, including the casting issues, the unilateral dialog rewriting going on in secret by the CD and some writer he had hired, and the forced change in animal trainers, I tended to ignore these rumors. I knew the situation was really bad, but I was facing seventy-two days of shooting on a six-day-per-week shooting schedule, mostly outdoors in the elements. I was just trying to keep my head above water and get through each day of work. We were shooting full twelve-hour days, so with lunch, the hour commute each way to the Simi Valley location, and the production meetings before and after work, I was averaging barely four hours of sleep per night, if I was lucky. On top of that I was sick—I had developed pneumonia and was living on antibiotics. Due to stress I wouldn't shake it for two full months.

To make matters worse, just prior to shooting, the CD had fired his assistant producer (remember Jeff, the guy with the black eye?) and then brought on a replacement, a new hatchet man to keep Paul and me in line. This new guy enjoyed his newfound sense of power and disrupted everything. All of the crew that Paul and I had meticulously hired were now in jeopardy of losing their jobs. He didn't know it at the time, but this hatchet man would, of course, ultimately find his own head on the chopping block as well. That was just the way our moneyman rolled.

Frequently, the CD would take over my office at our North Hollywood warehouse/stage while I was out shooting and use it as his own. Coming back after work one night after a long shooting day, I discovered a casually abandoned note on my desk with a list of replacement directors scribbled on it, along with their financial quotes. (Their fees were a helluva lot higher than what I was earning!) Was it forgotten? Or was it left there deliberately for me to see?

At the end of our first week of shooting, my cinematographer, John Alcott, got wind of the fact that production had decided to fire me. For reasons known only to him, John objected. Vociferously. John, without my knowledge, let it be known to production that if I were to be fired, he would immediately quit *The Beastmaster*. Despite the fact that John had relocated his entire family to Los Angeles, leased a house, and enrolled his son Gavin in school here. It was hard to believe John would suffer such financial hardship and disruption to his family's long-term plans just for the sake of a twenty-seven-year-old film director he'd only known for a few weeks. From that point on I intimately understood why, whenever I would see press about his career, John Alcott was always referred to as "Stanley Kubrick's loyal cinematographer." The operative and truthful word there was "loyal." John was one stand-up guy and I will always be grateful to him for that.

I made it through the first week of shooting and then, late on that Saturday night, I received the expected phone call. The CD was on the line and told me that after watching the film we had shot to date, he had decided that I did not know how to shoot action. I found myself in the humbled position of trying to protest to him that my previous film *Phantasm* was chock-full of great action and had been a critical and box office success. He simply ignored me and went on to say that he had magnanimously decided not to fire me (thank you again, John Alcott!) and instead had decided to hire a stunt director to oversee my action work. Of course I immediately objected vehemently and was informed by him that if I chose not to work with this man I would be summarily fired. I shot back that I was a Directors Guild member (DGA) and they would not allow him to force someone on me like that. (This turned out to be untrue; I later found out there were no DGA provisions that would protect me in this case.) The CD told me it was my choice, I would follow his instructions, or he would fire me. He gave me this guy's phone number and told me to call him.

Chuck Bail had a storied career as a stuntman and then migrated to actor and then director. He had a big success with his third film, directing the entertaining cross-country car chase film *The Gumball Rally.* His other credits were directing two of the so-called blaxploitation films, *Black Samson* and *Cleopatra Jones and the Casino of Gold.* He was also a longtime confidant and stunt coordinator for esteemed director Richard Rush. I called Chuck's number. He said we should meet and he volunteered to come pick me up.

When Chuck arrived at my house in Sherman Oaks, he was driving a 1955 Mercedes 300 SL with the futuristic gullwing doors. It was the first and only time I ever rode in one of these vintage, high-performance sports cars that today sell for well over a million dollars. On the drive I learned that Chuck also owned a Stearman PT-17 biplane, which he bought directly from his pal, actor Steve McQueen. Chuck was a big, larger-than-life, handsome guy with a disarming sense of humor. He hailed from Texas and broke into Westerns in the mid-1950s as a stuntman. He worked in television and films over the next two decades along with other stunt performers who later moved into directing, such as Hal Needham of *Smokey and the Bandit* fame. We drove over to our North Hollywood warehouse stage and I showed him around the *Beastmaster* interior sets. Chuck told me he was happy to get the gig and would enjoy helping me out with the movie.

I mulled it over that Sunday night. I was angry and frustrated. On my previous films the investors had no creative say whatsoever and I could make the films I wanted, the way I wanted. The call time Monday morning was at 6:00 a.m. I stayed up that entire night (which is a terrible thing to do when you are directing a picture) and after much soul-searching I made the decision to quit the film. I was not going to suffer the humiliation of being forced to have some random stunt director looking over my shoulder while I worked.

After my hour-long predawn commute, I arrived at our Simi Valley location up in Tapo Canyon Park. We were prepping to shoot the sequence in which Marc Singer uses his tiger to scare Tanya Roberts into falling into his arms. As I walked to the set I was assaulted by questions from the crew: "Where do you want the camera, Don?" "Don, do you understand that due to the cold temperature the tiger will be frisky and we all must stay on our toes?" "Tanya is having a wardrobe issue and we need you, Don." This is standard operating procedure for a director. In the mornings everybody has questions about the day's work and it's important to get those questions answered quickly and efficiently. It was a nice feeling to just ignore everybody. I wasn't directing this damn movie anymore because I was on my way to fucking quit. First stop, Chuck Bail.

I walked over to Chuck. "I need to talk to you." "What's up, Don?" "Chuck, I've thought it over and I've decided to quit the show."

"Wa-wa-wa-wait a second there, buddy." Chuck quickly slid his arm in mine and surreptitiously guided me around a stand of trees to where we could have some privacy. Chuck's intent, of course, was to stop me from quitting. But the most bizarre part of this conversation was that I had seen this movie before. Quite literally.

I don't know if I consciously remembered it at the time, but just the year previously Chuck Bail had a significant, featured acting role in Richard

Rush's classic film *The Stunt Man*. In that film actor Steve Railsback's character is on the run from police and hides out on a movie set run by a powerful and enigmatic film director played by Peter O'Toole. Throughout the film, as Railsback's life, reality, and even his sanity spin out of control, a sage and savvy stuntman is always there to take Steve under his wing, providing him guidance and counsel at critical moments. The memorable role of this important stuntman character was essentially a doppelgänger of Chuck Bail played by himself, only his on-screen name was Chuck Barton.

Now here I was at my wits' end and ready to quit my own movie, strung out just like actor Steve Railsback was in *The Stunt Man*. And right in my ear I can hear this same guy, "Chuck Barton," giving me confidence and hope. "Come on, Don. Don't do anything rash. This is gonna be a good picture. We've got a good gig here. It's your picture, I'll stay out of your way. I'm just here to help. Besides, it's a real good gig for me and I don't want to rock the boat. That executive producer of yours is paying me a hundred K to hang out in the trailer and be there when you need me. Plus he's buying me a new Cadillac for the wife."

I was thrown for a loop. I suddenly found myself as the protagonist in a Richard Rush film come to life. And Chuck Bail/Barton was convincing and assuring. I probably should have quit right there. But I didn't. I stayed on and finished the picture. To this day I still do not know if that was a good thing or a bad thing.

I actually learned a lot about the stunt world from Chuck Bail. Surprisingly, I ended up having a very cordial and easy working relationship with him. Having come up from Westerns his experience was invaluable since *The Beastmaster* was loaded with horse action. Chuck taught me how to work around horses without getting stepped on, which is a frequent director injury. He also taught me all about "falling horses." A rare few horses are born with the ability to lie down on cue. These horses are in huge demand; with a simple tug on their bridle, they will lie right down on the dirt. A good stuntman and falling horse can make it look like they've both been shot and get right up after the stunt with no injury. At that time stuntman Larry Randles owned the best falling horse in the business, and we were lucky to have him come work for us. The funny thing about these falling horses is that sometimes they are so prone to lying down that it can be hard to keep them on their feet. One day while we were waiting to set up a shot, I watched Larry try to ride his falling horse from the trailer to the set and the horse laid down and took him to the ground three times. Larry, muttering and cursing, finally had to get off and walk his horse over to the set.

Chuck also taught me a lot about working with stuntmen, being one himself. Sometimes I would get freaked when a stunt performer suffered a minor injury—and a *lot* of stuntmen suffered injuries on *The Beastmaster*. Chuck counseled me to not worry about it, as they were all skilled, knowledgeable, and very well-paid professionals. Chuck always said in reference to the injury, "Don't worry, they'll just rub money on it."

Practically every stuntman of note in Hollywood worked at some point on *The Beastmaster*. I learned from and worked with illustrious members of some of the legendary stunt families, including the Rondells, the Hookers, the Deadricks, and the Eppers.

Both Jeannie Epper and Tony Epper were featured in *The Beastmaster*. Jeannie is considered the greatest female stunt performer of all time and performed many dangerous gags doubling for Tanya. Her brother Tony portrayed the barbarian leader that Marc Singer battles on the fiery bridge in the finale. Choreographing that fight with Tony, Chuck, and stunt coordinator Steve Boyum was a genuine highlight. My brilliant production illustrator Nikita Knatz had designed the multibladed axe that Tony expertly wielded, and once he got that weapon flying through the air Marc Singer had to be quick on his feet to avoid a bloody haircut.

One of the major gags in *The Beastmaster* was blowing up the tar moat surrounding the walled city. The scene called for the barbarian horde on horseback to attempt to charge across the tar moat, and then for the townsfolk to ignite the oily contents. As written, the young prince Tal would run toward the moat with a torch but then go down with an arrow in his shoulder. The Beastmaster would vault over the gate, run to the stricken boy, grab his torch, and hurl it into the moat, which would cause the explosion. Tanya came to me and told me she felt that her character was left out of all the fun and wanted in on the action. I was also looking for something better, but stunt coordinator Steve Boyum was the one who came up with a terrific but complicated idea. Tanya would run to the stricken prince, grab the torch, and light a charging barbarian on fire; then the Beastmaster would leap through the air and kick the burning man into the tar moat, thereby igniting it.

Doing all of that at once seemed impossible and overwhelming, but directing is always about taking seemingly impossible sequences and carving them up into component shots that can convey the narrative—but are achievable. In fact, many of these component shots were very simple to shoot and we knocked those off quickly—the prince getting hit by the arrow, Tanya grabbing the torch, Marc Singer vaulting through the air. Now for the big enchilada: blowing up that tar moat.

I first met pyrotechnic effects wiz Roger George while working on *Phantasm*. We had to blow up a Cadillac hearse and Roger was recommended for the gag. He was a legendary special effects man and we were lucky to have him. The only thing that frankly was a bit odd about Roger was that when he first showed up on the set, one half of his face was seriously scarred from what appeared to be a pretty nasty burn. It actually gave us pause; there was concern as to whether he would be safe to work with. The cause of the burn was never revealed to us but I later heard a rumor that Roger was too close to a pyro charge that detonated prematurely. Roger had a jolly personality and he personally rigged the *Phantasm* hearse with black powder bombs, mortars, and lots of gasoline. Just before the take I saw Roger walking toward the hearse with a large package in his arms. He told me it was a "naphthalene bomb," which he had left over from a war movie he had been working on and that he had decided to place on the front seat of the hearse just for the hell of it. To say that Roger blew the bloody hell out of that *Phantasm* hearse is an understatement. Watch the movie and you can see the massive, fiery explosion he orchestrated.

For the tar moat explosion in *The Beastmaster* I wanted it done with the balls of that *Phantasm* blow, but times one hundred. So I, of course, hired Roger to do the pyro effects on *The Beastmaster*. Roger did not disappoint. He started with pipes submerged in the moat, through which diesel fuel would be pumped to bubble up through the water. For this one gag, Roger and his large crew of pyro techs placed dozens of steel mortars along the edge of the moat, each loaded with a black powder bomb topped with a bag containing several gallons of gasoline. It would be one hell of an explosion.

If you have watched any of my films you can quickly tell that I am in love with Hollywood movie fireballs. I try to put one in every movie (whether necessary or not!). Over the years I've worked with some great pyro effects technicians and in the process have learned that gasoline is definitely the only way to go. The black powder charge is simply used to lift the gasoline in the air, disperse it, and then, when it is fully atomized, ignite it. This creates the constantly expanding, roiling red-and-gold fireball effect. In colder weather the fireball stays low to the ground, and when warmer, it can lift very high. Prior to the shot, the challenge for the director and pyro tech is how to assess that temperature so as to correctly frame it for camera. Sometimes this just becomes a lucky guess, hoping the fireball won't just blow right through frame and not be visible. One hates to waste a good fireball!

Steve Boyum put together a crew of ace stunt players to double the actors in the explosion shot, including himself doubling for Marc, Jeannie Epper doubling for Tanya, and another legendary stuntman, Bob Minor, standing in for John Amos. A search was underway to find someone small enough to double our young prince. Steve finally found a volunteer, an ex-military, first-time stuntperson who was just diminutive enough to make a good match for young Josh Milrad. The challenge for all these stunt performers was that the actors were mostly clad in loincloths, so there could be no protective fire suits under their wardrobe. Usually for a fire gag, the stuntperson always wears a full Nomex fire-protective jumpsuit under the wardrobe. The only workaround was to cover the stunt players in Zel Jel, a specially designed and Academy Award–winning heat-absorbing gel that would allow them to get intimate with flames without their skin burning. The problem with the Zel Jel is that it sucked up heat, so once it was applied to bare skin, the stunt performers would quickly lose body heat. A funny thing I have noticed is that after burn stunts, the stunt performers will always be shivering—not because they are afraid, but because the Zel Jel causes hypothermia. These courageous folks brave not only fire but ice too, and frequently in the same gag. It was imperative that the Zel Jel be applied immediately before that shot, and there could be no delay.

John Alcott had five cameras in place to record the action. Everyone was ready and it was time to get serious. It sometimes feels a little morbid, but on major stunts it is essential to always have an ambulance with EMTs backed in as close to set as possible, doors wide open, engine running, with a clear path to the nearest highway. Our assistant director Jim Sbardellati gave the nod and the utility stunt guys started slathering gel on the stunt doubles. The set was cleared and Roger George armed his detonators. The stunt actors moved up to an area near the bridge that Roger had declared would be "safe" for them. Cameras started rolling and you could hear all the camera assistants screaming down the line, "A Camera speed! B Camera speed! C Camera speed! D Camera speed! E Camera speed!" It was time to shoot. Sbardellati cried, "Action!" into his megaphone.

Roger George thumbed the detonator and the night instantly turned to day. It was a simply humongous explosion and, amazingly, the stunt performers stood their ground. Well, three of them did. I later learned that the new stuntman, upon detonation, turned and ran for his life. And who could blame him? Roger George had created a veritable thermonuclear explosion right there on our set in Simi Valley. I felt the heat of the blast on my face and I was a good fifty yards away. Steve Boyum, doubling Marc Singer, heroically stayed right by the bridge alongside the stalwart Jeannie Epper, standing in for Tanya. The fearless Bob Minor, tracing John Amos's path, actually charged right toward the blast. Best of all, no one was injured despite the fact that after the blast, residual fiery debris rained down all around them. Once cut together it was the epic explosion sequence I always hoped for.

After we shot the explosion our fire work was by no means completed. Then followed a week of shooting action right beside the flaming moat. For a full week of nights we shot right in front of this flaming inferno as our heroes battled the marauding barbarian army. The actors had been especially bitter at the beginning of our shoot because they had to frequently work outside in cold windy weather wearing only skimpy loincloths. Frequently we had to interrupt takes due to their shivering. But for these night shoots, when Roger George lit the diesel jets, it warmed up quickly and you could actually see sweat on the actors' bare skin.

As we neared the end of the shoot we traveled to location on the Colorado River and the Valley of Fire for the final two days. Other than some scenic shots of the Beastmaster and his animal team running through the majestic rock formations, on the last day there we had two major sequences to film. One was the finale sequence in which Tanya surprises Marc and they embrace at the end of the film. The other was a vision sequence in which the Beastmaster sees through his eagle's eyes some of the bad guys transporting Tanya along the cliffs of the river. The challenge was that both scenes needed to be shot in late afternoon and the locations were eighty-seven miles apart.

The final sequence was shot at one of the most beautiful locations on the planet, Rainbow Vista, in the Valley of Fire State Park. John Alcott worked his magic that day to achieve some stunning imagery as Dar and his black tiger crest a rise and reunite with Tanya. As they kiss, my shot list called for a helicopter shot as the eagle swoops in over them and we witness their embrace through its eyes.

Paul and I had not had much luck with helicopters during location scouting. For our final scout we brought along Paul's wife Jacalyn and my fiancée Shelley for the ride. As we were flying through the Colorado River canyon, searching for locations, I remembered that when we had scouted the river by boat I had seen some vintage cable crossings where US Geological Survey researchers had stretched steel cable across, some thirty feet above the water. Our chopper was zooming down this same canyon, about thirty feet off the river, when I just casually mentioned to the pilot that I thought there might be some cables in the vicinity. Suddenly my stomach was in my throat as the helicopter shot straight up, just clearing one of these cables by mere inches. Upon landing, my future wife ordered that if I wanted to marry her, I was never to set foot in a helicopter again. I agreed and then unfortunately had to immediately break that promise, to get the final shot in the film.

That final shot, performing the "eagle-eye" view, called for the helicopter to fly up over a rock formation to reveal Marc and Tanya, and then swoop down at and around them as they kissed. Usually Chuck Bail would ride in the helicopter with second unit cameraman Joel King, who would hang out the door strapped to his Tyler mount. Since this was the final shot of the movie, I took over, wanting to make sure we got it right. I strapped in and we took off and did a rehearsal, which looked good. Since we were swooping in from above there was no place for an animal trainer to hide, so we had to leash the tiger to the rocks. The trainers wedged one of its favorite cooked chickens in between the rocks and the big cat ignored the helicopter and chowed down on some lunch during the shot. We did a take and it looked great, although later I found out that rather than kiss Marc, Tanya was screaming right in his face, terrified the prop wash from the chopper would blow them both off the rocks. Joel gave me the thumbs-up, so I called print and the pilot quickly set us down on the ground. I've never ridden in a helicopter since.

With the finale in the can our plan kicked into gear to get that last shot by sunset. The helicopter took off and started toward the location eighty-seven miles away. Meanwhile, over at the Colorado River location, Roberto Quezada, working as a one-man guerilla operation, had been there the entire day preparing. On his own he had recruited students from the nearby vicinity to stand in for the priests and slaves who would appear in the shot. Roberto had brought nine sets of wardrobe in his trunk and he handed them out to the students, including an auburn wig for the gal who would double Tanya. The location was a "miners walkway" in which planks had been bracketed into the sheer rock face about twenty-five feet above the river. Prior to the shot Roberto had to carry wood down to the location and lay new planks over the rotted old planks so it could be traversed safely.

As the helicopter left the Valley of Fire, Paul and I immediately took off by car, hoping to get within view of the location before the shot. We were pushing a hundred miles an hour on the desert highway in our rental car, convinced that with the helicopter stopping for fuel it would give us time to get there.

At the location, Roberto had a walkie-talkie and right on time he heard the chopper pilot informing him that they had arrived on the scene. As the sun was setting, Roberto and the students, wearing their robes, clambered down the cliff to the walkway.

About the same time, Paul and I arrived at Willow Bay Marina on the Arizona side of the border, hopped in a rental motorboat, and gunned it upstream toward the location.

The pilot informed Roberto they were ready for a take and Roberto lit four wood torches and handed them out to his student-extras. As the sun slunk below the horizon, the helicopter swooped in and Joel King rolled film as the extras marched along the planks on the canyon rock face. They did several takes and as the night closed in the torch flames became more visible. As they were doing the final take, our little motorboat rounded the bend and Paul and I were able to watch the marching torch-lit extras and the chopper swooping by. From where we sat it looked perfect.

The helicopter banked and headed back for home base as Roberto and his student crew packed up, heading for a nearby bar to celebrate. Bravo to Roberto for pulling off a terrific solo job!

Paul and I turned our little motorboat back downriver toward the docks. *The Beastmaster* had finished principal photography and Paul and I breathed a huge sigh of relief. Motoring down the Colorado River at magic hour, surrounded by its vast natural beauty, I suddenly realized a remarkable thing—for the very first time in my life, I had completely forgotten that this day was in fact my twenty-eighth birthday. The shoot was over, but the challenge of making a good movie of *The Beastmaster* was just beginning.

FERRET KISSES TIGER

One of the audience-favorite scenes at the very end of *The Beastmaster* is when the little baby ferrets pop up out of our hero's leather satchel. Audiences always go nuts for that one. However, there is a scene, right after that baby ferrets scene, that may have been one of the most absolutely harrowing scenes I've had anything to do with, ever.

We were in postproduction, about three weeks after shooting on *The Beastmaster* was complete, and busy assembling the cut. The plan was to go out and shoot some pickup shots to finish up and fill out our missing scenes. I always build into the budget additional money for pickup shooting days. I have found that these extra days are extremely important in crafting a good movie. You're able to come back, well rested after taking a few days off, you've seen all the footage, and can get those important shots you missed that can really make a movie great. Plus, it's usually a tiny crew of just a couple people and mostly relaxing and fun. No pressure.

We would frequently get orders from the powers-that-be who financed our film. This time the Commercial Director had decided that he wanted us to film a shot for the very end of the picture in which the mama ferret leans over and kisses the tiger. Paul and I immediately responded, "You can't do that. The tiger will eat the ferret!" Remember, we had just finished shooting seventy-two days of animal action; we had both been forced into becoming experts on the behaviors of these animals.

From the first day, it had been drummed into our brains that the animals could work together in only very rare circumstances and mostly not at all. The lesson we were taught, over and over by the trainers, was that if the eagle saw the ferret, it would attack and eat it. We were also taught that if the tiger saw the ferret, it would eat it. And if the tiger saw the eagle, it would eat it. And if the tiger saw a horse, it would eat that too. It was all pretty basic law-of-the-jungle stuff. To us this scene was a truly idiotic idea. Today, this kind of shot could be easily accomplished with 3D models and digital effects. However, back then it would require the ferret to get nose-to-nose with one of the largest predators on the planet. It was readily apparent this would not end well for the little ferret. Again we protested to our moneyman and were firmly told that we were not being asked, but told, the scene must be shot. No matter what.

So we went to the animal trainers. Their immediate response? "The tiger will eat the ferret."

We went back to this executive producer. "No can do. The tiger will eat the ferret." We were told to do it anyway. So I pulled out that trump card that all directors proudly carry in their back pocket. I climbed up on my soapbox. "If you insist on shooting that scene you will have to get someone else to direct it." The CD immediately responded, "No problem. Get the trainers, I will shoot the scene myself."

On the day of the shoot I had promised myself that I would not show up for the poor ferret's execution. But like a rubbernecker at a car crash I just couldn't stay away. The ferret was put into the Beastmaster's satchel, which was slung around one of the trainer's necks. The set was cleared and the process of bringing in the tiger started. The trainers started their standard tiger entrance speech. "Everyone on your feet!" "No menstruating women on the set!" "No children!" "No quick movements!" Out of instinctual fear, everyone scrupulously followed these instructions.

The tiger was led from his cage and escorted to his mark. Paul and I were watching from a dozen feet back. The camera rolled and the CD called, "Action!" I tried to close my eyes but try as I might I just had to watch, even if it meant witnessing the violent death of one of the loyal little stars of my film. The trainer with the satchel was hiding it from the tiger. He said, "Here goes nothing." Then, he swung around toward the tiger to reveal the ferret poking out of the bag. Shocked, the tiger just stared, stunned that this funny little creature was right there in front of him. Surprised, the tiny ferret fearlessly peered back up at the huge cat. The trainer leaned the bag toward the tiger. This was it, the poor little ferret was about to be tiger food. And guess what? The ferret and tiger kissed each other, then pulled back, then kissed each other again and the trainer quickly leaped away, clutching the little ferret. Dougie, our camera operator, switched it off and called out, "Got the shot!" And that was it. Meanwhile, the CD beamed with pride. Paul and I and the rest of the crew heaved a grateful sigh of relief. The tiger was taken back to his cage and rewarded with a cooked chicken.

Animal Trainer Note: If one wants to film a scary tiger snarl with a normally tame big cat, this is how it is done by the professionals. The trainer takes a cooked chicken, loops a line of steel cable through it, and then gives the chicken to the tiger to eat. The cameraman rolls film, and then, on a count of three, the trainer yanks on the cable. There is something about having your dinner snatched away that brings out the ferocious animal in any of us. In a tiger its stunning response is so terrifying that you immediately question why you would allow yourself to ever be in such close proximity to such a fierce predator.

REQUIEM FOR *THE BEASTMASTER*

During postproduction on *The Beastmaster* things quickly went south on many fronts. I was busily working with the editor Roy Watts to distill all the footage down into a coherent story. Traditionally the Directors Guild of America rules allow the director to supervise and create their own first cut of the film, which is then presented to the producers and studio. I was entitled to a month and a half cutting allowance to create my director's cut. Things were going well in the editing room when, a week or so into my cut, the Commercial Director's new assistant producer (he was on his third one now) came to me and asked me to meet with our moneyman. He had an idea.

The Commercial Director told me that since he, having final cut, would make his own version after I had finished my director's cut anyway, why not allow him to come into the editing room during my cut, sit beside me, and make suggestions? This way we could work together on a collegial basis and save time. I'm going to cop to something right now. I can be a gullible damn fool sometimes and this was one case. Nice guy Don responded, "Sure. That sounds logical. Why not?"

So I invited him to join me in my editing room a full month early and let him sit there right beside me and listened to his suggestions as I supervised the editor. The shoot was over, the pressure was off, I treated our moneyman as a creative collaborator. On exactly the Sunday night of the last week of my director's cut, this damn gullible fool got a big surprise. The

CD casually informed me that since my director's cut time allotment was now finished, there would be no need for me to come back to the editing room anymore. I was not needed.

It took a full, few moments for this to sink in. Had I allowed this SOB to participate in the editing for five full weeks during my director's cut to now be thrown out? But worse, it dawned on me that he probably knew it all along, from the time he originally asked me, that in just a few weeks' time I would be out on my ear. Have you ever seen those cartoons where the character's face turns red like a thermometer and then steam starts spewing out of its ears? That was me. I might have been slow on the uptake, but when I figured it out, it hit me hard. My mouth opened and without any conscious thought a torrent of profanity erupted like a fiery volcano. I took a step toward him and his third assistant foolishly stepped in the way. The only reason I didn't clock the guy right then was that I suddenly realized how and why that first assistant got punched in the eye all those months ago. I sidestepped the idiot and went right for the CD, but my dear friend Paul, who was much cooler under pressure, intervened and grabbed me and pulled me back. His quick thinking probably saved me from a massive personal injury lawsuit.

I didn't have any recourse but to call the Directors Guild. And they really couldn't do anything of substance other than to order my now-adversary and his minions to allow me to sit in the editing room whenever I wanted. I could talk, but no one was under any obligation to listen. So that's what I did. I sat there and watched as our moneyman made the movie he wanted out of the film I shot and ignored me when I complained.

Can you believe it got even worse? The CD decided to screen his new cut for an associate, a successful low-budget movie producer. After the screening the producer was asked for his comments. He said he liked the movie but it felt too short. I asked if he could be more specific. As he walked away the producer said it was an overall thing, he just felt the film moved too fast. Our moneyman nodded, he now understood all. He told the editor we must lengthen the movie. "Which scenes?" the editor asked. To his shock the editor was instructed to go through the entire film and lengthen every single shot. To any filmmaker reading this I don't need to explain what a travesty this order was. To randomly disrupt the inner timing and dynamics of each and every shot may by the worst instruction an editor could ever receive. And *The Beastmaster,* which would be advertised as "A Film by Don Coscarelli," would be ruined by this insanity that I had no control over.

Our moneyman was struggling to find a North American distributor for his new cut of my film. He finally made a deal with David Begelman, the notorious head of MGM. Three years previously, Begelman had left Columbia Pictures under a felonious cloud due to embezzlement by forging studio checks under actor Cliff Robertson's name and depositing them into his own personal bank account. Despite pleading guilty to a serious crime, this miscreant somehow managed to get himself installed as chieftain of the grand old movie studio that had fallen on hard times. Begelman was the perfect partner for the CD and proved it publicly by subsequently resigning from MGM moments after *The Beastmaster* contract was signed, leaving MGM completely leaderless for the release of our film. D'oh! It was oddly fitting that the rolling catastrophe that *The Beastmaster* had become would ultimately wind up at a rudderless studio with a half-baked marketing plan and little support.

When *The Beastmaster* opened to tepid theatrical business it was almost a relief for me. It may have been perceived as a career setback, but I would never have to see our moneyman again, let alone work under him. I have to admit that some of the critical reviews my film received did sting, especially when they blamed me for creative decisions that were forced on me. But best of all, I felt an odd contentment that this bastardized version of my film, forgotten, would disappear into the mists of time and I would be free of *The Beastmaster* forever.

Then a funny thing happened. The videocassette business exploded and *The Beastmaster* sold hundreds of thousands of VHS tapes worldwide. Then the cable TV business boomed and *The Beastmaster* became a staple on HBO and the Turner networks. HBO and TBS programmed the film in heavy rotation.

Despite all the damage done to my movie by my "collaborators," the heart of the movie that Paul and I created, the core concept of a lone warrior and his animal pals, struck a chord with fans. Family audiences loved it, despite its flaws. Moms loved the muscles of the Beastmaster, dads loved watching the swordplay and Tanya Roberts, and the kids loved the animals. *The Beastmaster* had become what Hollywood calls a "four quadrant" movie in that it played to everybody. HBO's acronym became known as "Hey, *Beastmaster's* On," and Turner's TBS was referred to as "The *Beastmaster* Station." All of this occurred with zero marketing help from the studio. I can only wonder what a franchise *The Beastmaster* would have become if a couple of years earlier Disney Studios had instead made the decision to produce the film, had allowed me to make the film I wanted to make, and put their marketing muscle behind it. Can you imagine the stores on Main Street in Disneyland pushing *Beastmaster* stuffed animals?

The very slow rollout of *The Beastmaster's* ultimate success was never acknowledged, other than years later by a generation of kids who watched it over and over on cable TV. Ultimately my film spawned two sequels and a television series that played for three seasons. I had nothing to do with any of them, and I was fine with that. Paul and I still own a large stake in the net profits of the original film and to date have never seen a dime.

The CD himself ultimately went on to cowrite and direct a sequel to *The Beastmaster,* which was entitled *Beastmaster 2: Through the Portal of Time.* That was the one in which the Beastmaster travels through time and drives around present-day San Diego in a red Porsche. His film really defies description—you should check it out.

In terms of my career, *The Beastmaster* was considered a failure in Hollywood, and nobody was beating down my door with offers. Until one Italian producer came calling . . .

DODGING A *SILVER BULLET*

iterally days after the disappointing theatrical release of *The Beastmaster* in North America, as I was digesting the less-than-stellar box office results and coming to grips with two years of creative interference on that film, I received a call from the world-famous Italian producer Dino De Laurentiis. I was summoned to meet with Mr. De Laurentiis at his very pricey family bungalow in the back of the Beverly Hills Hotel. I brought along Paul for the meeting.

A diminutive man with limited English skills, Dino had just finished cooking pasta for his extended family. As our meeting began, Dino told me how much he liked *The Beastmaster* and asked if I knew why he had summoned me. Knowing that he was producing the long-in-the-works major motion picture version of Frank Herbert's epic novel *Dune,* I half-jokingly responded, "So, director David Lynch has dropped out and you want me to take over and finish *Dune* for you?" Dino did not like my attempt at humor and shot me an irritated look. He said that he did indeed want to offer me a job to direct a picture, but it was not *Dune.* He told me he was producing a sequel to *Conan the Barbarian* entitled *Conan the Destroyer,* and it would be filming with Arnold Schwarzenegger in Mexico starting in just three months. Would I like to step in?

Great! My next project would involve months in another country filming another muscle-bound hero in a loincloth for another strong-willed international producer for whom English was a second language. Just my luck.

To say I was crestfallen to be summoned to meet one of the most successful film producers in the world and be offered another sword and sorcery movie right after finishing *The Beastmaster* was a serious understatement.

Later that night I read the *Conan* sequel script. It was immediately apparent that this predicament was even worse than I imagined it could be. The script was just downright lousy. Nothing compelling, cardboard characters, not even any unique action. It was just a dumb retread of the original. I didn't sleep a wink that night as I agonized over this situation. I was completely conflicted. How could I possibly pass up an offer to make an eighteen-million-dollar movie with worldwide studio distribution and get paid extremely well for it? *The Beastmaster* didn't exactly light the theatrical box office on fire. However, this new Conan project was pretty much the same kind of stuff I had been working on for two straight years, and with that script it would be supremely difficult, if not impossible, to make a good movie out of it. *The Beastmaster* reviews had been less than kind, and to add insult to injury, my film was skewered for being a *Conan* rip-off.

I had no idea where I would get funding for my next movie. Was it time to sell out? Two long days of agonizing and I made the decision that I had to turn down Mr. De Laurentiis. When I called Dino to inform him of my decision, he gasped in surprise. I told him I might consider directing Conan if he would give Paul and me the opportunity to rewrite the screenplay. He responded forcefully that he wasn't looking for writers or coproducers, just one director, and there was no time for a rewrite anyway. The phone conversation ended rather badly.

I wouldn't direct another film for more than three years. And during that time I would be lying if I told you I never second-guessed that decision. How could I have passed up the chance to work with one of the great action stars of my time on such a huge budget? (In my defense, *The Terminator* had not been made yet and Arnold was not yet taken seriously as an actor.)

To my surprise, several months later Dino called back and I was elated and relieved to hear that he wanted to submit another project for me to direct. I guess the lesson there is that turning someone down isn't always a bad strategy.

Dino had made a deal for several Stephen King books and this project was one of them. He didn't tell me anything about it—just said he would have the project delivered. I was an immense fan of Stephen King and was so excited for the opportunity to be involved with something this modern master had created! I literally sat by my front door, counting the minutes, waiting for Dino's messenger service to deliver the source material to me. My mind was racing. Would it be a book? If so, which one? A short story? Perhaps a completed screenplay written by Stephen King himself? How cool would that be! The messenger rang the bell and then a thick envelope was dropped into my hands. I tore it open to find . . . a calendar.

Well, it actually was a very short book inspired by a calendar that King had created with esteemed illustrator Bernie Wrightson. The calendar told the story in monthly format of a werewolf infestation in the small Maine town of Tarker's Mills. In the calendar, the werewolf would strike every month on a holiday. Much like *Phantasm* it had a young protagonist, Marty Coslaw, who is the only person in his town who understands the nature of this evil. Complicating things for Marty: he is a young paraplegic confined to a wheelchair. How could a boy in a wheelchair possibly confront this beast? The first werewolf attack is set on New Year's Day in January, the second is on Valentine's Day in February, et cetera. The final throw-down between Marty and the werewolf occurs, of course, on New Year's Eve. The title of the calendar/book was *The Cycle of the Werewolf*.

What a difference from *Conan the Destroyer*! This was a project I could quite literally sink my teeth into. There was no agonizing. I was in. I rang up Dino bubbling with enthusiasm, and told him without guile that I could make a great movie of this story. Dino grunted an OK. I asked if Stephen King might adapt the story into a screenplay and he told me no, that King was busy. Then he told me that he would send me the first screenplay he commissioned, which he did not like. So began the big problem of *Cycle of the Werewolf*—getting a screenplay.

I read the first-draft screenplay and did not like it at all. It was a rote retelling of the story without the monthly structure of the calendar. I was convinced that the calendar structure should be maintained and told Dino so. He invited me to come to New York City and meet and discuss.

Before being hired I had to pass muster with the Paramount Studios brass, who would be distributing the film. I arrived at the Paramount lot and was ushered into the plush offices of the studio boss. It was the easiest meeting I've ever had. Frank Mancuso was an approachable, nice guy. We exchanged pleasantries. He asked me if I thought I could make a good movie out of the property and I enthusiastically said yes, and that was it.

My wife Shelley and I arrived in New York and were put up at the Mayflower Hotel, a block from Dino's offices in the towering Gulf and Western Building. Shelley was six months pregnant with our first child, so it was an exciting trip on many levels. I lugged onto the plane with me my trusty Apple II computer, packed inside a cardboard box. I had stuffed the tiniest computer monitor I could find into my suitcase. I had owned the Apple II for a couple of years and had good results with an early word-processing program called Word Handler II. For the first time I was determined to try to write a screenplay on a computer, and *Cycle of the Werewolf* would be a great opportunity.

I met with Dino in his grand office overlooking Central Park and was introduced to his translator, Sergio Altieri. Sergio was a big, affable Italian guy and we became fast friends. Sergio told me that Dino required him to translate all submitted screenplays into Italian for Dino to read. It was a huge job and Sergio was constantly busy doing his translation work. Sergio was also an aspiring writer and later went on to a successful career as an Italian-language novelist with a lot of well-received sci-fi books to his credit. I think Sergio may have been lobbying Dino behind my back for the job, because Dino informed me that he had assigned his translator to cowrite the *Cycle of the Werewolf* screenplay with me. I really didn't mind the idea of working with him; I liked Sergio a lot and he was savvy about the inner workings of the De Laurentiis empire. I thought that might come in handy later.

I carried my Apple II over to the DDL offices and we began work in Sergio's little office. I don't think anyone there had ever seen a screenplay written on computer, so Sergio's coworkers frequently interrupted and I was forced to explain and demonstrate what we were doing.

I was very excited to be working on *Cycle of the Werewolf.* Stephen King, in my mind, was (and still is!) a national treasure and had crafted a horror story with real heart. What I thought could make this story great was really zeroing in on the capabilities of Marty, our young hero. Here was a kid who could not walk, who was doomed to spend his life in a wheelchair, marginalized and dismissed by everyone in his town as being disabled. Yet Marty was tough, resourceful, and probably smarter than anybody else around. This was a character the audience would root for.

I was not too keen on the title of the book. It made me think of werewolves on motorcycles. I believed we could do better for the movie. I had an idea that Marty's wheelchair might have a small factory insignia on its back that read SILVER BULLET MANUFACTURING, CO. And that is where the idea to title the movie *Silver Bullet* came from. I envisioned an opening title sequence featuring a blast furnace with fiery molten metal, where bullets made of liquid silver were being fabricated.

From the beginning Dino boasted that he had already hired Italian effects designer Carlo Rambaldi to create the werewolf. Rambaldi had garnered much success with his creation of the character E.T. as well as his work on the articulated head from the film *Alien*. A few years earlier Carlo had received tremendous notoriety for creating an infamous thirty-five-foot-tall mechanical King Kong, which Dino promoted relentlessly for his seventies remake of the original. I remember being terribly disappointed in the theater when I saw the finished film because Rambaldi's Kong was only on-screen for less than twenty seconds.

Despite Rambaldi, I was of the opinion that most movie werewolves looked terrible and were just not believable. As I began writing the screenplay, and even though I had not yet seen any of Rambaldi's concept art, I was determined to design the movie so that the werewolf was obscured as much as possible. In *Jaws,* they saved the shark for the third act. Why couldn't we?

This was the first time I was to butt heads with Dino. He could not understand my concern. I told him I did not believe that an animatronic werewolf would hold up on the big screen and that we should not show it until well into the film. He insisted we fully show the werewolf in the opening scene, just like in the book. Rather than immediately destroy my relationship with this powerful producer, I asked him to bear with me and let me write him a few pages of screenplay and read what I was thinking once I put it down on paper.

I had what I thought was a great idea for the opening scene, which might address both our concerns. King's story opens with Arnie, a railroad worker, drinking and working in the early morning darkness of New Year's Day, trying to clear snowdrifts off the train tracks. He is confronted and killed by the werewolf. In my screenplay draft, it's a full moon and we see Arnie through a mysterious point of view as something tracks him through the falling snow. Then we see glowing eyes, watching from the darkness, and finally reveal that the POV is from a menacing, and large, gray wolf, which is stalking Arnie through the woods. Arnie is oblivious, still drinking, as the large creature slowly moves in for the kill. Just as the wolf is about to pounce, suddenly a shadow crosses its face and the beast stops in its tracks. The wolf, startled, looks up, and suddenly two large claws snatch the animal, jerk it up into the air and, as the wounded creature shrieks in agony, it is torn in two. Arnie hears the mayhem, then looks around to see—the black silhouette of the huge werewolf—framed against the full moon—the creature howls in triumph. Cut to main titles.

In all humbleness, I thought this was an elegant solution to the dilemma and a great way to open the film. We start the movie with a misdirect by having the big, scary gray wolf threatening Arnie, but it turns out that scary animal is actually the little guy and there is a much larger beast to worry about. And best of all, we only show the werewolf in silhouette; we save the big reveal for later in the film.

Dino hated it. "No, you need to show the entire werewolf in the opening scene. Carlo Rambaldi will make a great creature. You will show it all." So my meticulously crafted opening was immediately scrapped.

Despite the setback, Sergio and I went to work to complete the screenplay. We found the easiest way to do this was to divide up the months of the *Cycle of the Werewolf* calendar. I took seven months and Sergio took five and we went to work.

I really enjoyed living in New York City for those few weeks and working there as a writer. As planned, Shelley returned to Los Angeles after a week and I remained at the Mayflower to finish the script. I loved that working on *Silver Bullet* gave me a legitimate reason to just hang out in such a vibrant city, but in my off time, I could be a tourist. Spring was around the corner and every afternoon I would walk along the south side of the park to get some exercise, and almost every day I would bump into Dino there. His offices in the Gulf and Western Building were on Columbus Circle, but he had a luxury apartment in Trump Tower on Fifth Avenue. Like clockwork Dino would return to the office along Central Park South after taking a midday nap in his apartment. Sometimes he would notice me and grunt a hello as we passed each other.

When Sergio and I were each finished with our drafts, we collated them and handed them in for Dino to review. The next day I received a disturbing call from Sergio. "Dino hates the script. He wants to see us in an hour."

I entered Dino's office with trepidation. He was grumbling and immediately launched into a ten-minute Italian and English rant about how bad our draft was. I really felt bad as he railed at us. He had spent good money to bring me out and put me up and I genuinely wanted to please the man. As I listened to him rant, something dawned on me. Dino was only criticizing Sergio's chapters and not mine. He was not aware of who wrote what. What should I do? A more politically astute writer might have immediately thrown Sergio under the bus and deflected the blame onto where it was deserved. But Sergio was a good guy and he had been extremely warm and welcoming to me. So I sat there and accepted the blame alongside him. Dino finished his rant and then informed us that Stephen King would be in the office the next day and we would all be meeting and discussing the project with him.

The next morning, I arrived early and was ushered into Dino's office. King had not yet arrived. A shoe-shine man was on his knees in front of Dino, buffing his black leather loafers. I sat quietly in my chair beside Sergio mulling over a simple question. How much would the most successful and possibly most wealthy movie producer in the world tip for his shoe shine? It's not often you get to witness how the mega-rich tip. Sergio kept pestering me with questions about the script, but I could not be bothered as I waited for the upcoming transaction. The shoe-shine man packed his gear and stood up. Dino reached in his pocket and laid one thin dollar bill in the man's hand. I figured that I had just witnessed the secret to financial success.

Stephen King arrived and I was surprised by what a kind, warm, and gracious guy he was. He was tall like me and dressed casually in jeans. Here we were, sitting with probably the greatest living writer in our lifetime, and he just seemed like the guy next door, the perfect pal to hang out with and knock back a couple beers. I tried to start some small talk about how much I liked his books but he didn't want to talk about himself; instead he generously shifted the conversation to *Phantasm* and how much he liked the flying ball.

Dino cleared his throat and the meeting began. I jumped in and confessed to Stephen how much trouble we had been having in adapting his calendar to a movie and, without asking Dino's or Sergio's permission, just blurted out a request for him to step in and write the screenplay for us. He graciously demurred, saying he was very busy on several other projects, but asked us where the problem areas were. Sergio and I listed out all our concerns and the roadblocks we were struggling with and he said he would think it over and see if he could come up with any solutions.

I had been in New York for over a month and had received the news that my air ticket home had been booked for two days later. I surmised that Dino had given up on Sergio and me as a writing team; then the hotel phone rang. Sergio said, "Don, get over here. A fax just came in from Stephen King." I raced over to Sergio's office and he handed me three pages of single-spaced text. King had gone through each of our concerns and had provided a solution to every one. His notes were brilliant. We could take his suggestions and easily rewrite the script and fix everything now. We were back in business!

I followed Sergio as we eagerly hustled over to Dino's office. We looked in to see Dino at his desk reading King's notes. He gruffly motioned us in and we sat down opposite him as he finished reading. I didn't completely comprehend it at the time, but I now believe his next utterances sealed my fate in regard to *Silver Bullet*. Dino scowled and uttered, "Humpf." And he tossed King's notes over his shoulder as if throwing out the trash. My jaw literally dropped open. It made no sense until it did. This guy was clueless. He had just been handed a gift from the greatest writer of our generation and was happy to trash it. And he was in total control of my movie.

The next day I flew back to Los Angeles and forgot about *Silver Bullet*. Shelley and I had more important things to focus on.

THE LAST IN LINE

Back in Los Angeles, counting the days until her due date, Shelley and I awaited the arrival of our first child. In the interim, I had heard nothing from De Laurentiis.

I received a mysterious invitation to a meeting over at Warner Bros. Records about directing a music video. The producers who greeted me there were two earnest young women, Francie Moore and Leslie Libman. They escorted me in to meet the Warner's executive in charge, Jeff Ayeroff. I learned that these three bright and intelligent people had been assigned to supervise the creation of a music video for one of the label's big-selling acts. The band was Dio, fronted by one of the most powerful vocalists in heavy metal, Ronnie James Dio.

Ronnie James's metal cred was impeccable. He had replaced Ozzie Osbourne in Black Sabbath; after that, he teamed up with guitar god Ritchie Blackmore in founding their band Rainbow. His new Dio band had previously released *Holy Diver,* a platinum-selling record, and now were looking for a director for the video of the title song of his new album. Ronnie James liked *Phantasm* and thus I was there.

Ayeroff popped a cassette of the song into his deck and we listened to it. "The Last in Line" was a damn good metal song. It had a soulful intro and then kicked into a hard edge on the strength of Ronnie James's vocal. It had a kickass guitar solo and lyrics of which I had absolutely no clue as to their meaning. Jeff told me he had a basic concept for the video: a teen falls down into hell. He then asked what would hell be like from a teen's point of view. I genuinely liked Dio's song and this project sounded interesting, so the next step was a meeting with Mr. Ronnie James Dio.

Ronnie was a legend who invented the heavy metal "sign of the horns," formed by extending the index finger and pinky while holding the middle and ring fingers down by the thumb. Dio's invention became the symbolic signal for hard rockers everywhere that is now so ubiquitous. The story goes that Ozzie used to flash the peace symbol onstage at Black Sabbath concerts; when Ronnie replaced him he wanted to honor but not copy his predecessor. Dio started flashing the sign of the horns, which he claimed his grandmother from southern Italy taught him could be used to ward off the evil eye. In person Ronnie was a supercool guy and did not affect a rock star swagger, although he never did dress in anything but jet-black.

Though born with an outsized voice, in person Ronnie James was a full foot shorter than I was. Ronnie quickly started describing to me what he was looking for in this video. He had a specific Dio philosophy in regard to the lyrics of the song and he tried to explain it to me. He told me that from birth we are all trapped in one long line, an immense line, that stretches from the day we are born until the day we die. He kept asking me, "But what if, what if you're the last in line? Think of the ramifications." Honestly, I never completely understood what he was getting at. However, I soldiered on and tried to reconcile Ronnie's ideas with WB exec Jeff Ayeroff's initial plan about kids in hell. Ronnie was dismissive of the record label ideas and insisted we incorporate his "line" philosophy. Ronnie then told me some background on his bandmates and their very important mascot, "Murray." "Who?" I asked. Dio patiently explained to me that Murray was a mythic and mystical demonic creature, which had appeared on the *Holy Diver* cover and now on *The Last in Line* album. On the album covers, Murray appears as a looming figure with a Greek god's body wearing the head of a cow skull with horns and red eyes. In the *Holy Diver* cover Murray appears to be drowning a priest with a heavy chain. On *The Last in Line* cover, Murray is lording over a fiery desert hellscape. Dio insisted that Murray appear in this video despite the fact that, between you and me, I never did understand his significance to anything.

I was then introduced to Dio's wife and manager, Wendy Dio. Known as a steely negotiator and always protective of her husband's interests, Wendy was also a producer of the video. I couldn't ignore the similarities to a movie I had seen just a few months before, which has since become a classic. With her long blond hair and British accent, Wendy Dio bore a striking resemblance to actress June Chadwick, who portrayed rocker David St. Hubbins's (Michael McKean's) girlfriend/manager in the satire *This Is Spinal Tap*. It felt like I had stumbled right onto ground zero of the heavy metal era with its strange philosophies, big hair, and demonic mascots. What could I do but crank that amp up to eleven and hang on!

I went home and quickly put on paper a scenario of a video that I thought might satisfy both Warner Bros. Records and Ronnie himself. In retrospect my storyline was truly ridiculous but it had enough of what each party wanted to get them all to climb on board.

The video would open with our young teen hero racing around town, working as a bicycle messenger. He enters an office building elevator and suddenly the elevator car breaks loose and plunges downward. Like an off-the-charts *The Wizard of Oz,* the elevator car crash-lands in a hellish underground landscape. Our plucky protagonist climbs out of the wreckage only to be confronted by some savage creatures with shock-rods who are part-human and part-mechanical. I called these enforcers "Mecho-Men." Our boy is grabbed and roughly shoved into a line of refugees, some really freaky-looking folks. He is now in "the line" and has no choice but to follow it. Ronnie James appears throughout the video at critical junctures dramatically singing the lyrics. Our hapless kid witnesses the following: a room full of teens playing video games and when they lose, they get an electrical punishment shock; another roomful of kids electronically jacked into guitarist Vivian Campbell's Stratocaster. As he plays they swoon . . . And then finally, our hero arrives to where the line is headed, of course, to an immense Murray, lording over the horizon. The kid turns and flees. Along the way he sees a roomful of captive teens watching Dio projected on a screen. Finally he makes a break back for the safety of the elevator car and just as a Mecho-Man is about to get him, Ronnie intercedes and zaps the Mecho-Man with his own shock-rod. The kid rolls into the elevator and it whisks our hero back to the safety of the surface.

Ambitious? Yes. Ridiculous? Yes. But it was the best I could come up with to satisfy everybody, and within days both Dio and Warner Bros. approved it. Francie and Leslie were terrific producers and assembled a crackerjack crew headed by director of photography Bruce Logan of *Star Wars* fame. In addition, they furnished me a surprisingly creative storyboard artist and for a week we worked together over at my Sherman Oaks house on the shots. This guy was a gifted artist and his boards ended up being extremely helpful. His name was John Dahl. A few years later he began his own directing career and to date has made some terrific films including *The Last Seduction* and *Rounders*.

Makeup effects were handled by John Carl Buechler and we worked together to design the look of the Mecho-Men. I am very proud of that makeup effect. Five years later it was flattering to see its resemblance reflected in the look of the evil Borg in *Star Trek: The Next Generation*.

A couple of weeks before shooting began, Shelley and I welcomed our son Andy into this world. It was a glorious time for us and we were both ecstatic with joy.

Production began on the Ronnie James Dio music video at the historic Charlie Chaplin Stage on the corner of La Brea and Delongpre in Hollywood. Working with Ronnie and the Dio band was great. They were cool cats, living the metal rock star dream. Their dressing room was tricked out with a fully stocked bar. The band had this mantra they were known for: "We never close." Even though it was an almost sixteen-hour shoot day those guys were still partying hard, well after we had wrapped.

I had a memorable *Spinal Tap* moment with Wendy Dio when I ordered my special effects tech to ramp up the wind machine. On my direction, he panned it over and hit Ronnie full force while we were filming. Dio's perfectly coiffed hair immediately shot back to reveal a rather deep receding hairline. "Get that machine off this set!" she yelled at me. It took a moment to register until it became apparent to me how valuable the image of hair was to the metal artists. I got the fan out of there, never to appear again on set.

In two long nights working with editor Don Wilson, we finished the video. This was before nonlinear video editing was in use, so once we made an editorial decision, the only way to make a change was to reedit everything you had done previously. It was a terrible way to work; in retrospect I can see why the final pace of the video now feels a bit plodding. At the end of the last night I received a call from Shelley telling me it was time to get home to help with our newborn son. Driving home that night it hit me that all the weeks of effort were simply in service of a heavy metal record company commodity. I had just made one very long commercial about something I didn't really understand or care much about. I decided there and then that I would never direct another music video. At the end of the day I needed to believe in my own work.

MTV dutifully placed "The Last in Line" video in rotation and the album was ultimately certified platinum, selling over one million records in North America. Sadly, Ronnie James Dio passed away in 2010 at age sixty-seven. But, amazingly, Dio lives on. The forward-thinking and irrepressible Wendy Dio has conjured up a wild retrospective concert tour featuring surviving members of the Dio band performing live while accompanying a holographic incarnation of Ronnie James Dio. I've seen clips and the resurrected metal god not only performs a profoundly stirring rendition of "The Last in Line" but simply kicks ass from beyond the grave. It will be coming soon to an arena near you. Rock on, Ronnie James!

A GOOD OMEN

n the aftermath of the Dio video I started to sense something might be wrong with me. I was having occasional night sweats and strange stomachaches without any obvious reason. I was slow to consult a doctor, as the symptoms seemed to come and then disappear in a completely arbitrary manner.

While in preproduction on the Dio video I had heard nothing about what was going on with *Silver Bullet.* One day I received a nice call from Stephen King himself to check on the status. I told him I loved his screenplay notes but Dino had rejected them, and Sergio had mentioned other writers were hired. I told Stephen I still hoped to direct his story but it was in Dino's hands and again encouraged him to step in and write the screenplay. He didn't think that was possible, but said he would discuss it with Dino next time they spoke.

A few weeks later I had a really bad night and set up an appointment with a gastroenterologist the next day. He checked me over and suggested a battery of tests. For a few days I felt like I was Regan in *The Exorcist,* having scientific procedures performed on me by disinterested technicians. It was a living horror movie. While I was getting a batch of abdominal X-rays, a traditionally noncommunicative radiologist came running into the X-ray room and without revealing results started interrogating me as to whether I had been out of the country in the past few days. Something serious was going on here.

A day later, in my meeting with the doctor, he informed me they had located a large mass in my abdominal region. He said there was a decent chance it was not cancer, but that I should prepare for exploratory surgery. I had lived a very healthy life and my only experience with surgery had been as a kid with a tonsillectomy. Yikes!

While I raced around getting second opinions and interviewing surgeons, I had a long-standing appointment on the books with Bob Shaye of New Line Cinema. Bob's company was on the rise; his film *A Nightmare on Elm Street* had been a hit and he wanted to talk. The meeting took place in their office at the American Film Market, which was being held at the Sunset Plaza Hotel on the Sunset Strip.

Over the years a lot of fans and critics have compared the similarities between *A Nightmare on Elm Street* and *Phantasm*. At the time I recognized that both films had an evil villain who moved through dreams but I didn't give the comparison theories much thought. Bob offered me the directing job for their planned sequel, *A Nightmare on Elm Street 2: Freddy's Revenge*. It was so unexpected, I really did not know how to respond. On the one hand it's always nice to have funding for a film, but on the other, much like the Conan sequel, I did not want to retread ground I had already covered. It just felt wrong. Also, my date with the surgeon pretty much dominated my thinking.

Back at home, the phone rang and it was Sergio calling from New York. He wanted to give me a heads-up that for no apparent reason Dino was now seriously considering terminating me and going with another director. Sergio suggested I have my then agent get right to work and try to resuscitate my chances of working on the film. With everything going on, I had a very laissez-faire attitude now toward working with De Laurentiis. I had no respect for him creatively and I guess he had even less for me. I loved Stephen King's *Cycle of the Werewolf* story, and to this day believe I would have made a great film from it—but not with Dino De Laurentiis calling the shots. So, I did nothing and a few days later was informed that I had been finally let go.

Surprisingly, Dino cast the resulting film well (with Gary Busey no less—more on him later) and managed to finally persuade Stephen King to write the screenplay. I think King's great story was ultimately let down by Dino's creative interference and Carlo Rambaldi's animatronic werewolf—which critic Vincent Canby of the *New York Times* described in his less-than-stellar review: "The werewolf, when it finally comes onto the screen, looks less like a wolf than Smokey Bear with a terrible hangover." By the way, in the opening sequence of their finished film, there is no appearance of the werewolf whatsoever, except for a single werewolf claw.

A couple of weeks later I was admitted into the hospital and was prepped for surgery. There was some kind of a delay in the operating room and I ended up waiting for an hour longer than planned. To say this was nerve-wracking is a serious understatement. I was newly married with a ten-month-old son, no job prospects, and I literally had no idea what the future held for me and my family. I was ruminating on my mortality, staring out the window at the overcast, gray morning, and then noticed something down in the back area of the hospital complex. Pulling up was a black Cadillac hearse, evidently to pick up the corpse of someone who had died. The sight of that long black funeral coach waiting down below brought a smile to my face. A good omen! The Tall Man was around. He would look out for me.

The omen proved true: the surgery went well, the infected mass was removed (with no cancer!), and I made a full recovery. During my recuperation I realized that it was a blessing in disguise to have been shown the door on the *Silver Bullet* project. Had I been in the process of shooting that film with my medical condition, there might have been a much more unfortunate outcome. Belated thanks, Dino.

THE SOUTH BAY FILM PACK

had always loved the outdoors and, from my youth, was fascinated with wilderness survival. I tried to combine that interest with my filmmaking and subsequently wrote a screenplay about an Outward Bound–style wilderness survival school in which the students get in trouble deep in the woods. In my story, I contrasted two forms of survivalism: one rooted in fear and weaponry and the other based in teamwork and self-sufficiency.

A previous investor agreed to contribute a significant chunk of funding to help me make this film, which I was calling *Survival Quest*. I asked Roberto Quezada, my veteran collaborator from *Phantasm* and *The Beastmaster*, to join me on the project and work as producer on the film.

I had done pretty well in casting the leads of my previous films with Gregory Harrison, Michael Baldwin, Angus Scrimm, and Marc Singer. All of these talents had been significantly responsible for the success of each movie. A film lives or dies on its leads. A poor casting choice could immediately doom a film. But now with *Survival Quest*, I was struggling. Who could I find to play mountain man Hank Chambers, the survival school instructor and the lead of our film? I had an early flirtation with actor Patrick Swayze, who was a solid choice until his agent informed us of his unaffordable (for us) rate. Then Roberto mentioned an actor he had admired while working on the low-budget biker film *Savage Dawn*. Lance Henriksen was a rugged and intense actor known for playing heavies in a lot of smaller roles. He had recently hit the mainstream with a powerful turn in James Cameron's *Aliens,* in which he portrayed an inscrutable android.

It is customary practice in Hollywood that once actors reach a certain level of success their agents will not allow them to audition for directors. They will take a meeting, but they will not read lines. From the actor's perspective this is understandable. Most have paid their dues and feel it is demeaning that as a known actor they would need to prove they can act, over and over again. From the director's perspective this can be especially frustrating as one must imagine what the actor might be like as the character. It frequently feels like you are being forced into buying the proverbial "pig in a poke." Lance came in for a meeting and did what smart actors do. He came in character. He was dressed like a mountain man in a warm flannel shirt and hiking boots. He exuded the strength and compassion of the character. Even though he didn't recite one line of dialog, it felt like I had just spent an hour with the hero of my film. Lance got the job.

Lance and I had a terrific relationship during the filming of *Survival Quest.* The intensity of his performance literally carried the film. Unlike most actors I had ever worked with, Lance had such a strong desire to see the film succeed that he wanted us to keep working together to refine the film even into postproduction. My bad experience on *The Beastmaster* made me gun-shy about giving anyone access to the editing room, and I think Lance was disappointed I excluded him. However, to this day I have nothing but the highest regard for Lance's talent and still hope we can make another film together.

Roberto and I were immediately overwhelmed trying to figure out the logistics of making this wilderness epic on a shoestring budget. We were in desperate need of assistance.

Our first task was to find some production assistants to help with all the details, hopefully for little or no money. Roberto mentioned two young production assistants he wanted me to meet. He said he had never met such dedicated workers, who would do literally *anything* to make the movie they were working on great.

Roberto had recently been working as chief lighting technician on an exercise video starring Dolph Lundgren, which had been shooting on a rather dirty section of Southern California beach. The sand was littered everywhere with dried dog droppings and the talent was complaining about stepping in it. The director of photography yelled at these two production assistants to solve the problem. Finding themselves without shovels, or even gloves, without hesitation these guys took it upon themselves to get it done and were on their hands and knees plucking the stuff up out of the sand with their bare hands. And worse, the crew had the audacity to laugh at them. Let me be clear: Roberto was not ridiculing them. He was in total awe that he was working with such eager young production assistants who were so dedicated to making this Dolph Lundgren workout video look good, they were will-ing to pick up dog shit with their bare hands.

Then one of these production assistants accidentally left some footprints on the pristine sand dune they were filming on. The director of photography again yelled at this PA and told him to fix it. Of course there was no rake. As Roberto told it, in order to fix the problem this eager young production assistant sacrificed his body and rolled down the sand hill so his rolling body would smooth out the sand. To produce *Survival Quest* we would be going into the wilderness, and our production would be a massive challenge and filled with hardship. I desperately needed some go-to PAs like this. I had to meet these two guys!

Roberto attempted to set up a meeting and invite these two PAs to join us, but he received an unexpected response. The two production assistants, Roger Avary and Quentin Tarantino (the one who rolled down that sand hill), had smartly decided they wanted to be filmmakers of their own and not production assistants for somebody else anymore. They had decided to dedicate themselves to getting their own films made. Obviously this was a good move. You can learn some things on a film working as a production assistant, but it's not a smart place to linger if your desire is to make your own movies. So Roger and Quentin very kindly introduced us to a couple of their best student filmmaker pals, Scott Magill and Rand Vossler, who came on board and became significant contributors in the making of *Sur-vival Quest*.

What I really admired about all these guys is that they had created a tight-knit pack of student filmmaker friends based in the South Bay area of coastal Los Angeles. There were about a dozen of them, and they would all work together on each other's film projects. They would screen each other's movies and read and comment on each other's writing. With Quentin employed at Video Archives in Manhattan Beach, they had access to a stellar movie collection to study.

It is so very hard to make a film on your own that to have a dedicated and loyal team of friends to back you up is just invaluable. Roberto and I enlisted a bunch of them to help out on *Survival Quest,* including Scott, Rand, Dov Schwartz, Alan Sanborn, and King Wilder. We referred to them as the South Bay Film Pack.

Our first hire was Scott Magill, an eighteen-year-old who became our first office assistant. During some downtime Scott offered to show me one of his student films. It was entitled *Portrait* and was a moody tone poem, shot in stark black-and-white Super 8 mm, featuring a troubled teenage girl. What most impressed me was that the finale of the film was a simple close-up of the actress as she stared out into the ocean. I think it was something like three minutes long, lingering on this actress's face. It was like the best early work of François Truffaut. Really impressive. Scott was one courageous filmmaker and these South Bay Film Pack guys really knew how to shoot film! I immediately gave Scott a promotion and he ended up working closely with me as my assistant editor. We spent almost a year in the editing room solving the puzzle of *Survival Quest.*

Despite the fact that Roger and Quentin had declined our invitation to work on *Survival Quest,* I got to know Roger well since he and Scott were writing partners. In the mideighties personal computers were not exactly ubiquitous, but we just happened to have a brand-new one at our office/editing facility. So after work, Scott would invite Roger over to use our office computer for their writing projects. I think during the editing of *Survival Quest,* Roger and Scott wrote something like three or four full screenplays on that computer. The two of them also assisted Quentin in filming his notorious early film *My Best Friend's Birthday.* Over the months of shooting they would trade off cinematography duties and Scott, Rand,

Roger, and even Roberto were all ultimately credited as cinematographers on that film.

During the editing process Rand told me he and Quentin were making progress on one of their projects. I invited them over to the office one day and we walked down to Greenblatt's Deli on Sunset and I bought them pastrami sandwiches for lunch. They had a line on some money to fund Quentin's script *Natural Born Killers* and Rand would produce. My understanding was that there were these twin bodybuilder twins, who billed themselves as the Barbarian Brothers, with a large chunk of money to invest in their project. Rand and Quentin needed to find cast and wanted me to give them a personal introduction to Lance Henriksen. Quentin told me in exacting detail how he was hoping to put his story on film. Even back then Quentin had a highly energetic and captivating way of telling a story and it sounded like it would make for a very cool movie. He wanted Lance to play the transgressive role of Detective Scagnetti, who was both a cop and a psychopath. I was happy to help but was up front with them that Lance and I had some disagreements at the end of *Survival Quest*. I couldn't really guarantee anything.

After they went home I left the first of several messages on Lance's voice mail telling him that I knew these great young filmmakers who wanted him to star in their first movie. After about a week with no response I really felt bad. I wanted to help these guys out and Rand had really worked hard on *Survival Quest*. So I called Lance's agent. I told him about these two great young filmmakers with an edgy script that I really liked and how Lance could do a lot worse than to at least meet with them. In typical fashion the agent was noncommittal, offering an "I'll get back to you." About a week later I called the agent again. And again. The agent refused to take my phone call! I called Rand and Quentin and gave them the bad news.

They never did get that version of *Natural Born Killers* off the ground. A year or so later I received a call from Rand, who told me that financing had just come through for another of Quentin's projects, *Reservoir Dogs*. *Natural Born Killers* was on hold and Rand told me Quentin had basically given the script over to him. Rand asked me if I would like to help him produce it with Rand himself directing. I was really busy at the time with other projects and had no choice but to decline. Later, somehow, Rand was maneuvered out of the project and ultimately replaced as director by Oliver Stone, who finally made the film. And of course, *Reservoir Dogs* launched Quentin's career into the stratosphere. Lance, I wish you would have called me back!

THE ACTOR'S QUEST

When I first started making feature films at the age of eighteen, I was intimidated by actors. Many of them were twice my age. The very nature of their job requires them to use their range of emotions more easily than the rest of us. This can be frightening to a newcomer if an actor unleashes a sudden burst of anger, sadness, or disgust in their direction. As I came to know more of them and understand the peculiar pressure they must withstand, I developed much more sympathy and affection for them.

Here's what you need to understand about actors in film. The process of filmmaking requires many collaborators to work for months, or even years, as they prepare a film to shoot—writing a screenplay, building sets, designing wardrobe and props, securing locations, constructing every detail of this grand pyramid of a film. Then on that first day of shooting our actor steps before the cameras and the entire pyramid of work is lifted up, turned upside down, and the point of it set on this actor's head. The director calls "Action!" and with the entire weight of all the hard work, hopes, and dreams of their collaborators bearing down, the actor alone must conjure magic and breathe life into this film. Let me tell you it's a helluva lot easier to sit in a director's chair or push a light around than it is to bring a character to life on cue.

So, I have made it my main task on set to take as much of this burden off the actors, to find ways to make the set a relaxing, fun, and pressure-free place to work and create.

Sometimes an actor will arrive on set questioning every choice by the director. While this interrogation can be intimidating, frequently it stems from simple miscommunication. All most actors want to know are the basics—where to enter the scene, where to deliver lines, where to interact with props, and when to exit. As long as the direction makes simple logic to them, the director can then get out of their way and let them act. If I notice an actor getting anxious or hostile, I've learned to quickly reset and walk them slowly and gently through the basics. It is surprising how that quickly tends to solve most problems.

Survival Quest was my first time working with a large ensemble of actors. For me it was more work than I had ever experienced as a director. There were an awful lot of them: Lance as the instructor; seasoned stage actor and *The Beastmaster* veteran Ben Hammer; rookie-with-a-lot-of-talent Dermot Mulroney; Shakespearean actor Dominic Hoffman; first-timer-with-promise Catherine Keener; eighteen-year-old ingénue Traci Lind; comic Paul Provenza; steady and talented Steve Antin; and another break-out star of *Aliens,* Mark Rolston. Whew! After each take I would need to tend to each of these actors and then listen to their concerns. Multiply that times eight and it was a heck of a lot of work.

DROWNING IN THE KERN RIVER

A major section of *Survival Quest* was written to take place on a river. The only real body of flowing water within a couple hundred miles of Los Angeles is the Kern River and its swift flow makes it extremely popular for white-water rafting. Sounds perfect, right? It was, except for the fact that this location was nicknamed the "Killer Kern" and was notorious as one of the most dangerous rivers in the region. On average, half a dozen people a year drown in the Kern.

While location scouting, Roberto and I learned this on our very first visit, the hard way. We were checking out a desolate stretch of riverbank for a location when Roberto casually stepped too close to the water. All the river rocks in proximity to the water were coated in a very slippery slime and, before he knew it, Roberto's feet shot out from under him and SPLASH, he was in the water. I busted out laughing because one minute he was standing beside me, and the next, right into the river. I reached down to grab Roberto's arm and my foot slipped on the same slime and SPLASH, I went right into the river. Within moments we both found ourselves submerged up to our necks in the cold Kern, hanging on for dear life to the slime-slippery rocks. No one else was around. We were on our own. And we had no clue about the level of danger we were in. We were still laughing at each other. Later we learned from trusted river guides that if we had lost our grip on those rocks on that stretch of the Kern we both would have drowned. The only way out was to crawl, so we slowly inched our way back up the rocks and collapsed on the riverbank. Welcome to the Kern River!

Once we started shooting, the process of getting to the selected river locations often required humping the camera and equipment half a mile over the rocky riverbank. I have always been of the belief that small crews where everyone is working toward the common goal is the best way to go. I actually find that lugging equipment makes me think more clearly and takes my mind off the day's problems. I've spent time in the luxurious trailers of director friends on big movies and I just think it's entitled bullshit. It separates you from everyone, including the actors and the crew. I like to be with them, working. And I love to see actors helping the crew. It makes us all part of a team!

One major action sequence required the actors to get into the river and, while hanging on to their backpacks, ride through a reasonably tame set of rapids. We stuffed buoyant foam rubber inside the backpacks for flotation. Each actor had a river safety guide waiting a hundred yards downstream to pluck them out of the water at the end of the shot. This was important because past the river guides was a Class 3 rapids, which ultimately led to a waterfall. We had planned the sequence carefully and everything was under control, until it was not.

When I was casting *Survival Quest,* a young actress came in to audition for me who had never had a featured acting role in a film. She came dressed demurely in a simple flannel shirt and hiking shorts. I was genuinely impressed with her quiet but strong demeanor and her simple, natural beauty. I cast her for the role of Cheryl in the film and as we started rehearsing, and then shooting, her dedication to the role became clearly obvious. She had a strong desire to get her performance right and was always focused on improving it. She was so dedicated to her role that she insisted on doing her own stunts; I can still remember her not flinching during a take as a three-inch wood splinter was impaled into her palm as she clambered over a fence. Catherine Keener has gone on to a highly successful career, receiving multiple Oscar, Emmy, and Golden Globe nominations, but I don't think she has ever risked her life for a role like she did in *Survival Quest,* her very first film.

I was operating the Arriflex BL camera from a large rock on the river-bank. My last instruction to the actors was to not let go of their backpacks as they rode them down the rapids. We rolled film and on cue the actors jumped into the river. Within moments they were caught up in the strong current and carried toward us in the swiftly moving water. The shot looked great!

Unbeknownst to me, there had been one mistake made by the crew, which we were all completely oblivious to at the time. The actors' backpacks were filled with flotation foam, but Catherine's had been mistakenly stuffed with rock climbing ropes from a previous scene. As the water flooded her bag, the ropes absorbed it and suddenly her backpack doubled in weight and started to sink. As always, Catherine was a dedicated actress striving for realism, and if her director instructed her not to let go of her backpack, come hell or high water she'd be damned if she released that bag. So as the actors swept by us, Catherine struggled desperately to keep that sodden back-pack from sinking and her head above water. She could not do both.

While watching through the camera viewfinder I could not tell that Catherine was in difficulty. It just looked like great, authentic acting to me. Roberto, my ever-vigilant producer, was standing right behind camera and he watched this impending drowning unfold. And then he made a huge mistake. Just as the take ended, Roberto dropped his walkie-talkie to the ground and hurled himself into the river to save the drowning Catherine. It was a noble act of courage and a foolish act of stupidity at the same time. All the other actors made it safely to shore or were picked up by their river safety guides. Even Catherine was plucked up by her guide and dragged onto his raft. But there was just a single safety guide for each actor and nobody looking after Roberto. Where did he go? No one had eyes on him.

We all ran down the rocky riverbank and around the bend to the exit point. On the walkie-talkies I could hear the assistant director screaming that they couldn't find Roberto. As we reached the exit point the raft guides were dragging Roberto up onto the rocks. He was unconscious. He had been trapped beneath one of the river guide's rafts for several frantic minutes. We got him up to the nearest road and into a car for transport to a hospital.

During preproduction Roberto had been interviewing candidates for his key assistant position and he was very happy with his final hire. His choice was a young woman named Celeste Beard. Although she had just started working in film, Roberto was impressed with her background as an intensive-care nurse. Roberto kept telling us her intelligence and experience with extreme situations made her perfect for the movie business. His instincts turned out to be right on the money.

As the car carrying Roberto raced over the dirt road to the highway, Celeste was searching for his pulse but couldn't find any. She immediately began CPR and during the forty-minute drive to the nearest hospital Celeste battled to resuscitate him. His heart stopped twice. By the time they arrived at the ER, Celeste had managed to revive Roberto and get him breathing and pulse stabilized.

Back at location we were all stunned by the turn of events. It was really hard to restart production after an accident like that. We managed to get shooting and limped through a few more land-based scenes before the sun set.

Once Roberto recovered, the final week of river shots went surprisingly smoothly. So well that the actors decided to have some fun with me. Dermot and Lance (and other unknown conspirators from the cast) decided to get a laugh at my expense. They bought half a dozen cartons of crickets from the bait shop adjoining our crew motel and proceeded to funnel them right into my motel room, under the door and through the window. I was just dozing off when I started to notice insects in my bed and when I turned on the lights was stunned to find thousands of the little creatures completely infesting my room. With no other choice, I spent the rest of the night sleeping in my car. Good actors should know that, as Shakespeare once aptly wrote, "Revenge is a dish best served cold." Even though a couple of decades have passed, my advice to those two is that they had better stay frosty.

A FIFTY-THOUSAND-DOLLAR GAMBLE

An important scene in *Survival Quest* specified that an airplane ferry the various characters up into the mountains and land them on a dirt airstrip. Our pilot of choice, Jan Arvik, owned a beautifully restored twin-engine DC-3, which he had recently purchased from actor and flying fanatic John Travolta. After some scouting, Roberto found us a suitably scenic location in the local mountains near Lake Arrowhead. A gentleman up there owned a large ranch with his own private dirt airstrip. On the tech scout, Jan walked the airstrip and tagged two small trees for removal that might graze his wingtips. Driving home our pilot dropped the bombshell on us. Due to the high altitude and short runway length he would need a fifty-thousand-dollar insurance policy to rebuild his plane in case he accidentally overshot the runway on landing. He also insisted that the landing must occur no later than 7:00 a.m. as the cold dense air would aid him in making as short a landing as possible under these conditions. We checked with our carrier and were presented with a quote for the insurance. For an up-front nonrefundable premium of twenty-nine thousand dollars, they would provide us a fifty-thousand-dollar insurance policy.

So suddenly, this landing scene went from costing less than three thousand dollars to almost thirty thousand. The only answer for a true indie? Self-insure. Roll the dice. Take the risk. I think I once had three hundred dollars spread out on a Vegas craps table but this was shaping up to be the absolutely biggest cash bet I had ever made in my life. It was going to be like laying fifty big ones down on that crap table and praying I didn't crap out!

Roberto and I drove up the mountain the night before and were out on the airstrip before dawn, just the two of us with our two Arriflex 35 mm cameras. We set up one camera at the end of the airstrip with a telephoto lens to close in on the action. The other was set up midway down the strip, which would be the wider angle to pan in the landing. Roberto had one of our field walkie-talkies with instructions to monitor channel 2.

Sure enough, at 6:59 a.m. we heard the drone of propellers. Jan came on the radio, informing us he was ready to go for it. I ran to my camera at the far end of the strip. Roberto gave Jan the go signal and we both flipped on our cameras. Jan circled the field once and then dramatically banked the aircraft and dove for the landing strip. As his wheels neared the ground, I was sweating bullets. Did I just put in motion a plan that would blow a huge chunk of our budget?

The wheels touched down and kicked up a cloud of dust as the big plane landed with a concussive impact and raced down the hard-packed dirt runway. It was going too fast! It was going for the cliff! I could hear metal-on-metal as Jan jammed on the brakes. Roberto and I kept our cameras centered, trained on the plane, determined to get the shot. There was no doing it again. The beast finally began to slow and rumbled to a stop—with two hundred feet to spare! The stunt wouldn't cost us a dime extra. We had rolled the dice and our fifty-thousand-dollar bet paid off, big time! The pilots safely disembarked just as the cast and crew arrived. We had our plane on the location up there in the middle of the forest and we spent the entire day filming some great shots.

Survival Quest ultimately had a very brief theatrical run and reached most audiences by way of home video. My initial screenplay featured a far more visceral take on the material in which the *Survival Quest* team squared off against a killer backwoods clan who called themselves "the Breed." A potential investor promised funding if I softened its raw nature, so I rewrote the screenplay into its current version. In retrospect I think this might have been a creative error on my part, and it also turned out to be a financial one as well, as that investor bailed just prior to production. The final film is a mixed bag, with some terrific performances by cast and superlative cinematography by Daryn Okada. But the writer-director (me!) made some mistakes and over the decades I've tried to solve them with a little reshooting and a lot of reediting. They say films are never finished, that filmmakers just finally abandon them. Well, I've finally given up on *Survival Quest*, but boy would I like to go back and start over from scratch on that one.

COLD IN JULY

Survival Quest was finished and it was time to close up the editing room. My trusty assistant editor Scott Magill was there as we packed up all the leftover supplies, dismantled the editing bench and Moviola editing machine, and loaded them all in the van for return to the rental house. Even today with digital editing, I get a melancholy feeling when the editing room officially closes. It symbolizes that the movie is over, definitively.

On this particular day, Scott was more reflective than usual. He told me that his good friend Roger Avary had flown off to Europe for the summer and that his mom had vacated the rental in Sherman Oaks that he had been sharing with her. She had moved back to the East Coast and Scott found himself alone for the remaining six weeks on the lease. After that he was at loose ends now that his job was over on *Survival Quest*. What Scott didn't know was that there had been some rumblings of interest in a sequel to *Phantasm*—from Universal Pictures of all places. I wasn't telling anybody about it yet. Until it was solid I didn't want to get anybody's hopes up.

I received a call a week later from a friend who had worked on *Survival Quest* who confided in me that Scott was severely depressed and had mentioned suicide. I immediately called Scott and asked him about it and he told me he had been feeling down but that suicide was not an option for him. I really didn't know much about depression and suicide back then so my words of encouragement were probably not very sophisticated; I just told him how much I valued his talents and how much I liked him and that at his young age of just twenty years old he had a lot to look forward to. We promised to meet up the next week. I saw him in Hollywood about ten days later and he was riding a brand-new motorcycle. I asked how he was feeling and he said he was good. He looked well and I intimated that we were making some progress on financing a sequel to *Phantasm* and that we might need to open an editing room again soon. To this day I wish I had told him then and there about Universal Pictures' interest and that I had been thinking of elevating him to full editor on the project if it went forward. But I didn't and we said our goodbyes and Scott roared off.

The Fourth of July holiday was the next week and I went with my family to a big fireworks and stunt show at the Rose Bowl. Early the next morning I was awakened by a phone call. A woman was on the line and she identified herself as calling from the coroner's office. She told me Scott Magill was dead. He had apparently killed himself on the night of July Fourth by leaping to his death from his six-story apartment building. I was stunned, but I remember informing her that I just couldn't believe this news and told her I needed to verify her identity. God forbid this was a prank call! She gave me her phone number and when I called back, my blood ran cold when the receptionist answered, "Los Angeles County Coroner's Office." The rest of the conversation was a blur. I remember something about the police finding a note in Scott's pocket addressed to several people including me, and then the very kind coroner's assistant reading it to me aloud. Something about how much he enjoyed working on *Survival Quest* with me and how he had loved watching my film *Kenny & Company,* that it was a great film, and how he was confident I would be making more good films.

Scott's death really hit me hard. I had just worked with him in the close quarters of our *Survival Quest* editing room for over a year prior to his death. Scott was so young. He had so much ahead of him. For years after, I was filled with regret. Why couldn't I have just said the right thing? Played up the potential new job on *Phantasm II*? Why didn't I tell him that I wanted him to be the editor? If only he could have lasted another few months we would have been in the thick of making *Phantasm II* for Universal, and he wouldn't have had any time for thoughts of killing himself. As the years passed I learned a lot about suicide, how there are people that threaten it and never do it, and the ones like Scott, who are in genuine pain and make up their mind and no matter what anybody says, they just go out and do it.

To this day, decades later, I still frequently ruminate about Scott Magill. I remember how much joy he was filled with on the day *Evil Dead II* opened in Hollywood. I gave him the day off and watched as he and Roger headed out from the editing room, bubbling with excitement about the new Sam Raimi movie. Whenever I'm at an opening night of a new horror film, I end up thinking about Scott as I wait for the lights to go down. Every Fourth of July when I'm watching fireworks, I think about whether Scott was watching fireworks from his apartment roof the night of his death. And whenever I go see a new movie by Roger Avary or Quentin Tarantino, I think about Scott and how much he would have enjoyed seeing his good friends thrive in Hollywood. He would have loved watching them win that Oscar together.

FUNDING ANOTHER *PHANTASM*

Throughout my entire career, finding the money to fund my films has been an excruciatingly difficult task. It has required countless meetings humbly seeking investors, and many times these so-called investors never had any money to begin with. The lure of Hollywood draws many strange people; frequently the easiest path to notoriety is to announce that you have created a fund to produce a slate of films, and independent filmmakers will lavish attention on you whether you have any money or not.

Phantasm II was the only film I ever made where the funding came easily. James Jacks was the junior studio executive at Universal Studios who was responsible for getting *Phantasm II* made. Well, not quite. Actually Jim was responsible for getting the project in front of his boss, the president of the studio, Tom Pollock, and he was the one who made the decision to put *Phantasm II* into production. I knew Tom; he had been my attorney while making *The Beastmaster*. Tom had been one of the first entertainment attorneys to focus on getting filmmakers an even shake from the Hollywood studios. Most famously, Tom had represented George Lucas on his first *Star Wars* film and assisted him in maintaining sequel rights in the series and helping him to create a literal empire of his own. It was ironic that Tom now ran a studio.

As head of the studio, Tom Pollock had one self-imposed mantra—to bring as many genre franchises into his studio as possible. During his tenure at Universal, Tom brought in directors like Wes Craven and Sam Raimi (another client) to work on films for the studio. He quickly bought the rights to the killer-doll *Child's Play* series from MGM. And then Jim Jacks mentioned to him that a sequel to *Phantasm* was in play. Tom jumped on in and literally within days we had the largest budget ever to be spent on a *Phantasm* film—just under THREE MILLION DOLLARS!

To the average person that might sound like a lot of money. And for this *Phantasm* filmmaker, who had made the original film for about 10 percent of that sum, it certainly was. But to put it in the proper perspective, Universal Studios had not made a film for three million dollars in a long time. Their idea of a low-budget movie at that time was more in the range of ten million dollars. *Phantasm II* was a killer deal for them.

After the original *Phantasm* was a success, I had no intention of ever making a sequel. In my mind *Phantasm* was a one-shot deal. At the end of my film the nefarious Tall Man won and everyone else lost. It was game over. However, after you make a successful film, all anyone wants to talk about is a sequel. "When's the next one?" I would go out on meetings, seeking funding for terrific new original film projects, and the subject of a *Phantasm* sequel would always come up. I would patiently explain that a sequel was never intended and that I had no idea how to write one.

A few years later, when I was seeking funding for *Survival Quest,* I was counseled by a film financier that if I had a screenplay for a *Phantasm II* and could offer that project along with the new one, the road would be a lot easier. Again, I had no clue where to begin a *Phantasm* sequel, but I love a challenge and put myself to work attempting to conjure up a legitimate plan.

One day, an idea came to me. It wasn't a sequel, it was simply an approach. What if I were to start *Phantasm II* the very moment after the original film ended? Such a simple concept, but for me it was mind-blowing. After all, while Mike is being attacked upstairs by the Tall Man and his dwarf-creatures, what's Reggie doing downstairs? And that question led me right into writing *Phantasm II*. Obviously, Reggie was still strumming the guitar, but then he would hear shattering glass upstairs—wouldn't our intrepid ice cream man hero investigate? He arrives at Mike's room to find the dreaded Tall Man in his house—what does he do? He runs downstairs of course to get his shotgun, but in searching for ammo he is confronted by a shitload of ornery dwarf-critters. Mayhem ensues and Reg goes mano a mano with the critters and must ultimately sacrifice his house to get his young pal Mike out of danger. The rest of the story would then be a road picture as our two heroes track the Tall Man. Bingo!

Once the deal with Universal was made I began assembling a crew to help me. After my *Beastmaster* debacle I swore I would surround myself only with friends I could trust. Unfortunately my longtime producing partner Paul decided to leave the film industry after *The Beastmaster*. Smartly, he had an exit strategy in place, right into a highly successful career in the financial world. I am so happy and proud of him and many times I wish I had followed his lead.

For *Phantasm II* my first hire was Roberto Quezada as producer. He had been there with me at the beginning with the original film. Backing him up was another key player from *Phantasm* and *Jim The World's Greatest*, Bob Del Valle, as production manager and associate producer.

Daryn Okada had been a kid, just sixteen years old, when Roberto brought him on board to work as a grip on *Phantasm*. In fact the first alcoholic drink Daryn ever had was Dos Equis beer during the *Phantasm* shoot in the bar set of the Dunes Cantina scene. Unfortunately, by the time we finished wrapping production that night, Daryn was passed out in the bar and the last crew out abandoned him there. I can only imagine what it must have been like for the teenage Daryn to wake up the next morning with a hangover in some strange bar and have to find his own way home. Now, ten full years older at age twenty-six, Daryn would be running our crew as the full-on director of photography on *Phantasm II*. Daryn would go on from our movie to a respected career in filmmaking, ultimately being elected by his peers to the prestigious role as president of the American Society of Cinematographers.

During preproduction Jim Jacks invited me to dinner in West Hollywood at the expensive Palm restaurant. Since it was on Universal's dime, I was happy to join him for lobster and steak (back when I used to eat that stuff). Jim was excited for me to meet a longtime collaborator of his, director Sam Raimi. It was fun to finally meet Sam and share war stories from the indie horror world. Sam expressed his admiration for *Phantasm,* and one scene in particular in which Mike finds Reggie's abandoned ice cream truck overturned in the fog. I in turn quizzed him on how he achieved all his marvelous effects in *Evil Dead II,* including the flying eyeball into the actress's mouth (reverse motion, just like our sphere impact!) and actor Bruce Campbell flying and spinning through the air (undercranked camera!). We both commiserated about our difficulties dealing with greedy and unscrupulous distributors. At that time in my career, I really didn't know many working directors so it was pretty cool to hang out with him. Sam was working with Jim on developing his new film *Darkman* at Universal. During dinner, Sam was kind enough to recommend to me two key crew members from his *Evil Dead II* movie: production designer Philip Duffin and special makeup effects artist Mark Shostrom.

I hired both of them, and in exchange Sam intimated that he would enjoy an acting role in *Phantasm II.* This turned out to be problematic for me as like the previous *Phantasm,* the sequel would take place in depopulated locations with a very small cast. There was no role for Sam! I came up with a way to include him in a sequence in which a creepy crematory assistant was preparing ashes and bone from a cremation for delivery. On the original *Phantasm,* I spent some time in working crematoriums and learned that after burning, the remains are not only ash. A lot of bones are left over that do not burn, and it is the job of the crematory assistant to smash them with a hammer so they will fit in the urn. (I also learned a lot of other interesting things about cremation if you are interested. When a corpse starts to burn, it causes the biceps and other muscles to tighten and its arms lift straight up above its head as if it is still alive. Freaky, huh? Did you know that breast implants and heart pacemakers have to be removed, otherwise they might explode during incineration?)

My workaround was to place Sam Raimi's name on a bag of ashes and bone that the Tall Man's assistant was hammering into dust in the crematorium scene. I thought Sam might like this "shout out" and that fans-in-the-know would enjoy seeing an obscure horror director's name referenced. Too bad Sam had to go on to such great success directing the *Spider-Man* films, among many others. Now when folks watch that scene and this world-famous director's name becomes visible, I think it's a real head-scratcher for most of them as to why it's there.

Just before *Phantasm II* received the green light, I received fantastic news that Shelley was again pregnant. We would be welcoming our second addition to our family during preproduction. This time it was a lovely little girl who we named Chloe. She was perfect in every way and Shelley and I were literally beaming with pride.

NOT CASTING BRAD PITT

U niversal put me in an awful predicament when they forced me to replace Michael Baldwin in the role he created in *Phantasm*. As casting began on *Phantasm II,* the Universal executives made it very clear to me that they expected me to cast a working actor in the role of Mike. This created a major problem as Michael Baldwin, who originated the role, had left the business and had not been working as an actor for a few years. I was in a very awkward position. I had known Michael for over a decade and had made two films with him. He was a dear friend. To try to change the executive's minds I even cajoled Michael into coming over and allowing me to videotape him reading for the part. In retrospect, this was hugely disrespectful. Michael had originated the role in a hit movie—why should he ever be asked to read for his own role? Well, I thought I could use his reading to convince Universal to allow him to play the role. It didn't work.

At the same time Universal forced me to look at other options to play Reggie. I had to waste valuable preproduction time interviewing almost every prematurely bald working actor in Hollywood. Finally the brass realized the obvious, that Reggie could not be recast. However they continued to insist on a new actor for Mike, arguing that the transition from twelve years old in the first *Phantasm* to nineteen-year-old Mike in part two could easily hide the change in actor. We ultimately cast James Le Gros, an exceptional actor who stepped into a difficult situation and performed the role admirably.

I sometimes wonder if I should have told Universal to take a hike when they suggested recasting. The harsh truth is they would have pulled the plug on *Phantasm II*. So I went ahead with the recasting, but to this day I still feel horrible about Michael Baldwin's treatment by the studio. The only thing that mitigates this whole mess is that on *Phantasm III* I had more control and was able to bring back Michael to star. After that, Michael went on to star in two more *Phantasm* films and he was terrific in all of them.

Sometime in the late nineties Michael told me an interesting story. He mentioned that he was over at a dinner party with actress Jennifer Aniston, whom he had been friends with since before she was famous. Her new boyfriend, actor Brad Pitt, suddenly blurted out, "Hey, you're the *Phantasm* guy." According to Michael, Brad laughed and said that he had auditioned for *Phantasm II* but didn't get the part. I didn't know how this could be. My memory must be failing me, but I never remembered meeting Brad Pitt. Well, Michael insisted that I did.

A while later, I came across some old VHS casting tapes from *Phantasm II* and started fast-forwarding through them. Lo and behold, there it was. On-screen, my casting director, Betsy Fels, opens the office door with a flourish and announces, "Don, meet Brad Pitt." And in walked Brad Pitt, who proceeded to read the cemetery scene from *Phantasm II*. "Reggie, every one of these graves is empty!" In my defense, Brad was young, twenty-three years old, had this Flock of Seagulls wraparound hairstyle, and at the time was wearing eighties parachute-style exercise pants tucked into his socks and hi-top Reeboks. In hindsight, I guess it was probably a huge mistake, but at that age, he had not matured yet into the Brad Pitt we know today. He gives it his best in the video audition and I am sure that he would have done just fine in the role. Can you imagine? Brad Pitt squaring off against the Tall Man? That would have been epic.

The Brad Pitt episode was not the only casting blunder I ever made. In my movie *Survival Quest* the character named Gray ultimately went to a fine young actor named Dermot Mulroney in his first feature film role. During casting for that film a diminutive, very young actor came in and read for the same role. I think my comment at the time was that if I sneezed he would blow away. I have taken so much flak over the years for my mistake with Brad Pitt, I am absolutely not revealing who this unnamed actor is. I will say, though, as he aged and matured into a seasoned actor—to my everlasting regret—his career has certainly rivaled Brad Pitt's.

PHANTASM II: WAR STORIES

We shot *Phantasm II* much like the original film, only we had a lot more money. We rented a huge warehouse in Chatsworth, the same city in which we shot *Phantasm,* and built a large mausoleum set just like before. I really enjoyed making *Phantasm II.* I was working with pretty much the same cast and some of the same crew, but this time we had the resources to achieve many things I was unable to in *Phantasm.*

It was a remarkable experience for me, shooting a sequel to *Phantasm* after all the years of professing publicly that I had no interest in making one. The more I worked on it the more I enjoyed it. It was so much fun that I have a distinct memory of one day walking through production designer Phil Duffin's magnificent mausoleum set and ruminating to myself out loud, "I could see making *Phantasm* movies for the rest of my life." Little did I know how prophetic that statement would be.

What was great about the making of *Phantasm II* was that in some respects it allowed me to remake aspects of the original film, only this time with the resources to amplify things and get them right. This was most apparent in the sphere scenes. This time I could have not one but *three* spheres, and one of them could be bigger, bolder, and gold. We nicknamed it the "Rambo-sphere." It was loaded with weapons and included a red laser and an assortment of new and improved cutting blades. I also had the opportunity to upgrade the makeup effects, some of which were pretty spectacular.

I hired Mark Shostrom to supervise the makeup effects. Mark had recently completed supervising on director Stuart Gordon's terrific *From Beyond*. A week into the show I got into a bit of a kerfuffle with Mark when I learned that he had concurrently taken on another big effects job on a creature film called *DeepStar Six*. I was concerned that he would be stretched too thin to cover our show. As luck would have it, two of his capable young assistants, Robert Kurtzman and Greg Nicotero, were fully available to us. These two brilliant makeup effects artists would go on the following year to cofound one of the great Hollywood makeup effects houses, KNB EFX.

One of the major differences between *Phantasm II* and the original was that, from the outset, I envisioned it as a "road movie." Instead of passively waiting for the Tall Man to strike, Mike and Reggie take it upon themselves to arm up and go after him, intending to hunt him down. What ensued was a dark odyssey through murdered towns following his trail of destruction. For me, this was a new and creatively exciting path.

One of the signature sequences in *Phantasm II* involved an exploding house. Despite the fact that we had somewhat more money to spend, how could we possibly find a house to completely destroy? Enter CalTrans, the California state department of roads and highways. They were in the process of extending a major freeway and had condemned an entire tract of postwar single-family homes not far from the Los Angeles International Airport, or LAX as it is known. These homes were all for sale, cheap. For a meager five hundred dollars one could purchase an entire house, but the catch was that you needed to move it off the property. Evidently the moving costs were tens of thousands of dollars, so people were not beating down their doors to buy these inexpensive homes. We gently asked CalTrans if we purchased one of their houses would they mind terribly if, using carefully monitored pyrotechnics, we might blow it up in place prior to moving it. They were happy to allow us to do so as long as we purchased the house in advance and all the wreckage was carted away at the end.

What made the gag ambitious was that I needed it to work for three entirely separate sections of the film. In the screenplay, Reggie is trapped by dwarf-creatures in his kitchen and decides to sacrifice his house to escape from them and the Tall Man. He extinguishes the pilot lights on his range and cranks open the gas on all four burners. With a roaring fire in his living room fireplace just a couple dozen feet away, Reg figures he will have just a few moments to grab young Mike and escape out a window before the creatures are all incinerated in a house explosion.

To film all the necessary action I needed the following shots: First, I needed young Mike and young Reggie to be seen running from the house as it explodes just moments after escaping from the Tall Man. Next I needed to see the Tall Man approaching his hearse after young Mike has escaped, as the house explodes behind him. And finally I needed to jump forward in time nine years to adult Mike and older Reggie as they return to the house and it explodes in a parallel timeline. The challenge was how to do these three sets of action at once, as we had just the one single house to blow up.

Here's how we did it: On the far right side of the house I found an angle using a telephoto lens in which the actual Reggie could run toward camera dragging our young Mike stunt double. Next, filming straight on, again using a telephoto lens to bring the background up closer, we positioned the hearse so Angus could walk to it as the house burst into flames behind him. And right between the two setups, we could film the final angle, set a few years in the future, in which we would film through the window of the 'Cuda as it motors toward the explosion and skids to a stop. We had just the one take at getting all three actions right. This was going to be one high-pressure night.

For weeks I had been badgering the *Phantasm II* effects team; since we had gone to the effort and expense to buy them a house to destroy, I was expecting them to fully blow the shit out of it in one hellacious fireball. I have to say that they took me at my word. I had seen the pyrotechnic schematics and they called for almost a dozen steel mortars, each with a half-pound black powder bomb and five gallons of gasoline.

There was one big problem. The fire marshal assigned to supervise the safety of our explosion was one of the tough ones. Most of the time, as long as one follows the safety rules the fire marshal will allow you to do whatever you want. This guy was a real stickler and was going around and demanding changes that would imperil our big explosion. After all the planning and effort it was so frustrating to have one person ruin everything. But then *Phantasm* worked its magic.

The fire marshal was talking to one of the crew and asked what this movie was. When he heard the word *Phantasm* his mood changed entirely. Was this a sequel to the horror film with the tall guy and the ball, he inquired? When that was confirmed, a big smile came across his face and he told our producer Roberto that we could do whatever we wanted and as far as he was concerned we could blow the holy hell out of the house. That was one fan who made a huge impact on our sequel.

The house was now essentially one big bomb ready to blow. There were so many explosives inside I think our pyro team's goal was to take that entire second story off. When a movie light inside the house fell over and needed to be righted, it caused a revolt on set by our electric crew. Prior to the explosion our director of photography Daryn sent an electrician in to fix the problem, but the guy only got a few steps in before quickly backing out. Daryn informed me his lighting crew would not go inside the house because the gasoline fumes were too heavy and he would not let them take the risk. One of the pyro team laughed, put out his cigarette, and ran inside the locked-and-loaded house and fixed the light.

We did the shot by countdown. As we started rehearsing the three sets of action, my assistant director Alan Connell would start counting down backwards from eight on his megaphone. After a few run-throughs every actor had their own count and all of them would hit their final mark on zero—that was the cue for the pyro techs to hit the detonator.

The FAA had been alerted of our intended explosion near LAX. Their approval came through and we had a five-minute window to shoot the shot with no jets in the vicinity. Alan gave the instruction to roll cameras and all five started burning through film. "READY! EIGHT, SEVEN"—the muscle car with James Le Gros and stuntman Reggie started to roll toward the house. "SIX, FIVE"—Angus Scrimm started walking toward his hearse. "FOUR, THREE"—Reggie and stunt young Mike began running from the house. "TWO, ONE" . . . and BAM! The house went up in a massive, concussive fireball. Mission accomplished!

Phantasm II was not without problems. We had one major incident that almost scuttled the production. We were filming one day up on the Angeles Crest Highway in the local Angeles National Forest. We had finished a couple scenes featuring Reggie Bannister and James Le Gros, then packed up and headed back down the mountain. Last to leave was our five-ton grip truck packed with not only our grip and lighting gear, but also our full Arriflex camera package, including a solid steel camera dolly. This was a big, heavy load.

Driving the truck down the hill in the encroaching darkness was a young grip named Shane who quickly noticed something was amiss with the truck, specifically the brakes. They didn't work! One can only imagine the thoughts that must have been running through that young man's head. Four miles to go downhill, three thousand feet of altitude to lose, no way to stop, and at the bottom of the mountain was a stoplight and a major intersection. Jump out? No way. Fifty miles an hour is far too fast to survive. So what did Shane do? He went for it, rode the truck all the way to the end of the line, determined to figure a way out of his predicament without killing anybody, especially himself. As the truck gained speed, Shane was able to maintain control of it through the hairpin turns and managed to avoid plummeting off a cliff. But coming right at him was that intersection where Highway 2 T-bones into Foothill Boulevard. As he raced toward a certain collision, Shane suddenly found himself with a choice: hit the soft target of two ladies in the crosswalk up ahead who were crossing Foothill Boulevard and then try to gently roll the truck on its side into the small park nearby; or aim straight for that brand-new Cadillac parked right there in the Denny's restaurant parking lot. Shane chose Detroit's finest and plowed directly into the Caddy. He totaled the luxury car, which absorbed the brunt of the impact and allowed Shane to walk away from the wreck relatively unscathed. The camera gear? Not so lucky. Total loss. Combining the truck, the Cadillac, and the lighting package, the loss totaled well over four hundred thousand dollars.

Later, the highway patrol inspection determined that the brake linings were worn and it was the responsibility of the truck rental company. And as we waited several months to get compensation, our production insurance was a true lifesaver, advancing money to keep us shooting. Our driver, Shane Hurlbut, went on to become a highly successful cinematographer in his own right, shooting some big movies. He shot the big-budget *Terminator Salvation* and had his own brush with tabloid notoriety when a voice recording of star Christian Bale screaming at him was accidentally released. I was impressed with how Shane kept his cool during that episode, but to this day am much more impressed with him riding that out-of-control grip truck down the mountain, without killing anyone, including himself.

For the first time since our amateur attempt at a research screening on the original film, *Phantasm II* was subjected by Universal to three rounds of professionally recruited audience research screenings. In the first of these screenings my cut was crude, and a few written comments said the movie might be "confusing." Despite the fact that the charm and the artistry of the original *Phantasm* was its nonlinear dream logic, a mandate came down from the Black Tower that I must remove all dream sequences; the audience must know where they were and exactly what was going on at every moment in the film. My arguments were ignored and that is why, still to this day, you can hear the character of Liz in the opening narration rather awkwardly say about the Tall Man, "He was a grave robber from another dimension." This was the truth, but we certainly never said it in the first film. We let the audience figure it out. While they were scrambling to figure out what the hell they were watching they might have been thinking, "Hey, wait! Is this tall dude a grave robber from another dimension?" It is so much more subtle to make the audience ask these questions of themselves rather than to come out and tell them.

Our second screening played much better, the cut was tighter, and the audience really liked it—so much so that Jim and the other junior executives decided they could take a gamble and invite studio chief Tom Pollock to the third one. During this screening, the film played through the roof. I knew we would be okay with the studio when, during the riotous gold sphere scene as it chewed through actor Mark Major as the hapless mortuary assistant, I saw Tom Pollock's bag of popcorn go flying in the air.

One of Universal's major summer movies was delayed, and in all their wisdom, they decided to release our little horror sequel in that slot. As we raced to complete the film in time, I received some devastating news. The Motion Picture Association of America had decided that *Phantasm II* was too violent to receive an R rating. It was the same roadblock we had run into on the original *Phantasm,* only this time the MPAA was resolute. I must cut the blood flow in two of the sphere scenes or I would be awarded the successor to the X, the dreaded NC-17 rating. Universal could not change the release date, so this made it impossible to schedule a formal appeals hearing. It was supremely frustrating for me to be in this position. Especially when I watched their approved version. The sphere sped down the hall and impacted the head of the victim who then struggled and fell to the floor in a huge pool of blood. But we never saw how the blood got there. The finished, *approved* version looked like the director had made a giant continuity error. I vowed then that if I ever made another *Phantasm* film it would be far more bloody and I would challenge them in an appeal.

Because we were suddenly opening in this new midsummer date, there was no lead time for proper promotion. For some unknown reason the studio marketing team did not follow the Avco Embassy playbook, so Angus and I did no touring and zero interviews together. *Phantasm II,* our small little horror sequel, would be running right into the teeth of the major summer "tentpole" releases with their massive marketing budgets. In fact, during that second week of July in which we opened, two major movies were each grossing over twenty million dollars in the marketplace, which was huge business at that time. Traditionally, lower-budget horror films played around Halloween or early spring to avoid big competition. And to top it off, when *Phantasm II* opened to just middling business, Universal already had us "closed-end booked" so that fourteen days after our release, their delayed film moved in and gobbled up all our theaters and we were done.

Even though my studio executive on the film, Jim Jacks, told me, "Remember, Don, you made a good movie," it was still a sad ending to a lot of hard work. I had been hoping that *Phantasm II* might give me that chance to finally break back into the studio system and leave the guerilla filmmaking world behind. It was not to be. Later, during a postmortem at the studio, Jacks quoted studio chief Tom Pollock as saying, "Unfortunately, we sacrificed *Phantasm II* to the movie gods of summer."

And then a funny thing happened. Much like *The Beastmaster* before it, *Phantasm II* went on to sell a shitload of videocassettes, which brought a big chunk of change back to the studio. Due to this success, I asked Jim to try to resuscitate my standing at Universal and see if he might find me a directing gig on another film over there. He agreed to try. A few months after that Jim confessed that he had tried hard to get me on one of their upcoming horror pictures, but a major agency pushed hard for a client and subsequently I lost out. I was thankful to Jim for the effort until I later learned that the film I wasn't good enough to get was the killer-doll sequel *Child's Play 3*. And in retrospect, that was probably a good thing.

HEY JOE

I t all started with an afternoon trip to my local horror bookshop in Sherman Oaks, California. It was a little hole-in-the-wall called Dangerous Visions, which is now long since gone. I was chatting up the guy behind the counter and casually asked him what was new and cutting-edge in horror. He said, "Follow me." He led me to the back of the store, to the "L" fiction aisle. "Texas author Joe Lansdale," he said, and stuck a paperback in my hand. "Good storyteller," he said, and, as I read over the back cover, he followed up with, "Joe Lansdale always has a high body count."

Well, I went home with a copy of Lansdale's *The Drive-In*. I was halfway through his funny, freaky, and horrific book when I realized it would make for a fantastic movie. Lansdale had an artistic proclivity for mashing up disparate genres and thereby creating something truly unique. My good friend Jeff Conner, who was once the publisher of the innovative and now-extinct Scream Press, managed to get me on the phone with Joe. I told Joe I was a fan and wanted to make his book *The Drive-In* into a movie. Unfortunately those rights had just been optioned to someone else, but Joe's response was to invite me down to visit him in Texas. He was sure we'd be able to cook up something for us to work on together.

About a month later I arrived in Houston and drove two hours north into Lansdale country, East Texas. Anyone who gets to know Joe R. Lansdale knows that his hometown of Nacogdoches informs his entire being. Much of his best work has been set among the mysterious pine forests on the border of Texas and Louisiana. Joe and I got along famously and although we did not find a project then to work together on, I had made a great new friend and was determined to one day make a film with this brilliant author.

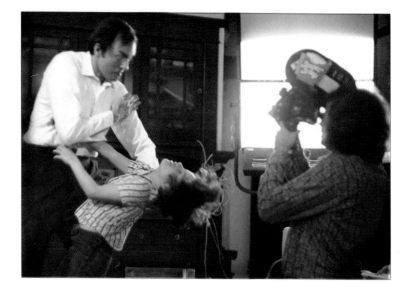

▲ Shooting a scene from my first film with Angus Scrimm. *(Courtesy of New Breed Productions, Inc.)*

◀ Receiving a big fat check! *(Copyright © 2018 Silver Sphere Corporation)*

▼ My first foray into indie film marketing with the Jim-mobile. *(Copyright © Paul Pepperman)*

◂ Sid Sheinberg and Lew Wasserman, titans of Hollywood. *(Photo by Lisa Rose/ Globe Photos, Inc.)*

▾ Me and the kids make the Tokyo front page with new pal, home-run hero Sadaharu Oh.

⏴ The *Kenny & Co.* cast. I still love these kids!
(Copyright © 2018 Silver Sphere Corporation)

⏴ Michael Baldwin—a good kid and a great actor.
(Copyright © 2018 Silver Sphere Corporation)

▾ The cast and I toast the success of *Phantasm*.
(Copyright © 2018 Silver Sphere Corporation)

▲ Ice cream man, friend, hero. Reggie.
(Copyright © 2018 Silver Sphere Corporation)

▼ Pondering the next shot. Note: Bill Thornbury behind me in position to get pulled into mausoleum wall.
(Copyright © 2018 Silver Sphere Corporation)

▲ Paul and I just hanging out with the Tall Man. *(Copyright © 2018 Silver Sphere Corporation)*

▼ The *Phantasm* brain trust on set. George Singer, Paul Pepperman, Michael Baldwin, and me. *(Copyright © 2018 Silver Sphere Corporation)*

Boooyyyyy! *(Copyright © 2018 Silver Sphere Corporation)*

▲ *The Beastmaster* at the Chinese Theatre on Hollywood Boulevard. *(Copyright © Paul Pepperman)*

◀ Guess which one is me? *(Copyright © 1981 Bill Richert)*

▼ The great pyramid of Aruk. Only Marc Singer had the agility to run up those steps. *(Copyright © 1981 Bill Richert)*

▲ Best cinematographer in the world. John Alcott! *(Copyright © 1981 Bill Richert)*

◄ Showing my dad around the *Beastmaster* sets. *(Copyright © 2018 Silver Sphere Corporation)*

▼ Actor John Amos on the bridge into the walled city of Aruk. *(Copyright © 1981 Bill Richert)*

▲ My mom (with my dad) enjoying her billboard on the Sunset Strip. *(Copyright © 2018 Silver Sphere Corporation)*

▼ The *Survival Quest* team is ready for some serious backpacking. *(Photo by Scott Redinger-Libolt; copyright © 2018 Silver Sphere Corporation)*

▲ Kerry Prior and coproducer Seth Blair with the brilliant see-through Plexiglas sphere rig, featuring a mirror to reflect the marble wall in the flying ball. 100 percent in-camera effect! *(Photo by Scott Redinger-Libolt; copyright © 2018 Silver Sphere Corporation)*

◀ *Thunk! Whirr! Splat! (Photo by Scott Redinger-Libolt; copyright © 2018 Silver Sphere Corporation)*

▾ That's me behind the camera as hearse slams into pipe ramp. Note: Stuntman ready to yank me to safety if things go wrong. *(Copyright © Bob Ivy)*

My dear friend Angus Scrimm. One of my favorite photos. *(Photo by Scott Redinger-Libolt; copyright © 2018 Silver Sphere Corporation)*

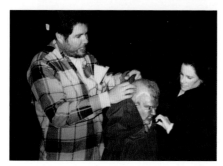

▲ The Demon Trooper (Bob Ivy) from *Phantasm Oblivion* has Reggie in his clutches. *(Photo by Scott Redinger-Libolt; copyright © 1998 Silver Sphere Corporation)*

▼ Shooting a fight with Reg and the Demon Trooper. *(Photo by Scott Redinger-Libolt; copyright © 1998 Silver Sphere Corporation)*

▲ Shelley and I prepare our daughter, Chloe, for her big scene. *(Copyright © 2018 Silver Sphere Corporation)*

▼ The smooth, marble mausoleum floors make for great dolly shots. *(Photo by Scott Redinger-Libolt; copyright © 2018 Silver Sphere Corporation)*

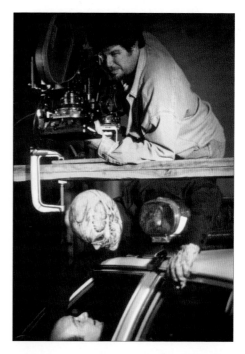

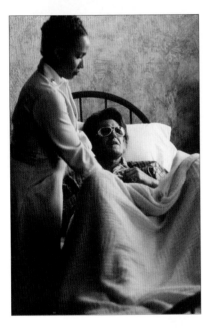

▲ Bruce and Ossie became fast friends on the set of *Bubba Ho-tep*. Here, they share a laugh before the camera rolls. *(Photo by Scott Redinger-Libolt; copyright © 2018 Silver Sphere Corporation)*

◄ Nurse Ella Joyce ministers to Elvis's faulty member. *(Photo by Scott Redinger-Libolt; copyright © 2018 Silver Sphere Corporation)*

▼ Bruce catching a little quiet time between takes at the Rancho Los Amigos set. *(Photo by Scott Redinger-Libolt; copyright © 2018 Silver Sphere Corporation)*

First Masters of Horror dinner (L to R). Front: Larry Cohen, Robert Parigi, John Carpenter, Bob Burns, John Landis, Tobe Hooper, Mick Garris. Back: Stuart Gordon, me, Guillermo del Toro, Bill Malone.

(Copyright © 2001 Robert Parigi)

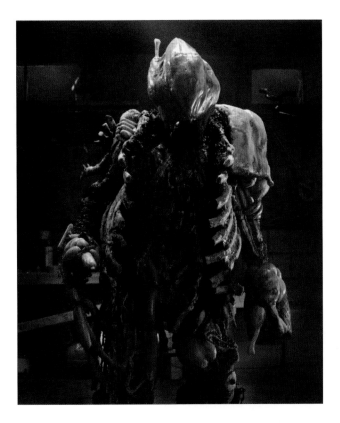

▲ The Meat Monster from *John Dies at the End.*
(Copyright © 2012 Silver Sphere Corporation)

▼ Dave (Chase Williamson) and John (Rob Mayes) from *John Dies at the End. (Copyright © 2012 Robert Raphael Photography)*

▲ The Battlecuda from *Phantasm Ravager*. *(Copyright © 2018 Silver Sphere Corporation)*

◄ Chunk (Stephen Jutras), Mike, and Reggie in *Phantasm Ravager*. *(Copyright © 2018 Silver Sphere Corporation)*

▼ The final day of shooting *Phantasm Ravager* (L to R). Reggie Bannister, A. Michael Baldwin, me, Bill Thornbury, and director David Hartman. *(Copyright © 2018 Silver Sphere Corporation)*

SCREENING ROOMS

One of the most immense changes in filmmaking in the digital age is the demise of the traditional Hollywood motion picture screening room. Out in front of the film labs filmmakers would congregate, waiting for their screening time and their room to become available. In the eighties, FotoKem in Burbank had a couple of much-in-demand screening rooms and the only place to wait was one cramped, narrow hallway. Frequently you'd run into indie filmmaker friends there, sometimes even major Hollywood stars waiting for their screening room to open up. Now you can watch your films right on your laptop or home TV or stream them to friends over the Web to get comments.

In fact, the entire nature of theatrical projection has changed dramatically. At the zenith of the multiplex cinema, a visit to the projection booth would be mind-boggling. A dozen large projectors would be whirring, manned by a staff of three projectionists—each with a six-foot platter system feeding thousands of feet of film per minute through these huge clattering beasts. But now? The projection booths are empty. And silent. A visit to a major multiplex theater projection booth today is eye-opening. No one runs the show. Just a single computer. And on Thursday night the theater manager alone loads no film, just the files of the new films into the server and everything else is automated—trailers, the feature itself, lights, and the curtains.

I received a call from Quentin Tarantino. He had booked a screening room to run the rough cut of his first film, *Reservoir Dogs*. There were just a dozen people in the audience, including Roberto and Roger, as Quentin gave a hilarious and heartfelt introduction about how happy he was to be there sharing his first film with us. Throughout the screening I kept wondering how a first-time filmmaker could make a film so accomplished and assured. It was simply stunning. Afterward we had to clear out of the screening room as another group was coming in. Out in the hallway with Roberto, Roger, Quentin, his producer Lawrence Bender, and editor Sally Menke, Quentin asked me what I thought. Of course I told him how much I liked it and how great the unconventional structure was. As a friend, and being the experienced director there, I felt obligated to give him some kind of constructive criticism since he was not finished with his cut. So, I had the temerity to ask Quentin if maybe he might think about trimming down some of that opening sequence dialog in the diner scene about Madonna and tipping and get on with the story. Maybe even lose it entirely and just get the story going? (Shows what I know. Those scenes are now considered by film critics worldwide to be some of the finest moments in the film.) Quentin politely declined my advice.

A year and a half later I was back in a screening room over at Raleigh Studios to watch the rough cut of Roger Avary's first film, *Killing Zoe*. Quentin had executive produced and helped secure the funding for the project, a brilliant, tough, and hard-edged little movie about a French bank robbery gone wrong. The entire South Bay Film Pack was there to watch another of their members' first feature directorial effort. Watching the film unfold, I couldn't help but wonder again how these two guys did it. Their very first films were so polished and made with such confidence. I was used to sitting through first films that were loaded with flaws and barely watchable. Quentin, and now Roger, made it look so easy!

And just a couple of months after that I was back in a screening room with Quentin and Roger again, only this time over at the Goldwyn Studios on Santa Monica Boulevard to watch the rough cut of Quentin's second film. Roger had cowritten the screenplay. This time there were some luminaries in attendance including Quentin's producer, Danny DeVito, and the great actor Dennis Hopper. Quentin and Roger were making the rounds, greeting all their friends and the luminaries. One thing I observed that night that I found really touching: As the lights went down, when it came time for the movie to start, Quentin and Roger didn't sit with the big shots. They went down to the very front row of the theater, off to the side, and sat together. I watched them. Even though they had now scaled the heights of Hollywood, they were still two fast friends from the South Bay Film Pack joking and laughing and filled with excitement as the screening of their new movie was about to begin.

Even though the cut was about twenty minutes longer than the ultimately released movie, *Pulp Fiction* was an even better movie than *Reservoir Dogs*. The structure was not only more audacious; the movie was funny as hell and had some extremely intense suspense sequences. Afterward, when Quentin asked me what I thought, remembering the *Reservoir Dogs* screening, I demurred and bit my tongue. I didn't want to make a casual comment that might inadvertently influence this great movie. Even though a scene or two might have been tightened I just told him how much I loved it, which was true.

As I was walking to my car I looked over and was surprised to find Dennis Hopper walking beside me. Usually I try to give celebrities their space and not bother them in public, but Hopper's *Easy Rider* had made a huge impact on me at a very young age and it was hard to contain myself. I decided to keep it simple and just said, "I really loved Quentin's film." Hopper stopped in his tracks and suddenly it was like I was standing beside Francis Ford Coppola's character the "photojournalist," right out of his *Apocalypse Now*. Just him and me. "Yeah, man. Quentin really did it, man. I mean really. He really did it." We both stood there in silent contemplation for a long moment, then wished each other good night and that was that.

The next day Quentin called and we spent an hour on the phone discussing *Pulp Fiction*. I went into specific detail about all the great moments in the film. Quentin averred that he was under pressure from the producers and Miramax to cut some scenes and asked for my opinion. He had been advised to remove a long sequence with actress Julia Sweeney. She was a friend of his and he was reluctant to cut it, but he felt that if any scene had to go, that one did. Even though a bit gun-shy after my "advice" about *Reservoir Dogs,* I did finally open up and told him I agreed that he could lose the scene and it would probably not be missed.

Pulp Fiction went on to become a huge critical and box office smash. In 1995, Quentin and Roger received the Academy Award for Best Original Screenplay. Roger Avary went on to write and direct some amazing films, including *The Rules of Attraction* and *Mr. Stitch.* And Quentin's career is, of course, legendary. It's interesting that Quentin always stayed true to film and always shot on film and, as of this writing, never strayed into digital territory. Quentin even personally funded one of the best revival movie theaters in Los Angeles, the New Beverly Cinema, which to this day bucks the trends and still shows movies the old-fashioned way . . . on 35 mm film.

LORD OF THE DEAD

After enjoying the luxury of the "huge" three-million-dollar budget on *Phantasm II,* I was hoping to make another movie with a deep-pocketed studio. I focused my efforts on writing two very different and, in my completely unbiased opinion, terrific screenplays, which I thought might appeal to studio sensibilities.

The first screenplay was entitled *Castle* and was set in sixteenth-century England. It told a historically fictional story about an intrepid band of mismatched mercenaries who must storm a near-impenetrable English castle to free an heiress to the throne. The conceit of the film was that our band of heroes comprised a young Englishman leading two savage Mohawks from the New World and two Samurai warriors by stealth into battle. Katanas and tomahawks versus broadswords—it would have been epic!

The other screenplay was a hard-core horror story that, much like *The Bad Seed,* concerned the exploits of a terribly evil child. Universal had no interest in either, and although the screenplays received a few nibbles from others, I was never able to land the funding necessary for either project.

I am not the fastest writer, so consequently I invested almost two years in those two projects with not much at the end to show for it. This is a perennial frustration for the indie filmmaker. Most every creative endeavor starts with investing time and sometimes money to jump-start a project on spec, with no guarantee of ever making a film, let alone being compensated. We are the ultimate entrepreneurs. Every film is a start-up! And after we finish a film, the entire process, including the inherent risk, starts all over again.

My loyal comrade-in-arms Reggie Bannister may have made the most important contribution to getting the next *Phantasm* sequel made. After *Phantasm II,* Reggie was focused on his music career and, weird as this seems, took a side job at a mortuary—Sunnyside Mortuary in Long Beach, where we shot the original film. Reg learned a lot about the funeral trade while working there and I always enjoyed it when he would regale me with his stories from the death factory. If you were a *Phantasm* fan attending a funeral in Long Beach around that time there was a chance you might spot Reggie carting off your beloved ones to their final resting place.

One day Reg rang me up and with great excitement told me about a huge and architecturally significant mausoleum complex in nearby Compton, to which he had just delivered flowers. Angeles Abbey was built in the 1920s and featured three major mausoleums on the same property. Reggie arranged a tour for me and I was suitably impressed. The marble hallways were immense, foreboding, and mysterious. The place was somewhat run-down, which added to its creep factor. This would make a fantastic setting for our next sequel.

Around this time I met Robert Blattner, who had taken over the helm at Universal Home Entertainment. Robert was impressed with the video-cassette sales numbers on *Phantasm II* and eagerly offered to fund another one. The numbers would not support a three-million-dollar budget, but they certainly could cover something in the vicinity of half of that. So I started thinking about what elements might interest me in a new *Phantasm.*

My first decision was to return Michael Baldwin to the fold. His unceremonious dumping by Universal on the previous picture was just not right. Bringing Michael back would provide some small form of justice, and for fans it would be epic. Then I began to think about what I wanted to accomplish with this new episode. What about doing a *Phantasm* in which Reggie could make a solo hero turn? And what about broadening the *Phantasm* ensemble to include some new characters? I was determined to go back to the roots and did this by introducing a young boy who might be reminiscent of Mike in the original. Also, how about something completely different for a leading lady? Maybe an African-American, nunchaku-wielding, karate-kicking love interest for Reg? And how about starting *Phantasm III* right where *Phantasm II* ended? The ideas started coming fast and furious and within days we were making a new *Phantasm*.

We blazed through preproduction and one of our best hires was D. Kerry Prior, who had been a key contributor to the sphere visual effects on *Phantasm II*. Kerry, a brilliant effects tech and filmmaker in his own right, agreed to come on board to handle the sphere effects on *Phantasm III*. The challenge for him was enormous. In *Phantasm II* we went from one sphere to three spheres. For *Phantasm III* my screenplay called for hundreds and possibly thousands of them. At that time computer-generated visual effects were in their infancy. (*Phantasm III* did feature three simple digital effects, which today you could do on your laptop, for which we paid tens of thousands of dollars.) Consequently, Kerry would be tasked with achieving these effects practically, in camera. Kerry sketched out some inventive and ambitious designs showcasing how he could build an elaborate Plexiglas rig that would support several different sphere models, all while being transparent to the camera.

About two weeks prior to the first day of shooting we received some terrible news. Our very supportive studio exec at Universal had died on Halloween night. Robert had been visiting a movie set in Utah and had taken a private plane home so he could be with his young children on Halloween and it crashed. This was a terrible blow. Not only was Robert a terrific guy who was willing to back me in a risky film project, but on the business side, we hadn't yet signed the final contract with Universal. Shooting started imminently and we were advancing money like crazy. A week went by and everyone on the crew was freaking out.

I was about to pull the plug on our film when Louis Feola called. Louis had just been selected to assume Blattner's position by the Universal brass. Louis revealed himself as a stand-up guy and told me that the policy he had instituted would honor all agreements Robert had negotiated, even if they were not yet signed. (Maybe there was a heart beating in Universal's formidable Black Tower after all.)

We leased a large warehouse out in North Hollywood and shooting began. As always, it was great to be working with the *Phantasm* cast again.

Reggie Bannister just seemed to get better with every film and in *Phantasm III*, with him now in the much-deserved starring role, we could take full advantage of his talents. Other core cast were back, including original star Bill Thornbury, who reprised his signature role of Jody in both corporeal and spherical form.

I was fortunate to find several new cast members, including Kevin Conners and Gloria Lynne Henry. Kevin was a tough little kid who performed his macho scenes with aplomb. Gloria was a joy to work with and a breath of fresh air for the franchise. Here was Reggie's sexy love interest, yet she had a badass streak and was a powerful force to be reckoned with. I also had some fun introducing three unique new characters, the "looters," down-market scavengers who were following the Tall Man's path of destruction and plundering the remains. These looters drove a pink hearse, which they used to carry all the gold and other booty they had "acquired" during their exploits.

The signature stunt of the screenplay was a concept that came to me early. I had seen a lot of pipe-ramp car stunts over the years, but never one featuring a six-thousand-pound Cadillac hearse. So I set about to fix that and wrote a scene in which Reggie, Mike, and their pals are accosted by the reanimated bodies of three looters they had previously killed. The undead looters arrive on the scene and a car chase ensues between Reggie, driving his restored triple black Hemicuda convertible, and the looters' pink funeral coach. The hearse loses control, hits a rock, and in true movie fashion is propelled skyward. How high and how far were the questions.

A quick explanation of how a pipe ramp works. Welded from tubular steel, the pipe ramp has three parts: a solid and heavy base staked right into the ground or asphalt with spikes called "bull pricks"; the main section, the ramp, which is just a single three-inch-wide steel bar designed at about a thirty-degree angle; and the "kicker," on top, which is just a small steel bar at the end of the ramp that is at a more severe angle of about forty-five degrees. The ramp is slathered with axle grease for lubrication. The task of the stuntperson is to get the car up to speed and aim directly for the ramp. The car goes up the ramp and hits the kicker, sending it almost straight up. At this point the stuntperson can no longer control the trajectory and, for better or worse, is just along for the ride.

One night I was watching a show called *Stuntmasters* where they had this daredevil stuntman ready to pipe-ramp a large school bus. Watching that yellow vehicle fly through the air was simply electrifying. This could be the guy who could jump my pink hearse! This Stuntmaster's name was Bob Ivy.

Imagine my surprise a few months later when my stunt coordinator, John Stewart, told me about a fellow stuntman he knew who was an expert at pipe ramps and a confessed *Phantasm* fan. Now, this was rare. Stunt guys just do not tend to be horror geeks. Then John told me the stuntman's name was Bob Ivy. I literally leapt out of my chair. "That's the guy who jumped the school bus on *Stuntmasters*!" John invited me down to San Pedro to watch Bob do a pipe-ramp gag. Bob was driving an SUV; he hit the ramp and crashed right into a boat on a trailer. It was a great stunt. Afterward I met Bob, who couldn't have been more gracious and unassuming. On the spot, Bob volunteered to do the hearse stunt and promised to make it a memorable event. Bob would turn out to be a man of his word.

The night of the stunt Bob was strapped into the hearse, inside a tubular steel roll cage welded inside the hearse's frame and clad in a full-body Nomex fire suit and crash helmet. I wished Bob luck, but I'm not sure he even heard me. Bob was a man on a mission and he was in the zone.

Everybody was there. All the cast, Angus Scrimm, Michael Baldwin, Reggie Bannister, the entire crew, including office staff and my family. Whether they were scheduled to work or not, no one wanted to miss Bob Ivy's hearse pipe-ramp stunt. It was a Saturday night on a quiet stretch of Mulholland Highway, which the city had granted us permission to close for the stunt. The lights were up and three cameras in position to film the stunt. About a half mile up one direction in the road, Bob was waiting patiently inside the hearse for his cue; a few hundred yards past the pipe ramp in the other direction an ambulance with EMTs was also waiting in case something went wrong.

We had three cameras set and the one I would be operating was right across from the pipe ramp. My task would be to pan with the hearse as it impacted the ramp and flew by into the air. I practiced the camera pan dozens of times. I could do this.

Bob was ready, and when the stuntman is strapped in and gelled up, it's time to go. I gave the nod to my young assistant director Jeff Shiffman and he called for cameras to roll film. Cries of "A Camera speed," "B Camera speed," and "C Camera speed" echoed down Mulholland Highway. I hunkered down next to my camera, and Jeff screamed into his megaphone, "Action! Go Bob, go!"

You could hear the hearse accelerate, and as it roared toward the ramp, building speed, one thing was certain in my mind. Bob was going to deliver on his promise. And you know what? He never took his foot off the gas pedal. He hit that pipe ramp fast and hard. Looking through the viewfinder of A Camera, I was the closest person to the ramp, and the sound of six thousand pounds of hearse hitting that pipe ramp was earsplitting. So much so that it caught me completely off guard. While looking through the camera viewfinder my eyelid instantly snapped shut! I went through the panning motion of the camera, which I had practiced dozens of times and memorized, but I had no idea if the hearse was correctly framed in my shot.

The hearse shot skyward and then tumbled through the air for over a hundred and eighty feet before crashing back to earth with a concussive and sickening crunch, rolling down Mulholland Highway until it stopped upside down.

A hundred people watched in stunned silence until stunt coordinator John Stewart broke from the crowd and charged into the road, racing down to the crashed hearse followed by literally everyone. I switched off my camera and made chase myself, stopping only to yank the battery cable of the 35 mm Eyemo "crash cam" that had been placed right in the middle of the road and was still rolling film. All the while I was mortified that while Bob had risked his life to create one of the most memorable scenes in the movie, I might have blown the shot.

The stunt team pulled the unconscious Bob Ivy out of the hearse wreckage and laid him out on the street. The EMTs swarmed around him and he was quickly revived. They checked all his limbs and nothing was broken. Bob got to his feet, gave the thumbs-up, and asked for a Coke. The assembled crowd cheered wildly. My cinematographer Chris Chomyn checked in, told me he got a great view from his camera and that the crash cam appeared to get excellent coverage of the stunt also. "How did it look from your camera?" he asked. "Just great," I replied sheepishly.

For two long days I waited to get the film dailies back from the lab, torturing myself that despite all the money we had spent and Bob's heroic efforts, I had blown the shot. Why didn't someone warn me there would be a huge bang when the hearse hit the ramp? I was in agony.

The film came back and my shot was perfect. Blind luck?! In any case when you watch this magnificent stunt in *Phantasm III*, consider these interesting facts. As the hearse soars through the air, Bob Ivy is strapped inside that thing, completely unconscious from the impact with the ramp, and the cameraman shooting it has his eyes completely closed.

When my terrific editor Norman Buckley finished our cut of *Phantasm III* it was submitted to the Motion Picture Association. And again, it was immediately slapped with the successor to the X rating, the just-as-restrictive NC-17, for bloodletting in the sphere sequence in which Taneesha (actress Sarah Davis) is drilled and killed. This time around I had the time to appear in front of an appeals panel and plead my case. My argument was strong: we had cut the length of the sequence, and bloodletting, to match exactly (to the frame in length) the original *Phantasm*. It seemed logical to me that if the original Phantasm received an R rating, how could they deny it to *Phantasm III*? The head of the rating system, Richard D. Heffner, presented his case at the appeals hearing, which was full of bluster and grumbling about how they had made a mistake on the original *Phantasm*, these sphere sequences were an outrage and he would not let me get away with it again. Blah, blah, blah. My argument persuaded a bunch of the panel members, but the deck was stacked against me. The rules required a two-thirds vote of the appeals panel to overturn and I came up one vote shy of that number. Again, I was forced to cut the sphere scene to the bone. The only consolation was that just a few years later, once DVD, Blu-ray, and then streaming became popular, my films could be seen anywhere in their original unrated form.

I was quite proud of the finished *Phantasm III*. However, I was in for a rude awakening when I submitted the final print to Universal for their consideration. After reviewing my film, one of their feature executives determined that *Phantasm III* did not merit a theatrical release and instead would be released direct-to-video. This was a horrible development. Back then, a direct-to-video release carried a terrible stigma and had the effect of turning your hard work into a "non-movie." Luckily I had asked for a clause in the agreement with Universal that if they decided not to give the film a wide theatrical release, they would fund a theatrical test market in two cities. I invoked this clause and a month later *Phantasm III: Lord of the Dead* opened in Grand Rapids and Baton Rouge. The weird part here is that the film did very good business in the test markets, and yet Universal still had no faith in it and we were relegated to the direct-to-video scrap heap. I was devastated after working for a full year and a half on a theatrical movie to have it disappear in an instant. It got worse, though.

At that time Blockbuster Video was the 800-pound gorilla in the home video world. A "brilliant" executive at Universal tried to knock them down a peg with an idea that Universal would sell videocassettes directly through McDonald's restaurants in a big holiday promotion. It was "buy a hamburger and get a videocassette for five bucks," and the tapes were flying out of McDonald's. Blockbuster hated this new sales channel; it bypassed them completely. So they retaliated. For the next quarter, Blockbuster unilaterally mandated that they would still take all the big star-driven movies from Universal, but they would refuse to buy any "second-tier" product. Guess whose film came out that quarter and was considered "second-tier" due to Universal's decision to send it direct-to-video? You guessed it! Universal Home Entertainment did not sell one single copy of *Phantasm III* to Blockbuster Video. This was a catastrophic event because, as indies, we had no control whatsoever in this clash of the titans and it guaranteed that *Phantasm III* would never recoup its investment. The sad truth is that the lowly indie filmmaker really has no control over the ultimate fate of their film.

A STUNT TO REMEMBER

n the early nineties, I was invited by Tony Timpone, the longtime editor of the great genre magazine *Fangoria,* to attend their Weekend of Horrors convention at the Hilton near LAX.

Actor Reggie Bannister was presenting our Tall Man, Angus Scrimm, with *Fangoria's* coveted Lifetime Achievement Award. Us genre guys don't get awarded Oscars, so this event is always a big deal in the horror fraternity. I brought the entire family with me and it was a genuine treat to see Angus up onstage receiving this well-deserved award. It was so nice to see Angus filled with such delight and humility as he received this honor. His on-screen nemesis, Reggie, gave a truly moving and heartfelt tribute and introduction to this man, who was so meaningful to us all and to the franchise. But a funny thing happened later as I was watching the rest of the show.

The star of the *Evil Dead* films, Bruce Campbell, was also in attendance to present an award. I had never met Bruce but had enjoyed watching the antics of his character Ash in the *Evil Dead* movies. When Bruce stepped through the curtains and walked out onstage to friendly applause he did something I would never forget. Without fanfare, as a treat for this crowd, Bruce suddenly performed an unexpected live stunt right out of *Evil Dead II.* Bruce wrapped his fingers around the back of his neck and threw himself forward, doing a complete somersault in midair and landing in front of the audience in a hard pratfall with a James Brown–inspired flourish. It was simply stunning. This was a damn dangerous stunt and it shocked everybody. A huge cheer erupted from the crowd and the entire audience jumped to their feet, clapping in delight. This guy was willing to risk his life to pay tribute to these horror fans and they responded with sheer adulation. I looked around at the cheering crowd and realized I had witnessed a connection between performer and audience of which I had never seen the likes before. That moment had a genuine impact on me and I would never forget it . . . and it would have a profound impact on my career a decade later.

PHANTASM 1999

When Roger Avary received the Academy Award for Best Original Screenplay with Quentin Tarantino for *Pulp Fiction* he probably ran into that annoying interviewer on his way out of the Shrine Auditorium. "Hey Roger! You just won the Academy Award. Where are you going now??" Well, Roger's appropriate answer should have been from the nineties theme park ad campaign, "I'm going to Disneyland!" But that's not Roger. In my imagination he said, "You know, I'm going home to start writing an epic, kickass, hyperviolent, balls-to-the-wall sequel to *Phantasm* for my friend Don Coscarelli to direct!"

With Hollywood at his feet after his Oscar win, Roger Avary had his choice of working on multiple big-money studio projects. He was the new kid in town and everybody wanted him to work on their projects. Instead, right after the awards, Roger invited me out for a Mexican lunch in Manhattan Beach and humbly and graciously asked if I would allow him to write the next *Phantasm* for me to direct. I tried to talk him out of it. I told him that our most recent *Phantasm III* had been tossed to the videocassette junk heap by Universal Pictures, and there was just no known business model for making a studio sequel after the previous sequel was sent direct-to-video. Roger was not to be deterred. He told me about how a decade previously, in the *Survival Quest* editing room, I had once told him and Scott Magill an idea for a *Phantasm* sequel in which Reggie set out into a wasteland decimated by the Tall Man, looking for his friend Mike. He wanted to take that idea and go crazy with it.

Roger had this incredible notion of an alien virus unleashed by the Tall Man that was 100 percent fatal. The Tall Man would be ensconced underneath Utah's Great Salt Lake, mining the Mormon Mausoleum—where every Mormon going all the way back to Joseph Smith was interred—for corpses. Millions of them! Salt Lake City would be ground zero of the "plague zone" and the intrepid Reggie would enter in search of Mike. He would drive an armored "Battlecuda" and be accompanied by his loyal sidekick, a squirrel monkey named Titi. On a parallel track, one badass military strike team commando, Colonel Heckleman, has received orders with his "S-Company" (S = Suicide) to enter the plague zone, find the Tall Man's lair, and cross into his dimension and detonate something called "the Quantum Phase Device." In the plague zone, S-Company gets in deep trouble and Reggie bails them out and they team up. Massive mayhem ensues.

It took Roger just three months to craft his epic script and I had a blast visiting at his house and encouraging him as he worked. His ability with creating dialog scenes just amazed me. He even gave the Tall Man his own inscrutable language, which he cheekily described in the script as sounding like Vietnamese spoken backwards. In reading his brilliant final script, I found it true to the original films while being original, epic, and violent in its own right.

In our minds we believed only one company had a real shot at getting *Phantasm 1999* funded. The first person Roger sent the script to was Bob Weinstein at Miramax. When Miramax dismissively passed on *Phantasm 1999*, I know Roger was shocked and dismayed. Roger had just won an Academy Award for cowriting their breakout hit *Pulp Fiction*, and he expected more loyalty and respect from them. Miramax had a reputation for being ruthless and unscrupulous; their actions in this regard spoke volumes.

We had one other realistic shot at getting the film made. A scrappy independent company expressed serious interest from the get-go. It was strongly suggested that if Roger and I came to that year's Cannes Film Festival in France, we could seal the deal right there on the Croisette. We paid our own travel costs and in many ways it was a terrific trip. We were able to hang out with Roger's longtime pal from his video store days, John Langley, who was the co-creator of one of the most-watched TV documentary series of all time in *Cops*. Roger also introduced me to his star from his great film *Killing Zoe,* French film actress and director Julie Delpy, and that was a genuine delight.

On a sunny afternoon in a quiet café in Cannes, we made a deal with the big boss of the company and shook hands on it. He told us we would reconvene on the phone in one week and firm up the terms of the deal. Roger and I were elated. Our trip had been worth it, mission accomplished!

One week to the day later, back in Los Angeles, I opened the *Hollywood Reporter* to read a story featuring the big boss, in which he stated that he had just closed a lucrative deal to sell his company for an astronomical price and he and his entire executive staff would be resigning immediately. It took awhile for the shock to wear off and the news to sink in, but something became immediately clear. These guys shook our hands and looked us right in the eye and told us they would be making *Phantasm 1999* and yet they had no intention to do so. I never did figure out why they would summon us across the world to do this, but in any case it pretty much was the death knell for *Phantasm 1999.*

A COUPLE OF WEB-SLINGERS

L ong before DVD and Blu-ray, Bruce Venezia and Sergio Leeman at Image Entertainment approached me about assisting them in creating a high-quality laser disc box set of *Phantasm*. Frustrated with the poor-quality VHS releases of my film, I realized this might be my golden opportunity to finally improve the viewing experience for fans. (The quality control of early VHS was so bad that a tape operator once erred and omitted a thirty-second sequence in the third act of *Phantasm*. For a decade this "short version" of the film was all that was available on VHS.)

In the midnineties, the laser disc format had a passionate fan base of cinephiles who were avid collectors of these expensive disc sets. Inspired by some great early laser disc editions, including Robert Rodriguez's *El Mariachi* and David C. Fein's production of *Aliens,* I threw myself into collecting as much value-added material as possible to create a memorable and tangible keepsake for our fans. The edition was limited to 2,500 units, which were signed and numbered by both Angus and myself. In addition to improved video and a new stereo soundtrack created by future Academy Award–winning sound editor Dane Davis, the release was chock-full of trailers, deleted scenes, and all kinds of *Phantasm* ephemera. It even featured a 24-carat-gold CD copy of the soundtrack music.

I thought the Image laser disc would be a one-off item and hoped it might have resonance for a short while. The edition quickly sold out. It was my first experience with the allure of the fan object and why these items can be such an important, immersive, and tangible legacy that connects a film to its fans in an authentic way. Over the years as technology improved, I have been able to participate in a number of cool collector editions, including the first MGM DVD, the phabulous *Phantasm* Sphere Set released only in the UK, and most recently working with home video industry aces Cliff Macmillan and Tony Vandeveerdonk on the *Phantasm Collection* in HD Blu-ray from Well Go USA. This one was limited to ten thousand units, yet it quickly sold out. As technology keeps improving, it's my goal to always keep *Phantasm* current. Definitely keep an eye out for that long-awaited 8K Holographic 4D Dolby Insanity Edition, which I am sure will be coming in the near future. It will be mind-blowing!

Around the time of the laser disc project, I had a brilliant friend named Sam Gasster who graduated from MIT and was, no joke, an actual rocket scientist. Sam worked in the aerospace industry on insanely complex space-related projects—supporting the Department of Defense, NASA, and other government organizations—that were so top-secret that he was never at liberty to discuss his work with me. We had a lot of fun together when our sons were young, taking them way out in the desert and shooting off model rockets. One thing Sam was definitely good at was building kickass model rockets.

In 1994, Sam mentioned this thing that he had available to him at his office, which he told me was called the "world-wide-web." He said I should come out there and check it out, as it was an efficient way of transmitting colorful pictures and text between computers. I had been an early member of the America Online Internet community and had been using it for email for some time. AOL had a large button on its splash page labeled "Coming Soon! WWW!" AOL promised that one day soon they would allow connectivity to this brand-new world-wide-web thing. A month or two later, when I finally gained access to the Web, I could see the potential to connect with film fans and determined that we absolutely needed to create a *Phantasm* website. With Sam as my technical guru we put together a detailed website with a dozen different sections, containing everything from a custom audio greeting from Angus Scrimm, to "the Tall Man's Tomb" with a history of the films, to "Epitaphs" with biographies of the cast and crew.

The most exciting aspect of the site was the "Tall Man's Guestbook," in which fans could publicly post their comments about the films. For a filmmaker, this was a completely novel and unprecedented experience—to have fans of the *Phantasm* films communicate their thoughts directly to me. Previously the only feedback I ever received was in rare audience screenings or by reading a film critic's opinion in print. Now, every single day, random people worldwide would post their sentiments online about my *Phantasm* films. (Remember, social media would not gain traction for another decade and a half.) Until the dawn of the Web I really had no idea how meaningful *Phantasm* was to so many people. It was a truly incredible and wonderful revelation and blessing.

But Sam and I really blew one big thing with this Web stuff. We had established a "Crypt Collectibles" page on the site in which we could sell leftover items of memorabilia directly to fans. *Phantasm* star Michael Baldwin had written a short book that his mother Pat published as one of her "miniature books." These were collectible limited-edition art books of no larger than three inches in height or width. *Sleep Achiever* featured an inventive design encasing Michael's two-inch-by-two-inch book within a tiny brass rail bed frame.

Believing *Sleep Achiever* to be an interesting *Phantasm* collectible—it was star Michael Baldwin's first published work and, much like *Phantasm,* concerned the subject of dreams—I purchased two copies. I mentioned to Sam that it might be fun to auction a copy off on Phantasm.com. Sam took this idea to heart, went to work, and designed a brilliant and original piece of software to conduct an online Web auction of the book. Sam uploaded the program and we watched in amazement as bids started coming in. Just like a real auction, Sam had even included a method to create a "reserve," so the bids would need to hit a certain price threshold before the auction could be completed.

History now tells us that the *Phantasm* Web auction went live a full month earlier than a small site called AuctionWeb—which was the original name of the Web auction giant now known as eBay. Sam had built an auction page on Phantasm.com before eBay was even invented! If only Sam and I would have had the foresight in 1995 to patent his auction software! Would we now be billionaires?

JOURNEY INTO *OBLIVION*

I t had become apparent that *Phantasm 1999* would never get funded. At the same time I continued to receive almost daily solicitations from *Phantasm* distributors around the world asking me to please make another *Phantasm* film. And every day on Phantasm.com I was hounded by "phans" demanding to know, "When's the next one!"

A few years prior to this I received a phone call from Metrocolor, MGM's esteemed film laboratory. During the production of *Kenny & Company* I had gone through a lot of grief working with another Hollywood film lab, so much so that when it came time to film *Phantasm*, I moved the work to Metrocolor. It also didn't hurt that Metrocolor was director Stanley Kubrick's lab of choice. Metrocolor was calling to inform me of the sad news that their lab was closing down and they had found some film cans of mine. I dutifully went over there and took possession of dozens of cans of film negative. I was thrilled to discover that these cans contained all the outtakes and lifts from the original *Phantasm* shoot, still in pristine condition.

As I gave serious thought on how to make a fourth *Phantasm*, I was always conscious of budgetary challenges. Based on the sales of *Phantasm III*, I doubted I could get even a million dollars to make the new one; it probably would be a lot less. It was a real challenge figuring out how to make another *Phantasm* at half the budget of *Phantasm III*. And here's where those cans of negative came in . . . what if I were to take a select few of the very best scenes excluded from the original *Phantasm* and wrote a new screenplay around them? Might it be possible to start making a film with 10 or 15 percent of it already in the can? The more I thought about this idea the more exciting it became. *Phantasm* by its very nature was illusory and disconnected temporally. How cool would it be to shift back and forth thirty years in time with your lead actor playing his role at both age thirteen and thirty-five?

As I began working up a scenario for the film that would ultimately be titled *Phantasm Oblivion,* I determined to go back to the basics of the tone and atmosphere of the original film and not be afraid to create something mystifying and challenging. It was time to reveal more of the Tall Man's endgame and to bring a conclusion of sorts for our three heroes, Mike, Jody, and Reggie. The film would start, of course, right where the previous film ended: with the Tall Man releasing Reggie from his imprisonment and then using him as a stalking horse to flush out and subdue Mike. The location for the final throw-down would be in the most appropriate place of all, the barren and beautiful Death Valley.

It was extremely gratifying that all of the *Phantasm* actors agreed to join me in this small labor of love. Michael Baldwin even made me an offer that was hard to refuse. He had always been interested in working on the other side of the camera and asked if he could assist me as a producer. Michael was smart, eager, and talented and would be a great addition to my production team. I had literally known him since he was a child and he would be someone I could trust and rely on. Along with savvy production manager Rosa Gonzalez, assistant director Jeff Shiffman, and dedicated production coordinator Jason Savage, Michael would be instrumental in bringing our project in on time and budget.

Phantasm films traditionally take place at night. Night filming is always more expensive due to lighting requirements and general lack of productivity as everyone (including me) is always half-asleep. For the fourth *Phantasm,* I wanted to find a way to let a lot of the action unfold in the daylight and still be eerie and creepy. The stark vistas and strange environments of Death Valley and its environs were perfect for this.

With our small crew, we relocated up to the tiny town of Lone Pine on the eastern side of the Sierra Nevada mountain range to shoot our exteriors. Lone Pine was adjacent to a geologically interesting rock formation called the

Alabama Hills, which was the scenic location for dozens of Hollywood films from the thirties and forties, many of them classic Westerns. During the shoot we all bunked at the vintage and inexpensive Dow Villa Hotel in the same old rooms that John Wayne, Hopalong Cassidy, and Tom Mix had bunked down in.

Our Death Valley locations were about eighty miles east—stark, empty, and beautiful. We used the *Phantasm III* muscle car for this one and getting it to the Death Valley location was a severe challenge. Its 426 Hemi engine was a major gas-guzzler and prone to overheating. During the *Phantasm III* shoot the powerful Hemi had thrown a rod and almost destroyed the engine. So on this trip our 'Cuda mechanic, Greg Buhlinger, always departed well before us to make the long predawn drive so it was cool enough to get it over to Death Valley safely.

When my daughter Chloe was just ten years old, she had several very memorable appearances portraying multiple hooded creatures in *Oblivion*. The creatures she played were crushed by a huge boulder in one scene and killed twice by Reggie in others. It was great fun for her and I remember she enjoyed the attention from the cast and crew. Chloe ultimately pursued her passion for cooking and her love of animals to create a career for herself as a top vegan chef, restaurateur, and cookbook author. It may be unseemly, but this horror filmmaker is a dedicated vegetarian and I highly suggest you give it a try yourself.

After we shot out our locations up north, we retreated to our *Phantasm* studio (and I use that term loosely). Due to budgetary concerns we rented a tiny workshop, just fifty-five feet by nineteen feet, not far from our favorite district of Chatsworth, where we filmed all of our interior sets. It was so small we could only fit one set in there at a time. Consequently we shot outdoors as much as possible.

Trying to raise the production values of *Phantasm Oblivion,* I decided to attempt the audacious and ambitious for two sequences. For the first one, I was determined to re-create the American Civil War. Most microbudget films would not even *consider* attempting such a sequence; the most they might attempt would be a couple of actors talking in a room. But I'm proud that the *Phantasm* films have always been exceptional in that regard. An indie filmmaker's reach must exceed their grasp!

I was budgeted for one single Steadicam shot of Mike's Civil War nightmare: he envisions a pitched battle and winds up seeing himself prone in an embalming tent as Angus embalms this doppelgänger alive. It was one of those challenging shots that invigorates the entire crew to make it work. The sun was setting, so we had at most fifteen minutes to get the shot. We had a dozen friends to play dead Union soldiers and they were scattered around the set, covered in blood. Even Roger Avary got in on the fun playing one very effective stiff. Then we enlisted a crack squad of Civil War reenactors who brought along costumes, rifles, and props from the era and were extremely knowledgeable about battlefield action and formations. We had just the one horse, with, of course, a uniformed Bob Ivy astride it. So, on action, our camera would come out of a cloud of smoke and move through all the dead bodies; meanwhile the reenactors were racing by camera, bayonets fixed, toward the fighting. The horse would come right at camera, rear up, and then more smoke and we would duck into the embalming tent to find Angus at work. We did nine takes in rapid-fire succession. It was a total adrenaline rush and so satisfying to finally get the perfect shot just as the sun dipped below the horizon.

The other major and ambitious scene in *Phantasm Oblivion* went down like a military operation, but guerilla-indie style. The script called for Michael to cross through a dimensional portal and land on a major big-city boulevard, completely devoid of people. He would scan the empty city in astonishment and then find the Tall Man striding down the empty boulevard toward him. I always enjoyed these sequences in other films like *The Omega Man* and *The Devil's Advocate,* but those movies spent literally fortunes on police and street closures to achieve their shots. How could we pull off a shot like that in the central district of one of the largest cities in the world with no money for a permit, let alone police?

For the entire year before shooting, on major holidays like Easter Sunday and Independence Day, I would roust myself from bed before dawn and tour the major boulevards of Los Angeles to see what kind of traffic was on them at that hour. I witnessed that on these major holidays, in the moments before 6:00 a.m., there would be about a ten-minute window when there was absolutely nobody out on the street. No cars. Nothing. And just enough light to shoot.

So, on Thanksgiving morning, we all met up at Michael Baldwin's apartment at 4:00 a.m. and got Angus into makeup. When he was ready, we loaded him into our makeup artist Melanie Kay's car and the rest of us piled into my van. Cinematographer Chris Chomyn had a hand-held Arri IIC in his lap as we arrived on Wilshire Boulevard at Cochrane Avenue in Los Angeles's Miracle Mile district. Camera assistant Justin Zaharczuk had a changing bag on his lap and was furiously loading additional film magazines. We parked and waited for the sun to come up. We looked like criminals in a heist movie. Every few minutes Chris would stick his light meter out the window and take a reading. Melanie parked her car down the street; the plan was that when she received the go signal from us on her walkie-talkie, Angus would exit the vehicle and stride down Wilshire. Chris took a reading and whispered, "We're good to go." We all surreptitiously exited the van and moved out into the center of the desolate Wilshire Boulevard. It was completely empty. This major boulevard was ours for the taking.

We quickly shot the scenes of Mike tumbling through the portal and onto the street. Now it was time for Angus. Chris rolled film, I whispered action into the walkie-talkie, and Angus stepped out from the shadows—the Tall Man strode down the center of Wilshire Blvd. The scene looked glorious. It was the magic hour just before dawn and the cityscape looked eerie and foreboding. There was no one else in the shot . . . until an LAPD squad car swerved around the corner and zoomed down the street straight at us. Oh, fuck. Busted!

The cops pulled right up to us, eyed us harshly, then turned and looked over at Angus standing there in his pale makeup and black Tall Man suit. Angus glanced over at the police and gave them something completely unexpected . . . a broad, sweet smile.

The cops didn't know what to make of this and then suddenly hit the gas and accelerated away, without a word. I yelled at Angus to run back to first position and that was a sight, the Tall Man running in his elevated boots. We shot the scene again and again . . . except for an occasional delivery van or jogger we had all of Los Angeles that morning to ourselves. We got the shot.

I had been cutting my films on the venerable Moviola film-cutting machines for my entire career. Not much had changed since their invention in the 1920s. The Moviola was now headed for extinction and in its place were the new computer-based, nonlinear editing systems. On *Phantasm Oblivion* we used a Lightworks and for the first time had the luxury of easily assembling, cutting, and recutting our film with just a few keystrokes. We used this system to great effect when I encouraged my creative editor, Scott Gill, to create a new kind of prologue to the film. Back in my student filmmaking days I loved cutting using a technique called kinestasis, in which dozens of rapid-fire cuts could tell a story quickly. Scott used this technique expertly to quickly tell the backstory of the *Phantasm* films and bring the audience up to speed in an illusory and ephemeral way.

MGM had inherited distribution rights to the original *Phantasm*. When their home video division heard about our new movie they eagerly snapped up the *Phantasm Oblivion* rights so they could market the films in unison. They released the film around Halloween with the tagline, "THE NIGHTMARE LIVES ON, BUT HUMANITY MAY NOT!!!" VHS and DVD sales were strong for both titles and the fan response to our new film was excellent. Even if it was mostly in their homes, it was satisfying to know that a lot of folks watched *Phantasm Oblivion* on disc and tape. Our new Phantasm.com website was inundated with praise from fans, which was incredibly gratifying. Fans appreciated the darker tone, the return of the original cast, the time loop ending, and their first view of the original *Phantasm* sequences.

While I was preparing to shoot *Phantasm Oblivion*, tragedy struck the Coscarelli family when my mom was diagnosed with a devastating disease called amyotrophic lateral sclerosis, or ALS. Beyond being a source of endless love and support to me and my sister Anne, she was also an inspiration to my career in so many ways. Her love of books and reading was contagious. I was so proud of her when in her midfifties she willed herself to become a *New York Times* best-selling novelist; St. Martin's Press executive Sally Richardson and CEO Tom McCormack took a chance on her and published her first book, *Fame & Fortune*. A treasured family memory was the day we all congregated on the Sunset Strip to witness the unveiling of an immense billboard for *Fame & Fortune*, which Richardson and McCormack had so kindly purchased. Born Shirley Mae Tyer, she ultimately published six acclaimed novels under her nom de plume Kate Coscarelli before this wicked disease robbed her of the ability to write.

My mom's impact on *Phantasm* was immense. It would not have been the same film without her contributions. She actually wrote the only novelization of *Phantasm*, which unfortunately was only published in a translated edition in Japan.

A year after *Phantasm Oblivion* was released, my mother, author Kate Coscarelli, finally succumbed to the effects of her terrible illness.

EVERYTHING I EVER NEEDED TO KNOW IN LIFE, I LEARNED FROM PRO WRESTLING

In the midnineties, when my son Andy was younger, he got me hooked watching professional wrestling on TV. While perceived by many critics as juvenile, silly, and inane, I'm not ashamed to admit that I reveled in the deeper dramatic and comedic elements and was captivated by many epic storylines and feuds which could play out on a nationwide canvas over months, and even years. It basically is an immense, endless soap opera with shining heroes and loathsome villains who can surprisingly switch roles at the drop of a hat. The compelling characters can spout captivating soliloquies and frequently the violence can be sudden and shocking. William Shakespeare would have loved this format!

Andy and I dived deep and pretty soon we started following some of the more underground and radical promotions, like the original Extreme Championship Wrestling (ECW) out of Philadelphia and, more close to home, the hardcore Xtreme Pro Wrestling (XPW), which are both sadly now long gone. Lately we enjoy a newer local promotion in Pro Wrestling Guerilla (PWG). Along the way we've had some memorable experiences, including Shawn Michael's plummeting from the arena roof at Wrestlemania 12 and landing right in front of us (you could see us on TV!), amassing a spectacular collection of ring-used and head-dented chairs used by ECW's "hardcore chair-swingin'" freak Balls Mahoney, and attending one of Dwayne "The Rock" Johnson's early appearances in WWE (more on this great performer later).

Sadly, there are few true pro-wrestling fans in Hollywood (I guess most feel it's beneath them) but one was studio exec Jeff Katz, who personally introduced me to some greats, including Chris Jericho, Diamond Dallas Page, and Paul Heyman. On social media I've interacted with a bunch of them who were fans of my films, including the legendary CM Punk.

My love of wrestling and film collided when Roger Avary and I began collaborating on a dramatic series pitch set in the world of pro wrestling. Unfortunately, our brilliant pitch went right over the heads of all the TV big shots we met with. At the time, Roger was represented by the powerhouse agency CAA, and they informed him there was a job opening we should hear about. We went over there and were introduced to Eric Bischoff, the CEO of Ted Turner's now-defunct World Championship Wrestling. He was in Los Angeles and desperate to hire some Hollywood writing talent to shore up his sagging promotion. Roger and I were the only ones who jumped at the chance to meet with him. Bischoff was debuting a major new character just a few days later on his Monday Nitro show and wanted help with booking (screenwriting) the introduction. The rock band KISS would be performing at that show and would introduce their new spawn, a rookie wrestler, called DEMON.

Roger and I batted around some ideas but he was fully occupied on another writing project. Faxes started coming fast and furious into my office from Bischoff, asking when he would receive our material. Not wanting to miss my one golden opportunity to have a real creative impact at a major wrestling promotion, I sat down with Andy and in one long evening of work, we came up with what we thought would be a clever, dramatic, and exciting way to introduce DEMON and his gimmick. We wrote out a script describing the angle (fictional storyline) with some spots (series of actions) and faxed it off to Bischoff. Again, would it dash your hopes if I told you the guy never responded and they didn't use our material? Unfortunately that's what happened. Monday Nitro went with another angle and all I can say is that charitably it was a major blunder. If you look it up on the web, DEMON's debut has gone down in history as one of the ten worst debuts of a wrestler ever. And Eric Bischoff was fired from WCW a few weeks later. Eric, you should have used our script!

UNRAVELING A MUMMY

Almost a decade after my original journey to Nacogdoches, Texas, to meet author Joe R. Lansdale, I found myself in a bookstore holding a new book of his. Over those years nothing concrete had materialized in terms of my making a film of one of his stories. *The Drive-In* had been optioned to somebody else, and then I had a brief flirtation with his crime novel *Cold in July* but ultimately decided not to pursue it. Together Joe and I had gone through a long and frustrating journey trying to get his book *Dead in the West* mounted as a film. Essentially a horror Western, *Dead in the West* had classic elements from Clint Eastwood's best work in that genre, along with a healthy dose of what George Romero had popularized. Unfortunately no one shared our vision that the material could make for a great movie, so that project cratered.

The book I was holding in my hand was Joe's new story collection entitled *Writer of the Purple Rage,* and on the dust jacket a log line for one of the stories grabbed my attention. "*Bubba Ho-tep,* in which Elvis battles a mummy." That single short sentence was all it took to hook me.

Before I ever read Joe's story, I had a subconscious and ephemeral belief in Elvis Presley as a heroic figure. Of course he *was* the King of Rock and Roll, but it was the nuances of Elvis's character, his respectful Southern manners, his loyal devotion to his mother, and yes, those martial arts poses that led me to believe he had an innately heroic nature. So when I read that log line, I literally thought to myself, "Hot damn! I could see Elvis kicking undead ass."

Joe had been inspired by the numerous tabloid headlines of Elvis sightings after his death. "ELVIS SPOTTED IN WAL-MART BUYING POCKET COMB!" His novella, *Bubba Ho-tep,* told the "true" story of what happened to Elvis. We find him as an elderly resident in an East Texas rest home. The staff and other residents believe him to be an aging Elvis impersonator, but our protagonist insists he is the real deal and switched identities with an Elvis impersonator years before his "death." Due to the results of a trailer park fire, Elvis then missed his chance to switch back. The only person who believes Elvis's story is an elderly African-American fellow nursing home resident named Jack, who believes himself to be President John F. Kennedy, dyed black. They become fast friends, and when Jack investigates a series of deaths only Elvis believes his theory that a four-thousand-year-old mummy may be crawling up from the local creek at night to suck the souls of their fellow residents. The two valiant old codgers team up and sally forth to battle this evil Egyptian entity, who has chosen their long-term care facility as his happy hunting grounds.

In the context of this audacious tale, I saw a moving meditation on old age and death, an elegy to friendship and courage, and a realistic portrayal of what we all face at the end of the road—disinterest and abandonment in the warehouses of the nursing home. I could immediately see it as a framework for a fantastic movie and was ready to do whatever it took to get it made.

I focused all of my efforts on *Bubba Ho-tep* even though everyone thought I was crazy. Joe's initial response was that of all his work he never saw this story as something that could be made into a movie. Many of my friends echoed that response. A frequent comment was, "Why do you think a youthful movie audience would want to spend ninety minutes with two old geezers in a rest home?" I received many suggestions that I add some young characters to make it more relevant or change the setting to a more conventional venue such as a mental hospital. I also received a lot of pushback on the title; many found it inscrutable, and one good friend kept mistaking it as "Bubba Hotel." Once I started writing, I found it to be a fairly

easy adaptation to screenplay. Since it was based on a novella it did not require much cutting, just additions of new material.

The Hollywood big shots I submitted my screenplay to did not get it. At
all. The screenplay received poor comments such as "ridiculous," "won't work
with a younger audience," "not an Elvis fan." Despite these snubs, I had an
unshakeable confidence that I could make an accessible, hilarious, and moving film out of it. It was now pretty obvious that my only option was to
make the film as an indie, and I would probably have no choice but to invest some of my own money.

The great thing about the *Bubba Ho-tep* screenplay was that it was basically so simple. Many of the best scenes in the film were simply Elvis and
Jack sitting and talking in their bedrooms, and two actors talking in a room
is very inexpensive to shoot. It became apparent to me that it just might be
possible to make *Bubba Ho-tep* efficiently as a low-budget indie movie.

I started thinking about actors for the starring role. I had an early desire
to cast an actor who had some musical credibility so I initially reached out
to Michael Lee Aday, whose stage name was Meat Loaf. It did not work out
with him, so I went to my second choice, which was actor Gary Busey. Now
you may think I had lost my mind on that one, but, in my defense, Busey
had been nominated for an Academy Award for his critically acclaimed performance as rock-icon Buddy Holly. At that time it may have been outside
the realm of possibility that Busey was capable of giving a restrained performance, but I always thought a credible version of Elvis might be within
his grasp. Unfortunately (or possibly fortunately), my conversations with his
agent devolved into an argument over whether we had the resources to provide his actor with a pop-out luxury dressing room trailer, which we certainly did not.

A decade later I had the strange opportunity to be in close proximity to
Busey when we both appeared at a horror convention. He was starring in
an oddball little horror film entitled *The Gingerdead Man,* providing the
voice for a killer cookie. We rode in from the airport on the same minivan,
but it wasn't until after check-in at the hotel that I had my up-close and
personal encounter with him in the hotel gift shop. He was scouring the
shelves of drinks and candy searching for something. I moved up beside him

to grab a bottle of water, with no intention at all of interacting with him, when Busey spun around and pinned his glare on me. I shrank back. "The drugs, man." I had no idea what he was talking about or how to respond so I just grunted a "Huh?" "The drugs, man, the drugs." I had to play this out with him but I really had no clue what the heck he was talking about. "The drugs, man. The drugs. They're everywhere." And he walked away without another word.

ONE CRANK CALL

One afternoon I returned to my office on Hollywood Boulevard to find an odd message waiting for me from my hardworking assistant Melanie DuBose. Director Sam Raimi's office had called and left a message with an invitation for me to join Sam at a retrospective screening he was hosting in Westwood for *Close Encounters of the Third Kind*. I hadn't heard from Sam for a couple of years and didn't realize he was such a fan of that film. So I called Sam's office to RSVP and got his assistant on the line. The assistant was immediately flummoxed. He didn't know of any screenings that Sam was hosting, certainly not one in Westwood of *Close Encounters*. He told me to hold on and a minute later Sam came on and wanted to know all about this "supposed" screening he was hosting. Well, we realized it must have been some kind of a strange phone prank. We both had a good laugh about it. We started talking about projects we were working on. He told me he was prepping a movie based on the *Spider-Man* comics and then asked me what I was up to. I told him about this crazy Joe Lansdale novella I had just optioned about Elvis battling a four-thousand-year-old Egyptian mummy in an old folks' home. Sam volunteered, "You should cast Bruce Campbell. He's a great actor." My immediate reaction to Sam's suggestion was that it reminded me of myself: I would pitch actor pals Angus Scrimm and Reggie Bannister to any director friend who would listen. But then an image popped into my head of Bruce risking life and limb to entertain the crowd at that *Fangoria* show a decade ago. Sam was relentless. "I'll have him call you."

Sure enough, ten minutes later the phone rings and it's Bruce, in that inimitable style his fans know and love. "Don, I hear you're making an Elvis picture. I want to hear all about it." We had a nice chat and scheduled a breakfast meeting for a few weeks later. We met up at Jerry's Famous Deli in Encino. Seeing him in person, I was truly surprised how striking Bruce was with his dark-haired good looks. During breakfast, it sure seemed to me that, except for the chin, Bruce had a passing resemblance to the King. We were still a ways away from shooting the project but we promised to keep in touch.

In those intervening months I even came back to Bruce about costarring in Roger Avary's *Phantasm 1999*. However, once *Bubba Ho-tep* was a go, I submitted the final draft to Bruce with an offer. He quickly called me back and told me that it was the "weirdest script he had ever read." He also said that before he gave me an answer he had one question. "Are you going to show it?" I asked him, "Show what?" He said, "You know. It. The penis. Are you going to show Elvis's cancer-riddled penis?"

One of the themes in *Bubba Ho-tep* is that old Elvis is tormented by a mysterious infection, or as the character describes it, "a growth on my pecker." In the film Elvis is convinced that it's cancer and that his days are severely numbered. In actuality, I hadn't really yet given this subject much thought. The guys at KNB EFX had told me that they still had the plaster mold at their studio for the large penis that Mark Wahlberg wore as porn star Dirk Diggler in *Boogie Nights*. They volunteered it would be no problem to cast that thing up and sculpt a wicked tumor on the head of it. I could tell Bruce was a bit apprehensive, and I knew that getting full frontal nudity past the MPAA ratings board would be a long shot anyway. I also had learned that hiding an effect off-camera would give it more resonance if the audience was forced to look closely at the actor's response. So, quickly considering all these factors, I told Bruce we would not show it and rely instead on his acting skills to convey what was going on off-screen. Bruce immediately responded, "Count me in." And Elvis was in the building.

MUMMY BUSINESS

From my first reading of the *Bubba Ho-tep* novella, I firmly believed only one actor in the world could play our African-American President John F. Kennedy, and that was the great Ossie Davis. Mr. Davis, in my opinion, was an authentic national treasure with a long and storied career, not only as a celebrated actor on stage and screen, but also as a director, author, poet, playwright, and social activist. His career as a director included the very first of what became the popular and durable "blaxploitation" genre with his film *Cotton Comes to Harlem*. Ossie was an important civil rights activist in the sixties. In addition to the honor of being selected as the emcee at the legendary 1963 March on Washington, Ossie also attended the funeral for human rights activist Malcolm X and delivered his eloquent and moving eulogy.

From the get-go, I believed Ossie had the presence and gravitas to ably portray a character of presidential stature. While I was writing the screenplay, I learned that Mr. Davis, with his gifted wife actress Ruby Dee, would be making a public appearance not far from my home at a bookstore in support of their new memoir. At the reading that night I studiously watched Ossie from the small audience and was dazzled by his charm, grace, and warm sense of humor. He even looked presidential in his tailored gray suit. I stood in line to get a book signed but as I got near I couldn't think of the right words to say and said nothing and just nervously smiled.

It took some serious convincing with Ossie's agent. His agent said he didn't like the script much and didn't think it would be appropriate for Mr. Davis but that he would let me know what his client thought. Desperate, I even imposed on friend Mick Garris, who had directed both Ossie and Ruby Dee in his epic TV miniseries *The Stand*. Mick was kind enough to write Ossie a letter telling him that I was a good guy and he would enjoy working with me. I dutifully called the agent back week after week and finally received the news I was hoping for: "You know, I don't really like your script, but my client does."

We rounded out our *Bubba Ho-tep* cast with some very fine actors to play the key supporting roles. Ella Joyce played our nurse with a sass and verve that lit up the screen every time she appeared. After working on *Phantasm Oblivion,* Heidi Marnhout enlisted for a second tour of duty with me as an appropriately sullen beauty, the daughter of Elvis's deceased roommate. Edith Jefferson portrayed the elderly lady down the hall with spunk and larceny in her heart. Larry Pennell, a star of Westerns and many favorite TV shows from my youth, including *Outer Limits* and *Ripcord,* played our gunslinging Kemosabe and was terrific in his showdown with the mummy. And actors Daniel Roebuck and Daniel Schweiger provided grim comic relief as the two clueless hearse drivers.

I was blessed again by coming across a terrific location in which to film *Bubba Ho-tep.* The expansive and ancient south campus of Rancho Los Amigos Rehabilitation Hospital in Downey, California, had been shuttered and abandoned. A few years previously I had driven by it while attending my son's high school football game and had noted the creepy old place. My resourceful young producer on *Bubba Ho-tep,* Jason Savage, made friends with the local county police who had jurisdiction over the property and we were allowed the run of the place to shoot our film. It had everything—old bedrooms and hallways, an exterior for the rest home, and even a field to blow up Elvis's trailer park. Production designer Daniel Vecchione and art director Justin Zaharczuk literally took up residence on the property and worked round-the-clock for several weeks to transform the facility into the

Mud Creek Shady Rest. When they finished, we took occupancy and over the course of thirty challenging shooting days created the world where old Elvis would spend his final days.

On the first day of shooting *Bubba Ho-tep* we had a serious problem. Our star Bruce was forty-three years old playing Elvis in his seventies. Howard Berger at KNB EFX had created a terrific old-age makeup for Bruce, but it was literally falling apart as we filmed. His wrinkled neck makeup was delaminating from his skin. We raced some early film we shot over to a screening room at FotoKem to view it up on a big screen. It looked pretty bad, but what to do? Howard and the team at KNB, including crack makeup artist Melanie Tooker, came up with a fix in the method of application that seemed to solve the problem. But Bruce came up with what, in my mind, was the real fix. He gathered me, the camera, and lighting crew around in a huddle and said something profound. "Gents, we need to shoot Elvis's makeup as if it were an aging starlet." He was right on the money. From then on we took extreme care to softly light the makeup and remove any possible harshness. We would do a makeup rehearsal in which Bruce would walk through the camera setup and all of us would scrutinize how the light played on his makeup. This process allowed Bruce to work his acting magic without the fear of being saddled with bad makeup.

Bruce had made his bones battling supernatural creatures of all shapes and sizes in his *Evil Dead* films. I decided to write a scene to service his fans that was not in the original Lansdale story. A key icon of Egyptology is the scarab beetle, and it seemed to me that wherever our mummy showed up, a few of those buggers should too. Many months before shooting, I was lucky to enlist effects genius Kerry Prior to create the bugs. He had done such wonders with the various *Phantasm* spheres he had designed, I figured flying scarab beetles would not be that big of a stretch for him. Kerry certainly did not disappoint. Much like he did with the spheres, Kerry created separate bug models that each would do a different action. One would crawl, one had a retractable head that could pop out, and another had flapping wings. Though Campbell had previously fought some supernatural entities on screen, I tailored this one specifically to the context of *Bubba Ho-tep*. Consequently, Bruce would go into battle against this evil Egyptian insect armed only with a fork, a floor heater, and a bedpan.

I think one of the most enjoyable aspects of making my film was the research and planning that went into Elvis's wardrobe. Shelley had volunteered to create the wardrobe on *Phantasm Oblivion* and did a fantastic job. Consequently I drafted her to take on the challenge of designing the wardrobe for *Bubba Ho-tep* as her costuming skills were terrific. The King was a renowned clothes horse, so assembling his opulent wardrobe on our budget would be Shelley's largest challenge. She made contact with the costumer on an Elvis-themed film, *3000 Miles to Graceland,* hoping to borrow some of their Elvis jumpsuits. Unfortunately they were last seen in a warehouse in Canada, their fate unknown. Next on her list, she tracked down the greatest outfitter of Elvis tribute artists, Butch Polston of B&K Enterprises, and worked a deal with him to create several authentic jumpsuits for Bruce to wear in the film. Butch owned the original designs of the most famous Elvis jumpsuits, so these were guaranteed to be the genuine article. Shelley also supervised the creation of an extralarge version of the jumpsuit for when old Elvis goes into battle, which accommodated the "fatsuit" that KNB EFX created for Bruce to wear underneath.

To add some authenticity to Bruce's performance, we brought in Tim Welch, a notable Elvis tribute artist from Las Vegas. Tim spent a few minutes working with Bruce but then left pretty quickly. "Forget it, man. You're on your own." Bruce didn't give up; he was determined to get those moves right. He spent hours scrutinizing the King in his movies, including the MGM classic *Elvis: That's the Way It Is*.

Even though our ancient mummy would be moving slowly, the creature would be involved in a lot of on-screen action. For that reason, and because he was a student and fan of the Universal classic monsters, I asked stuntman extraordinaire Bob Ivy to play the role of our mummy, Bubba Ho-tep. Bob was a huge fan of the great Boris Karloff and dedicated himself to channel the spirit of the master in his approach to this performance. One of our key creative collaborators, the brilliant Robert Kurtzman of KNB EFX, sculpted an eerie desiccated face for our mummy, then took full plaster body molds of Ivy and designed and fabricated several fabulous formfitting, full-body mummy suits for his use.

Once Bob was inside the suit he would be trapped in it for the entire day. It was a similar situation for Bruce. Once his old-age makeup was applied and he was strapped into his fatsuit, he was stuck as old fat Elvis for well over twelve straight hours. This was genuinely entertaining for those of us on the crew as Bruce stayed in character; off-camera, he was almost as funny as grumpy old Elvis as he was on. I am so thankful to have had such a dedicated cast who put up with this ongoing discomfort for our entire shoot in support of making a good movie.

Ossie Davis had confided in me that he had fraternized with several genuine American presidents, but he certainly never expected to be asked to portray John F. Kennedy. While filming the denouement of *Bubba Ho-tep,* in which our JFK fights to the death with the murderous mummy, I witnessed the absolute high point of the shoot. The entire experience felt right out of Tim Burton's *Ed Wood.* Ossie was down on the grass outside his rest home with a large prosthetic mummy bearing down on him and trying to suck out his soul. As we started, I was thinking to myself, "This is completely ridiculous." But then on cue, Ossie grabbed that rubber mummy and clawed at it, he fought it, he battled that vicious creature, and in doing so he brought the thing to life. Ossie conjured up pure cinema magic!

We worked with a lot of seniors while shooting *Bubba Ho-tep.* One of the challenges I was completely unprepared for was that, as we age, one of the first things to lose its edge is memory. It became a constant battle: remembering sections of the script could be so challenging for many of our senior actors. For the first week I was tearing my hair out because many of them could not remember their lines from one take to the next. I finally developed a technique to give them "triggers" to spark their memory, in which I would cut every long monologue down to no more than two or three lines without another actor responding with something. The other actor's line would "trigger" their memory and they could much more easily continue with the scene. Sometimes, on scenes with a single actor, I would hover right outside of camera frame and whisper short trigger phrases that would spark them to keep going. It was a slow process to shoot in this manner, but working with these fine actors was one of the genuine highlights of my career.

The sad part for me is that the themes of aging and loss in *Bubba Ho-tep* have played out for me in real life with my cast. As I write this, just a few years later, every single one of our elderly actors and background players has passed on. As I look back on the experience, I realize how honored and just plain lucky I was to work with them all. From Larry to Edith to Ossie, I can truthfully say that they will be in my heart forever.

HEARTBREAK HO-TEP

With editors Don Milne and Scott Gill, I worked on the cut for almost a year. They taught me Final Cut Pro and *Bubba Ho-tep* was one of the very first feature films edited using that Apple software. My favorite music recordist from *Phantasm*, Paul Ratajczak, now owned a terrific film audio studio, Mercury Sound, and we worked together for months to create a superlative soundtrack. However, the true hero of *Bubba Ho-tep* was composer and key collaborator Brian Tyler. His guitar-based score was the soul of the film and was so good it made audiences forget we had no real Elvis music at all.

The letter read, "I must regretfully inform you that we did not select [*Bubba Ho-tep*] for inclusion in the . . . Sundance Film Festival." A rejection from the Sundance Film Festival can be catastrophic news to the indie filmmaker. Despite the festival's best efforts to position itself as the most prestigious and artistic film festival in the world, which in many respects is true, it is no secret that Sundance is the best, most visible, and potentially most lucrative sales market for independent films in the world. If you are denied entry into Sundance, the financial prospects for your indie film plummet precipitously.

Even though *Bubba Ho-tep* was not my first feature film, it was my first submission to Sundance. I was like a starry-eyed newbie when I dropped off a screening copy at the festival office on Wilshire Boulevard for consideration. Like most idealistic indie filmmakers, I had big dreams of immediate acceptance, a gloriously received premiere up in the snowy mountains of Park City, and a big-bucks distribution deal. At the festival those top talent agents from the premiere agencies would circle the lucky few, dangling offers of major studio directing gigs and the prospect of riches beyond imagination. I believed *Bubba Ho-tep* was my best movie yet and honestly believed that the festival powers-that-be would recognize my true indie cred and reward me for all my years of laboring to make films in the indie trenches.

Traditionally, Sundance announces the chosen few the week after the Thanksgiving holiday. It's generally known that the lucky winners are notified in advance in the three days prior to that Big Thursday. Unfortunately for *Bubba Ho-tep*, it was not to be. It was a quiet Thanksgiving with no phone call. At the time I thought there was something wrong with my film, but I did not understand how the odds were stacked against all indie filmmakers.

It's all in the numbers. Using their own analytics, the odds are less than 1 percent in being accepted to Sundance. That means that for each film invited to the big dance, more than ninety-nine features—think about that—ninety-nine films that indie filmmakers have slaved over and poured all of their hopes, dreams, and in many cases gone into serious debt for, are not going to be selected.

It is common knowledge that you can increase your odds of selection in most film festivals if you can submit through a friendly programmer. The problem for most newbies, though, is how in the heck could you ever know a programmer if you have never been to a major film festival? By no way does this guarantee selection, but it certainly does improve the odds. In the case of *Bubba Ho-tep*, Roberto Quezada introduced me to his writing partner, and director friend, Kayo Hatta, who had a history with Sundance including the premiere there of her beautiful indie film *Picture Bride*. Kayo was kind enough to contact Sundance programmers Trevor Groth and Mike Plante and put in a good word on our behalf, and we submitted under their auspices. However, we didn't get accepted and things were looking pretty grim for *Bubba Ho-tep*. How would we find distribution? It was time to generate some publicity.

Looking back it is hard to convey just how powerful blogger Harry Knowles and his *Ain't It Cool News* website was at that time. Harry was the original Internet tastemaker and was the first to wield his power over the studios. They truly feared him. The Hollywood studio big shots literally quaked in their boots when they heard Harry was writing about their unfinished movies. Being the first person to publish advance reviews by sneaking into studio research screenings gave him tremendous power. And with a worldwide network of geek "spies" Harry was everywhere. A bad review of a work-in-progress film could literally destroy it before it was even finished.

His site became an incubator for several well-respected film writers including Eric Vespe, who wrote under his pen name "Quint." I met Eric when he was nineteen years old on my first trip to Austin for the Phantasmania weekend held at the original Alamo Drafthouse, in which we screened four *Phantasm* films with the cast over a very fun weekend.

Having confidence that *Bubba Ho-tep* was a good movie, and with the comfort that Bruce Campbell was so great in this role, I decided that *Ain't It Cool News* would be the first outlet to get a look at it. I contacted good friend Eric and offered to give him and Harry an early preview of my movie. At the same time, Tim League, owner of the Alamo Drafthouse, generously offered to let me use his theater for a private morning screening. Hand-carrying the twin fifty-pound film cases, I eagerly flew down to Austin for this private world premiere.

I arrived at the Alamo Drafthouse Village theater for the 10:00 a.m. screening. To my delight and everlasting gratitude, Tim greeted me warmly at the front door and I learned that he would personally be threading up the film and running the projector for us. Eric was waiting along with author Joe Lansdale. I was very excited to share the movie with the author of the novella it was based on but I have to admit, I was a bit nervous. God love him, but Joe is a very confident man and does not suffer fools, or foolish pursuits, gladly. I was the first to bring one of his stories to the screen and if Joe didn't like it, I knew I would hear about it directly from him. The final guests arrived as Harry and his father Jay took their seats. With just five people in the otherwise empty theater, Tim rolled film.

After the film finished I nervously stepped out into the bright Austin afternoon to learn its fate. The normally taciturn Tim told me he loved my movie and said that he looked forward to booking it in every one of his theaters. Then Joe Lansdale approached, gave me a hard look, and said, "I liked it. Don, you made a damn good movie." I breathed a huge sigh of relief. Eric told me how much he liked it too and promised to do everything he could to get the good word out about *Bubba Ho-tep* on *Ain't It Cool News.* The trip was a success.

I was working furiously on finishing up the final postproduction on the film, still smarting from the disappointment of the Sundance rejection. Then the phone rang. It was Sundance programmer Trevor Groth.

I have to admit I was a bit perturbed. Why would the guy who had passed on our film want to talk to me? Sundance was over and all the opportunities with it. Trevor was very friendly and told me how much he liked *Bubba Ho-tep.* I was not very nice. "Then why the heck didn't you invite us to Sundance?" Trevor, having dealt with a few disgruntled indie filmmakers in his day, stayed upbeat and gave me the pitch for a new film festival he was programming for in, of all places, Las Vegas. Trevor wanted me to bring *Bubba Ho-tep* to Sin City and premiere our film at CineVegas. He believed it would be the perfect place to premiere *Bubba Ho-tep,* especially considering the longtime connection Elvis had with Las Vegas. Trevor got me with that one. I immediately flashed back to one of the most thrilling moments of moviegoing in my entire life—when my ten-year-old self witnessed Elvis on-screen at my local Fox Rossmoor theater as he belted out "Viva Las Vegas" with the alluring Ann-Margret go-go dancing beside him. That was the first moment I actually "got" Elvis and for me, he was linked to Vegas forever. Trevor made a point. Elvis was the King of Las Vegas, and what more fitting tribute than to have our premiere there?

Along with producer Jason Savage and my entire family, we went into overdrive to prepare for the screening, including arranging for key cast and crew to attend and blanketing every comic book shop in Vegas with flyers and posters to announce our screening. Trevor promised he would do everything to invite acquisition executives to the festival, including offering free travel and accommodations at the Palms Hotel and Casino where it was held.

My entire family and a bunch of cast and crew drove out to Vegas for the big premiere. I even brought along my supportive Australian horror director pal Jamie Blanks (*Urban Legend*) and his gorgeous wife Simone for moral support. It was going to be a great weekend.

The movie played to a completely packed house and it was a smash. I was waiting with Bruce and Joe Lansdale up near the screen as the end credits rolled, ready for the filmmaker Q&A afterward, and something incredible happened that cemented it for me. Since the film ended on such a melancholy and downbeat note as Elvis closes his eyes at the finale, to raise the audience's spirits and give them some hope, I inserted a line in the end credits that read, "Elvis returns in . . . BUBBA NOSFERATU—Curse of the She-Vampires." As a kid I always got a thrill watching the James Bond movie end credits where they would announce the next 007 that way, so I figured why not try that with Elvis. As this announcement rolled onscreen, suddenly a guttural roar erupted from the crowd and they burst into riotous applause. Three hundred people wanted a sequel, like, immediately.

After the screening as we exited the theater, I was swarmed by wellwishers. The entire audience loved the movie and were genuinely enthusiastic about *Bubba Ho-tep*. It was also pretty damn exciting to learn that our film played well across all age ranges—our younger, black-T-shirt-wearing *Evil Dead* and *Phantasm* fans in attendance loved it, but so did a bunch of older folks in the crowd. In fact, Trevor grabbed Bruce and me and excitedly explained that his parents were in the audience and told him it was the best film of the festival.

But our joy was short-lived. Where were the distributors? Big problem. It turned out that there were no acquisition executives at our screening, and the ones that did attend CineVegas were busy at the gaming tables and didn't make it to any screenings.

I returned to Los Angeles and started hand-carrying the film print around to several distributors to only tepid interest and no offers. Friend Roger Avary, who was shooting his terrific film *The Rules of Attraction* at the time, managed to entice executives from his film's distributor, Lionsgate, to attend a private screening of *Bubba Ho-tep*. After the movie ended, I positioned myself at the screening room door in order to speak directly with the distributors on their way out. I got the bum's rush with just some platitudes tossed over their shoulders about it being cool and they'd think about it. It was nervous-time in Bubba land.

Colin Geddes, the ultracool programmer of Midnight Madness at the Toronto International Film Festival, rang me up and invited us to bring *Bubba Ho-tep* up north for its Canadian premiere in his well-respected section. I knew that TIFF, as it is known, was a near equal to Sundance in terms of visibility and distribution opportunities. I was determined not to waste this valuable opportunity so I immediately went about filling out our team with a festival publicist and a real film sales agent from a major talent agency.

Linda Brown was a well-respected indie film publicist. With her partner Jim Dobson, she put together a smart and scrappy strategy for the festival. Her intuitive plan was to do anything she could to line up interviews with Bruce and me with the large daily Canadian newspapers in Toronto. Her belief was that all acquisition execs would read the *Toronto Star* and *Globe and Mail* over breakfast; if we could get well-placed articles in them, it would create targeted buzz for our film. With the assistance of a couple of Canadian journalists who happened to be *Evil Dead* and *Phantasm* fans, we got major interviews placed in their newspapers. Bruce even did a great photo shoot among the real Egyptian mummies in the Toronto Museum. If nothing else, every horror movie fan in Toronto was primed for our premiere.

Our sales agent, however, turned out to be a bust. I did not realize until it was too late that, in addition to representing *Bubba Ho-tep,* he also had been assigned to set up their agency party at the festival. It was his job to arrange this festivity, to make sure the food and booze were flowing, and to be sure it was populated with lots of beautiful actresses. Oh, did I tell you that our agent just happened to schedule this party at the very same time and date, five miles away, as our premiere screening? There were Bruce and me at our agent's glorious agency party with all the inebriated distributors and actors and actresses, and as we left for our premiere we actually waved goodbye to several acquisition executives from major distributors as they stayed for the party and skipped our screening. Major bummer.

Prior to the screening Lionsgate, based on their previous viewing, made the only offer we were to receive at Toronto. At the major festivals you frequently read about the big money sales in which eager distributors offer millions of dollars to secure distribution rights to the films. Well, Lionsgate told us they were eager to make *Bubba Ho-tep* the first sale of the festival and they came up with a novel approach. They offered zero dollars in advance with a poor net profits backend deal, and required an immediate answer prior to the start of our screening to preclude anyone else from bidding. They quickly received their answer, which was a big fat no. I had risked far too much and worked too damn hard to throw my film away for nothing. It's not as if Lionsgate had no money. Three days later they made a deal with my friend, filmmaker Eli Roth, and paid him five million dollars for his debut film, *Cabin Fever*. I was flummoxed. Was there something wrong with *Bubba Ho-tep*?

Our Canadian premiere screening at the Uptown was sensational. It was a grand old movie palace, built at the turn of the twentieth century, with its one thousand seats packed with rabid horror movie fans. Midnight Madness is one of the best elements of TIFF and their rowdy late-night screenings are truly something to behold. They loved *Bubba Ho-tep* and we received sustained applause throughout. But no theatrical distributors were in attendance to witness this genuine love from the crowd, and our agent was back at his party, so he didn't see it either.

Back in Los Angeles I found myself in the same situation as with *Phantasm*, decades previously. I was sitting on what I believed was a good movie, with no viable distribution opportunities. A very smart distribution consultant, Alex Nohe, approached me and graciously suggested that he could make an introduction to the folks running the American Cinematheque in Los Angeles. The AC was running a series every month of recent independent films and Alex believed they would be interested in including our film and screening it at their flagship Egyptian Theater on Hollywood Boulevard. He felt that staging a big Los Angeles premiere with cast in attendance in the six-hundred-seat Hollywood movie palace could gain some notoriety and interest for our movie with the local film community. Hell, our movie was about a mummy, what better place to screen than at the Egyptian!

We again went into overdrive to publicize the upcoming Los Angeles premiere, hoping this would be the one to snag us a distributor. My good friend Jeff Conner reached out to a veteran *Los Angeles Times* writer and convinced him to give us some coverage. David Chute's story, entitled "Bubba Unites Cult Heroes," was terrific and featured some great photos of Bruce and me posing among the Egyptian statuary and hieroglyphs in the front of the theater. Between our good word-of-mouth coming from CineVegas, Toronto, and now this, you could feel the buzz building about *Bubba Ho-tep*. It felt like we just might have a shot.

The morning the *Times* article ran, the phone rang. It was the assistant to the president and CEO of one of the biggest major studios. The studio boss came on the phone and told me that from the article, our film looked very interesting and that he would like to screen it. It was a long shot but I asked him if there was any way he could come down to the Egyptian Theater the following night to our screening so he could see it with an audience. Studio bosses traditionally would never attend an indie screening and this guy was no different. He demurred and said he was unavailable that night. With no other choice, I relented and sent a DVD screener over to his office.

The *Bubba Ho-tep* screening at the American Cinematheque that night was epic. Practically every Bruce Campbell, Don Coscarelli, Joe Lansdale, and mummy-loving fan in Southern California descended on Hollywood Boulevard. We sold out two shows at the Egyptian and for years afterward the Cinematheque brain trust would remark how it was the biggest money-making night in their history. All the ticket sales went to the AC, of course, which was fine by us because they are a terrific organization. The movie played beautifully again, and after the screening Bruce and I did a Q&A. Well, it started out as a Q&A but Bruce grabbed the mic from the Cinematheque's host, Margot Gerber, and quickly turned it into a comic *Bubba Ho-tep* lovefest. Bruce is terrific in front of a crowd, very quick on his feet and hilarious. If you have never seen him live onstage, put that one on your bucket list. When someone from the audience asked if we had filmed in a real rest home. Bruce responded, "What's the matter with you? Yeah. Right. We took over an old folks' home, kicked some old people out of their beds, and shot some flying bug scenes." The audience roared with laughter.

Director Sam Raimi, who directed Bruce in the *Evil Dead* films, was in the audience. Bruce spotted him and put him on the hot seat. Sam responded with tongue firmly planted in cheek, "Don, I think you have made a good picture here. But Bruce, your performance, well it really calls into question my previous decisions and I don't think we will be working together again." This got another huge roar of laughter from the crowd.

The only somber note from the screening was that unfortunately our agent was unable to attend. It's too bad he never saw what a large crowd *Bubba Ho-tep* drew or what a powerful impact it had on the audience. We were told he invited some distributors, but unfortunately none that I could tell made it to the show. Again I was stymied. Would I have no choice but to send Bubba to an early grave in the trash heap of "direct-to-video"?

The next day, I realized that I had never heard back from that major studio president. I followed up with a phone call to the studio and the studio boss was kind enough to answer it. He wasn't gushing, so I had to put myself out there and ask him what he thought of my movie. He said that he watched it and that he liked it and wished me luck with it. I decided to press it a bit and asked if he, as president of one of the big studios, had any advice for me as a filmmaker about what I should do with my film, and if there was any chance that his studio might want to distribute it. He said that his company distributing *Bubba Ho-tep* wasn't really a possibility but that "You should just keep doing what you're doing." With that, he said goodbye and we hung up. As Charlie Brown would say, "WTF?"

We had one last stop on the festival tour. Texas author and friend Stephen Romano had submitted *Bubba Ho-tep* to the South by Southwest Film Festival and they had kindly invited us to screen there. The screening at South by Southwest was the only disastrous one we ever had. I had been provided a nice seat in the center of the festival theater as the amped-up crowd filed in. Every seat was quickly taken and the festival staff placed some additional folding chairs along the walls to accommodate the standby line outside.

I noticed a guy coming in late with a mass of dreadlocks and standing in the aisle searching around for a seat. I realized it was Elvis Mitchell, the then film critic from the *New York Times*. I watched as he walked down toward the front of the screen and sat down in one of the folding chairs. The most important film critic in the country was sitting in the absolute worst seat in the house, ten feet from the screen and with a terribly angled view. I immediately went into a panic. Should I help him find a better seat? Should I give him mine? By the very act of approaching him will I cause him to dislike my film?

I knew I had to act. I took a deep breath, jumped to my feet, and hurried over. "Hi, Mr. Mitchell. I'm Don Coscarelli and I made this movie and you've, well, you've got the absolute worst seat in the house here. Please, would you like to sit in my seat? I've got a good one, right in the middle." He looked at me like I was an alien. "No, I'm fine here." "But, I'm more than happy watching from the back anyway. Please, take my seat." "No, I'll be fine here." I sheepishly made my way back to my seat and sunk down into it as the movie began.

It was playing well, and it being a midnight show, I started to relax and enjoy the movie and the great crowd response. But around 1:00 a.m. I witnessed something really strange and thought I might be hallucinating. As Bruce and his nurse, played by the great Ella Joyce, were bantering on-screen, I started noticing some small bubbles floating around the actors. I had never seen an anomaly like that in a screening. Had I drifted off to sleep? Suddenly the image jerked, snapped to a stop, and SMOOSH! The film melted before my eyes. The lights came up and I immediately bolted for the projection booth. The projectionists were racing around the booth trying to figure out what had happened. Later I learned that there had been a freak projection bulb explosion during the previous screening. They had not focused the new projector lamp correctly, which ultimately caused the projector lens to crack. This caused the print to slowly burn (the bubbles!) until the lens cracked open completely and incinerated the film.

It took a full twenty minutes to get the movie back up and running. In a regular evening screening that might be tolerable, but in this case it was disastrous; it was well after one in the morning. I actually saw audience members dozing off in their seats during the break! *Bubba Ho-tep*'s momentum was completely lost, and while the audience still enjoyed the movie, it was just a more sedate experience than the previous screenings. As the movie ended I watched Elvis Mitchell exit the theater and had a serious hunch we would not get a great review. And I was right. As Mitchell wrote in the *New York Times,* "There is a grungy high spirit during the first third of this film, but then it dissipates like a mist from an aerosol can."

I was truly disappointed that a seasoned professional at the *New York Times* like Elvis Mitchell could not see beyond a technical problem that was completely outside the filmmaker's control. That "dissipating mist" had nothing to do with *Bubba Ho-tep*: It was a twenty-minute-long projection snafu at one in the morning, which drained the energy out of that audience and that critic. It was so pathetic that Mitchell couldn't comprehend this and chose to take it out on my film on the pages of the most widely read newspaper in the country. I still find it remarkable that a veteran film reviewer would not understand that there is one hard truth that all filmmakers and many film viewers are forced to learn quickly—the only person with ultimate control in the movie business is the projectionist.

IT'S NOW OR NEVER

(Self-distributing *Bubba Ho-tep*)

had been selling international rights to my films at the American Film Market in Santa Monica and various other international film markets for over a decade. In fact, I had found it to be the best, and maybe only solid, way for an indie filmmaker to make any money in the game. I never understood why so few filmmakers actually sold their films themselves at the markets. Most license their film rights to sales agents who charge exorbitant fees and commissions and rarely return any revenue to them. It's pretty simple actually. You just book a room at the market, hang a poster out front, play a trailer inside, and then spend the week haggling with international distributors about their interest and the terms they might pay. If you have a movie with the right elements it's possible to do well. If not, you are in for a long market.

I was sitting on the seventh floor in my office at the AFM in the center of the action, the Loews Santa Monica Beach Hotel, commiserating with distributor-friend Ted Chalmers about the dearth of legitimate buyers. I was doing my best to license international rights to *Bubba Ho-tep* and it was really tough going. There were certain territories where Elvis was popular and others where horror films were in demand—and even some with both. A bunch of international distributors had interest, but they all had the same question: "Who is distributing your picture in the States?"

Having your North American release contracted in advance increases the value and raises the comfort level of the buyer. My typical response, after some hemming and hawing, was that we had a lot of serious interest and were close to making a deal but had nothing we could talk about officially yet. I had one very solid offer from my favorite UK distributor, Mo Claridge of Anchor Bay UK. Mo had been the visionary behind the best DVD package ever, the "Phantasm Sphere Set," in which he had created a way-cool plastic chrome sphere on a stand, which held the actual discs. It even had blades! I loved working with Mo and his business partner and wife, Liz, on that spectacular edition and was heartbroken when Mo suddenly passed away just a couple years later.

A guy strolled into the AFM office uncharacteristically clad in board shorts and flip-flops. His name was David Shultz and he told me that he was an associate of the folks at the American Cinematheque, that he had attended the Egyptian screening, and that based on the huge turnout and fan passion for the film he witnessed, it was his opinion that it might be possible for us to set up a nationwide theatrical release of *Bubba Ho-tep* and get the film into theaters around the country. He also confidently announced that he was the man to help me do it. What followed was an intense series of meetings over the next several weeks as he laid out his intrepid plan.

Dave, through his company Vitagraph Films, had an excellent relationship with the honchos at the Landmark Theatres chain, Ted Mundorff and Mike McClellan. He believed they could be staunch allies in placing our film in dozens of their theaters. I told Dave about my friendship with Tim League and his offer to book Bubba into his Alamo Drafthouse Cinemas chain. Dave felt that if we could launch the film in a few good theaters in key cities and if we were able to attain decent grosses, he was confident that offers from independent theaters would pour in. Our film had also received rave reviews and many "pull quotes" that could be used for marketing. Nick Digilio of WGN Radio, who also happened to be a longtime *Phantasm* fan, gave us a sensational quote in which he called *Bubba Ho-tep* "an important piece of American cinema." And in David Hunter's review of our film in the *Hollywood Reporter,* he celebrated our star's work by writing, "Bruce Campbell in a performance for the ages."

It all looked quite promising, and then Shultz mentioned just one more item—we would need some money to launch this endeavor. The roughed-up budget for this independent *Bubba Ho-tep* theatrical release came in at about a hundred and thirty thousand dollars. Yikes! But Dave Shultz firmly believed that if luck was with us, we could easily gross multiples of that number and actually turn a profit.

For me it was an extremely tough decision. I had made a huge investment from my savings to pay for the production costs of *Bubba Ho-tep*. My dad in loyal fashion had also kicked in a chunk of change. With his background in financial planning he had always taught me that the best investments are when you invest in yourself and the principles you believe in. In making the decision to invest in the production of the movie his advice guided me. To now have to cough up these additional costs was still a fairly daunting proposition. However, I had personally witnessed the love the film received when it played at all the festivals and I firmly believed that if given a chance, audiences would flock to it. All these distributors who had ignored *Bubba Ho-tep* or avoided screenings of it, or who didn't get it—were they right? Had I been wrong to make *Bubba Ho-tep* in the first place? I firmly believed that the answer to that question was a resounding HELL NO.

I rang up Tim League at the Alamo Drafthouse and he agreed with Shultz's assessment that an independent distribution of *Bubba Ho-tep* could work. Tim also gave me some important practical advice in advertising and marketing. So, with my wife and family's full faith and confidence, we once again stepped up to the movie craps table and I laid a hundred and thirty big ones down on the pass line. The dealer handed me the dice and I rolled.

Dave Shultz quickly booked the first three weeks of openings. Weekend no. 1 we would open in the northwest at Landmark's Varsity theater in Seattle and at the Cinema 21 in Portland. Weekend no. 2 would be Southern California with Los Angeles, Irvine, and San Diego, and Weekend no. 3 would be the Big Apple itself, New York City. If the film managed to play well in those first few cities we could then think about moving on to the rest of the country.

My agreement with Shultz was that he would create the release plan and book the theaters; me and my team would do everything else. My team???

I moved quickly to create a team around me to assist with the launch. Bruce gamely agreed to appear at theaters to publicize the openings in many cities. In addition to Linda Brown, I hired two additional publicists, Sasha Berman to handle New York City and Margot Gerber to supervise national publicity. I brought in my longtime web designer, Aaron Lea, and he created the magnificent art for our one-sheet poster and several mini-posters. Shultz turned us on to an inexpensive printing company and we ordered a couple thousand of the one-sheets. The day of the print run was a nightmare. We were struggling at the last minute to make a final decision on the tagline for the poster. At the very last moment, good pal Jeff Conner came up with a brilliant tagline for *Bubba Ho-tep* for which I will be ever grateful: "YOU KNOW THE LEGENDS, NOW LEARN THE TRUTH."

This was a genuine grassroots distribution operation. Looking back on it, I doubt any movie has ever been released nationwide in this manner. Members of my immediate family were key players in this crazy endeavor. Shelley volunteered to help me manage the release, and my kids, Andy and Chloe, eagerly worked on it in between their college and high school studies. Shelley recruited an immensely bright young senior from nearby UCLA, by the name of CJ Yu, who came on board to help.

We had no choice but to work out of my house. We quickly moved the couches out of the living room to clear the decks for our distribution operation. We then filled our "War Room" with workstations, shipping materials, and even a section for print storage. CJ arrived bright and early every morning and we would all take our places and get to work.

Shultz impressed upon me that we had to get trailers to the theaters early because most of them, including the Landmarks, would be happy to play them as long as possible. Except for shipping and print costs, these trailers were essentially free advertising so it was critical that we get them into theaters. To save money I cut the trailer myself, based on a web promo created by Aaron Lea and his associate Phillip Howard. Once it was replicated one of our daily tasks was to pack and ship trailer prints out to all the upcoming theaters. Every afternoon, Shelley, Andy, or myself would have to lug at least a hundred pounds of film to FedEx.

One of the unmentioned assets we had going for us was a legion of *Evil Dead* and *Phantasm* fans nationwide, who we quickly learned were eager to assist us with the release. Though social media had not yet made a significant impact, we were able to find and communicate with these kind folks through email and the Web. My son put himself in charge of recruiting "street teams" in every city to help us with the release. Once he had made contact with a recruit who seemed dependable, we would ship them a kit of flyer handbills, mini-posters, and postcards for them to post in appropriate places in their city. First up was the Northwest, where a dedicated chap named Steve Tenhonen out of Portland flooded the city with *Bubba Ho-tep* flyers and posters and hounded the local radio stations and newspapers to drum up publicity for us. This guy really worked his ass off for us and it definitely paid dividends.

Film prints were a significant cost to our release. Shultz figured we would need a minimum of ten prints to start, with a plan to order more if things heated up. My print cost in bulk from our supplier FotoKem was about twelve hundred dollars each, so this ultimately added up to a big chunk of the budget. Today, movies are delivered on hard drives in the DCP (Digital Cinema Package) format and each "print" is much less expensive, and small enough to be tucked in your back pocket. The 35 mm prints also weighed a lot so there was a grunt labor factor to consider and significant shipping costs to budget.

Around three weeks prior to our opening date I received a telephone call that threatened to entirely upset the applecart. Jack Turner, a bright young executive over at MGM/UA, called with a stunning proposition. He and his boss, Bingham Ray, had heard about what we were doing and the great buzz around *Bubba Ho-tep,* and he was calling to inquire about acquiring the film. *Arrrghhh!* Where were these guys a few months back when I was literally begging distributors to come to our festival screenings?! I detailed for Jack all the plans we had in motion about our upcoming theatrical release. Jack told me that he and Bingham had been brainstorming and wanted to throw out an idea. What if MGM/UA were to take our *Bubba Ho-tep* trailer and affix it on their upcoming major theatrical release of their horror sequel *Jeepers Creepers 2* and get it playing in two thousand theaters across the country? Then, a few weeks later, they would release *Bubba Ho-tep* in at least a thousand theaters with a large marketing budget. They wanted to know what I thought of that idea. Obviously this would be a dream situation, but because our indie opening was literally just days away, I told them that with prints already on their way to theaters, ads placed, and street teams working, the *Bubba Ho-tep* train was leaving the station. MGM would have to make us an immediate offer and be ready to close a deal within hours. Jack said he would get right back to me.

Thank God MGM/UA decided not to move forward with this plan. We would have never been able to pull out of our self-distribution at that late date. But what they did come back with was even better. Since they now believed in *Bubba Ho-tep* and were convinced our theatrical self-distribution plan would be successful, MGM/UA offered to come on as a partner and distribute our film in all the other media, including DVD and television. My trusted longtime attorney, Peter Bierstedt, immediately started negotiating a deal with their sharp distribution executive Malik Ducard, with assistance from their ace studio counsel Greg Julian. This gave us the terrific advantage of having a major studio handling all these ancillary rights.

It now became apparent to me that the main goal of all our publicity and theatrical marketing going forward was not only to make money at the cinema box office, but was also about creating impressions with the general public so that down the line they would purchase that *Bubba Ho-tep* DVD! This became the mantra of our theatrical release.

As our release date in the Northwest neared, I contacted Bruce to arrange for his travel to Portland and Seattle and received a terrible shock. Bruce informed me he had just been cast in a new movie entitled *The Woods* for director Lucky McKee and would be shooting that same weekend in Montreal. Our release plan revolved around Bruce making in-theater appearances to help draw in theatergoers and bump up those first few weekends' box office grosses. Bruce would still make his appearances in LA and NYC, but what the heck would we do now at our Portland and Seattle world premieres?

I had something up my sleeve. Portland and Seattle were the first cities in which I implemented a marketing tactic that Tim League had schooled me on. Back then, local, late-night cable TV advertising was cheap. What

Tim would do for his Alamo theaters was to buy local thirty-second spots on the youth-demographic cable channels like Cartoon Network and MTV and run them between midnight and dawn. Bought in local packages, these late-night spots were quite inexpensive, sometimes as low as ten or twenty bucks a pop. I went ahead and bought a thousand-dollar package in each city.

The opening weekend of September 23 was shaping up to be a genuine nail-biter for us. Would all this work and financial risk pay off? On that opening Friday night the phone rang and it was our loyal street team leader in Portland, Steve Tenhonen. He was reporting in from right in front of the Cinema 21 theater. He proudly told us that there were hundreds of people lined up in the street outside the theater for the show. When the box office numbers came in Monday morning we were astonished. *Bubba Hotep* had performed terrifically in both Seattle and Portland, grossing $34,943 and $25,805 respectively in their first week of play without the benefit of Bruce's in-theater appearance. These numbers were huge for us. Shultz was already swamped with calls from exhibitors looking to play our film in cities everywhere. Yippee Ki Yay, Motherfucker!

Once Bruce got into the act, our numbers went even higher. We were quick to perfect the art of scheduling appearances so we could target more than one screening. In Manhattan, Shultz had booked us into the Angelika Film Center on West Houston. He had taught me that it would be extremely difficult to make money in New York City. The theaters there charged a premium and at the Angelika our floor share would be only 20 percent of the box office gross. Everywhere else in the country you could be guaranteed a minimum of 35 percent in your opening week. Because of the dearth of good theaters in prime Manhattan we had no choice but to accept these onerous terms. On top of this, at that time print advertising in newspapers was very pricey; we had to spend over twenty thousand dollars just in ads to launch in the Big Apple. However, working directly with management and with Bruce's enthusiastic participation, we figured out a way so that in about three hours at the theater he could do an introduction and/or Q&A in six different screenings. All these screenings sold out and our first week's gross was a huge $41,995.

On the next weekend in Southern California we really went to town.

On Friday night, at Landmark's Nuart Theatre in West Los Angeles, Bruce arrived early to introduce the first screening and then stayed on for a Q&A after. He stayed through the break to introduce the later show to an entirely new audience. Both screenings sold out. Meanwhile, I was down in Irvine in Orange County at the Edwards University Town Center theater to host both screenings there. On Saturday night we switched theaters and Bruce appeared in Irvine with actor Reggie Bannister while I hosted the screening at the Nuart. And then on Sunday, Bruce made the drive to San Diego to appear at Landmark's Ken Cinema. The Nuart's first week gross was a stellar $46,959! Big crowds. Big grosses. We were on our way.

Now, every independent theater in America wanted to play *Bubba Ho-tep*. For the next four months it was like going to war. I relinquished my occupation as a writer and director and became a full-time film distributor. I quickly learned that this movie distribution business was almost as difficult as making the damn movie in the first place! Every Monday morning would start with hours on the phone in the early morning with Shultz as we assessed the previous weekend's performance. Then we would make critical decisions as to which runs would end and where we would move our prints to next. Dave would leave to confer with all the various exhibitors and I would marshal our troops in the War Room (my living room) to prep the next weekend's release. It was a nonstop whirlwind of publicity, promotion, print and materials shipping, advertising purchase, and local interviews.

Meanwhile, Bruce continued to support the film, trekking cross-country for appearances in Washington DC, Chicago, and even to his hometown of Lansing, Michigan. His support for the release of *Bubba Ho-tep* was unflagging. The fans loved meeting him in person and his genuine enthusiasm for our film was contagious. He made a memorable comment in front of the crowds, which I think summed up the entirety of the distribution experience of *Bubba Ho-tep*. As Bruce so aptly stated, "*Bubba Ho-tep* is a film that didn't get released, it is a film that escaped."

It's common knowledge that indie films rarely make much money from theatrical distribution. In retrospect it was actually a blessing that all those lazy and disinterested distributors ignored my pleas and passed on *Bubba Ho-tep*, forcing us to go out and make some serious money in the theatrical marketplace.

THE MASTERS OF HORROR

irector Mick Garris had an idea. Why not invite some of his horror
director friends out to dinner? He made a reservation at Café Bizou, a
nice French restaurant over in Sherman Oaks. Mick quickly assembled
a guest list, and I was lucky enough to be on it.

I had no idea what to expect as I arrived at the restaurant. I had been
friends with Mick for a while but had only a passing acquaintance with a
couple of the other horror directors. Here was his guest list: John Carpenter
(*Halloween, Escape from New York*), Tobe Hooper (*The Texas Chainsaw Massacre*), Stuart Gordon (*Reanimator*), John Landis (*An American Werewolf in
London*), Larry Cohen (*It's Alive*), Guillermo del Toro (*Cronos, The Devil's
Backbone*), and Bill Malone (*House on Haunted Hill*).

I was excited as I entered the restaurant to find Mick and John Landis
waiting by the bar. Cries of "Don, Don!" came from the two and I was
warmly greeted by them both and offered a drink. This pattern would repeat itself as each invitee arrived; quickly it was like a gathering of old, dear
friends. As we sat down to dinner I noticed a remarkable thing—no one
wanted to talk about themselves. Everyone was asking questions about the
other directors' films. It quickly became apparent that more than just horror directors, I was sitting with a group of diehard horror geeks!

Also in attendance were a young director friend of Mick's, Robert Parigi,
and the greatest movie prop collector on the planet, Bob Burns. It was fitting that Bob had been invited, as his home was a world-renowned museum

of sci-fi and horror geekery containing rare memorabilia and props from all of our favorite genre films. I had recently visited what is referred to as "Bob's Basement" and was fortunate to be allowed to personally sit in the actual *Time Machine* prop from George Pal's epic 1954 film. This original time machine was lovingly and meticulously restored by Bob and was a stunning work of art. Sitting in this amazing craft made me feel as if I was Rod Taylor traveling back through time. Bob's home museum, which was a large two-story addition onto his modest Burbank home, was packed to the rafters with cool stuff. The front section was filled with screen-used *Alien* and *Terminator* props. Digging deeper were pieces from the original *Outer Limits, Creature from the Black Lagoon,* and the absolute prize of Bob's collection—the original armature model from Universal's 1933 *King Kong*. While wandering through Bob's massive collection, I also managed to accidentally trip over something in the passageway. I suddenly realized I had kicked the one-of-a-kind "Mankind" sphere prop from one of my favorite sci-fi films of all time, *Invaders from Mars*. I gently put it back in its place and nobody realized I had dislodged such an irreplaceable and valuable prop. Sorry about that, Bob!

This directors dinner was the first time that I had met several of my favorite horror movie directors, including the irrepressible Larry Cohen, who was one of the great indie writer-directors from New York working in the genre in the seventies and eighties. Larry created the terrific low-budget 1974 film *It's Alive* about a killer baby, which was a personal favorite of mine. He told some great stories about the difficulties of shooting the opening sequence of that film, in which a woman gives birth only to watch her newborn slaughter all the doctors and nurses in the delivery room.

We did not only talk about movies. John Carpenter had recently been taking helicopter flying lessons and taught me the ins and outs of levitating the whirling contraption using the "collective" and other flight controls. And I told him about my misadventures with helicopters on *The Beastmaster*.

Tobe Hooper was the antithesis of what one would expect for the director of *The Texas Chainsaw Massacre*. He was such a sweet and gentle man, with a deep baritone Texas drawl. I told Tobe about how much I loved his *Salem's Lot* miniseries and what a great series of scares he created with Austrian actor Reggie Nalder as the vampire master.

I enjoyed meeting Bill Malone, who had recently done an excellent job directing the remake of *House on Haunted Hill*. Like Bob Burns, I was fascinated to learn that Bill had a large collection of movie props himself, including major pieces (Robby the Robot) from the classic sci-fi film *Forbidden Planet*.

John Landis was the raconteur of the bunch, with wild stories of major Hollywood legends that he had met over the years, from Alfred Hitchcock to Don Rickles to even Jerry Lewis. John was a student and a fan of movies his entire life and made a point of meeting as many screen legends as he possibly could while they were still alive. He knew everybody!

Stuart Gordon and I had met previously and I was a huge fan of his work on great films like *Reanimator* and *From Beyond*. Stuart had a great sense of humor and I was surprised to learn that he had been collaborating on theatrical productions with writer David Mamet since their college days.

I had never met Guillermo del Toro. He was a very sweet guy with an ebullient and gregarious personality who had started his career as a makeup effects artist in Mexico City. He was about to depart the next day for Prague to direct a new film entitled *Hellboy* so the dinner also served as his send-off. I told Guillermo what a fan I was of his early films, including *Cronos* and especially *The Devil's Backbone*. I was extremely flattered to hear from him that *Phantasm* had been an inspiration for him and that our sphere prop had influenced his design of the scarab-shaped mechanical objects in *Cronos*.

Mick's dinner was such genuine fun for all of us that Mick would go on to schedule many more of them over the next decade. Along the way his dinner list grew to include some of the greatest genre filmmaking talents of our time, including James Wan (*Saw, The Conjuring*), David Cronenberg (*Scanners*), Dario Argento (*Suspiria*), Wes Craven (*A Nightmare on Elm Street*), Mary Lambert (*Pet Sematary*), Greg Nicotero (*The Walking Dead*), Rob Zombie (*The Devil's Rejects*), Ernest Dickerson (*Juice*), Quentin Tarantino (*From Dusk Till Dawn*), Edgar Wright (*Shaun of the Dead*), Eli Roth (*Hostel*), James Gunn (*Guardians of the Galaxy*), Tom Holland (*Child's Play*), Katt Shea (*The Rage*), Robert Rodriguez (*Planet Terror*), William Lustig (*Maniac*), Lucky McKee (*May*), Joe Lynch (*Mayhem*), Adam Rifkin (*The Dark Backward*), Adam Green (*Hatchet*), and many more.

At the end of the night when it came time to pay the dinner tab, I think

Mick was stunned to find that when he counted up the contributions from everybody he had a couple hundred dollars in overpayments. His guests were having so much fun that all the directors kicked in way more money than we had to. Out of gratitude, we insisted that Mick keep the overage money, but Mick dutifully promised to hang on to it and apply the additional funds to the next dinner.

Some might say that the moniker applied to this group of directors is unseemly and smacks of Hollywood ego. Not so. Let me tell you where the name came from. At that first dinner there was a table nearby with the family of a young woman celebrating her birthday. It was getting a bit raucous over at the directors' table and the laughter and hilarity probably impacted her birthday dinner in a negative way. At the end of the evening, as this woman's birthday cake was being delivered to her table, Guillermo interceded. He jumped up and, with a deep chivalrous bow and tongue placed firmly in cheek, profoundly announced to her, "Please accept our felicitous best wishes to you on your birthday from the . . . Masters of Horror." The woman blushed and we all burst into cheers. The name stuck.

THE LATE GREAT *BUBBA NOSFERATU*

By the time theatrical distribution had finished and the *Bubba Ho-tep* DVD was successfully launched, it was past time for me to take off my marketing and distribution hats and write and direct a new movie. As *Bubba Ho-tep* had been both a critical and box office success, and there was no question that fans of the movie wanted more, it seemed like the smart move for me would be to make the sequel. How was I to know that this would turn out to be one of the great setbacks of my career?

An interesting thing I figured out early was that if you took the word *Bubba* and added a monster name after it, you would have a sequel. For a while I was seriously thinking about making *Bubba Sasquatch*. I liked the idea of old Elvis relocating to a rest home up in the Northwest, and lurking in the tall pine forests surrounding the place would be a tribe of killer big-foots. I even mentioned it once at a screening Q&A when asked about se-quels and remarked, "There hasn't been a good bigfoot movie for a while." Joe Lansdale, who was with me, shot back, "Don, there hasn't *ever* been a good bigfoot movie."

I had read a lot about Elvis's fascination with the occult and it seemed logical to me that the King had probably had quite a few interactions with the supernatural prior to his residency in that East Texas rest home. I had also seen the photos and videos of Elvis demonstrating his obsession with the martial arts and it immediately sparked an idea that the King and his "Memphis Mafia" boys might team up to lay down some serious whoopass on the forces of darkness. We had already established that seventy-year-old Elvis was one tough old geezer and now I started thinking about the possibility of younger Elvis kicking undead ass as well. Could a prequel to *Bubba Ho-tep* be in order? The more I thought about it, the more it seemed right to combine the best elements of the two. What if old Elvis was forcibly relocated to another rest home and along the way he reminisced to his nurse about his youthful encounters with evil? The best of both worlds!

Another topic that dominated my thinking about a sequel was Elvis's unscrupulous manager, Colonel Tom Parker. The Colonel was reputed to have a Svengali-like control over Elvis, dominating him and his career; he has been vilified relentlessly by Elvis fans almost unanimously. Many fans blamed Parker for Elvis's downward spiral into drugs and held him accountable for the King's untimely and ignominious death. I read as much as I could about the Colonel and came across some astounding "facts" about his murky past. As a young man it was reputed that he fled his homeland of the Netherlands under suspicion of a woman's murder and entered the United States under mysterious circumstances. He reportedly spent a decade traveling the country as a carnival barker and con man. It is believed that the reason Elvis never performed outside the USA was due to Parker's illegal immigrant status. The Colonel cashed in at Elvis's expense, reputedly taking commissions as high as 50 percent. As I ruminated on Elvis, his interest in the occult, and the Colonel's unholy sway over the King, I could only come to one obvious conclusion. It had to be vampirism!!! How the hell else could one explain Elvis paying fully half of his income to the Colonel for simply being his manager?

I took all of these ideas and conjured up a nine-page treatment of the *Bubba Nosferatu* story I wanted to tell. Much like my *Phantasm* sequels, it would start right from where *Bubba Ho-tep* ended. Elvis's loyal nurse would find him dying on the creek bank, dutifully jump into action, and resuscitate his sorry ass. Both of them subsequently expelled from their residence at the Mud Creek Shady Rest Home, they would head down to New Orleans to a new rest home, and on the way we would learn about Elvis's past and ultimately confront his very dark future.

In the course of their travels, Elvis would confess to his nurse about his reticence to revisit the Big Easy. He would relate that he had memories of witnessing some bad mojo down there in the seventies working on a studio movie that had been abandoned under mysterious circumstances. The story then flashed back to 1974, with the Colonel convincing Elvis it was time to resuscitate his acting career, and his best move would be to star in a "horror picture." We then would find Elvis shooting MGM's *Curse of the She-Vampires* at a spooky old mansion in New Orleans. Elvis would co-star with an elderly, Karloff-like horror star by the name of Claude Kilgore. (One of the tragedies of the demise of *Bubba Nosferatu* was that I conceived this role for Angus Scrimm, who would have been simply fantastic in it.) My screenplay would ultimately reveal that the Colonel was attempting to re-pay a debt to a coven of real vampires he had crossed paths with in his youth, and the bloodsuckers had smuggled him out of Europe ahead of the Nazis into the American South. These vampires were now based in New Orleans and the Colonel owed them big time.

Meanwhile, in present day, Elvis and his nurse would encounter this same vampire clan in the vicinity of their new rest home. We would contrast two ongoing battles: one in 1974, which we referred to as the "Blood Riot," in which Elvis and his Memphis Mafia buddies would have to go mano a mano with the vampires, beat them back, and escape with their skins and souls intact; and one battle in the present day, in which Elvis, his nurse, and his new comrade-in-arms, a Native American rest home neighbor who believed himself to be the great chief Sitting Bull, would finally vanquish the vampire threat. Cue the tomahawk action!

I was genuinely looking forward to filming the final showdown, which featured old Elvis battling a four-hundred-year-old rotting and decrepit vampire queen in a crazy, low-speed joust on mobility scooters. It was a terrific yarn very much in the spirit of the original, but with more action and horror.

Meanwhile, I had been in touch with Bruce about the story concept of the sequel and told him about my idea. We could do both a prequel and a sequel in one movie. Bruce told me he liked the idea, as he had long been a proponent of doing a prequel about Elvis's early years fighting the undead. I sent him a copy of the treatment to read.

Bruce and I started the funding process by accepting an invitation to meet with Jack Turner and Danny Rosette, executives working at MGM and its affiliate United Artists. They were eager to stay in the Bubba business. Bruce and I went over to the MGM offices and pitched the project to them based on my *Bubba Nosferatu* storyline. Jack and Danny loved it. I gave them a copy of the treatment and within a week received a written offer from United Artists to fund a screenplay and produce a movie based on it. We were going to make *Bubba Nosferatu* and they were offering to put up five million bucks to do so. This was too easy!

And of course, it turned out that it wasn't. To my utter shock, two weeks later, as my attorney Peter was reviewing their proposed agreement, I read an alert in the Hollywood trades that MGM had suddenly shuttered United Artists and decided they would not be making movies there anymore. It mentioned that both executives we had met with would be leaving the studio.

Into the void stepped Jeff Katz, an enterprising young studio executive who worked for Bob Shaye over at New Line Cinema. Jeff approached me about doing a remake of *Phantasm* and, as an added bonus, to put into production a sequel to *Bubba Ho-tep*. I went right into negotiations with New Line. During this period I started to put some serious work into the storyline for the sequel.

My first decision was to enlist author Joe Lansdale in the process. I came to a tentative agreement with Joe's agent for his services but then learned that Joe had deadlines in place for some other major writing projects; it did not appear to me that this would work in our time frame. Joe's very successful literary career had heated up quite a bit. It seemed the most prudent approach would be for me to finish the screenplay myself.

Around this time an article in one of the trade papers came to my attention. It was during awards season and it was a profile on celebrated actor Paul Giamatti. In it they asked him which director he would like to work with one day and he had answered "Don Coscarelli," saying he was a huge fan of *Bubba Ho-tep*. At first it was flattering that such a great actor would express such sentiments, but then it started percolating in my mind that maybe Paul could be the perfect Colonel Tom Parker. I managed to secure his email address from a colleague and wrote to Paul. We met up a few weeks later for coffee at the Farmer's Market in Los Angeles.

I found Paul to be an extremely intelligent, superfriendly, down-to-earth guy. He also was funny as hell. An avid reader, he was also, surprisingly, a big-time horror fan. He told me a favorite story about how his older brother Marcus had sneaked him through a back door into a theater to see the R-rated *Phantasm* when he was twelve years old. I mentioned to Paul that I might have a project we could possibly team up on together with Bruce Campbell, and he was immediately enthusiastic. He loved Bruce's work and said he would definitely be into it. Paul had just started a small independent production company with his college-friend Daniel Carey and offered its services to assist with seeking funding and distribution for any projects.

I went right to work on the *Bubba Nosferatu* screenplay. To speed things up I hired Stephen Romano to help me finish it. When it was complete I let Giamatti read it. He loved it. The Colonel was in!

There were some problems over at New Line. While they liked the *Bubba Nosferatu* screenplay, the *Bubba* offer was tied up with the *Phantasm* remake, and I was having cold feet about doing a reboot of my film. I had submitted to them an inventive script for a new *Phantasm*, which I thought was quite clever and worked as both a remake and a sequel rolled into one. My plan was to have Angus reprise his role as the Tall Man, and feature a new cast in a new town. Yet in the third act, just as our new heroes fall into the Tall Man's clutches, Reggie and Mike appear with the cavalry to save the day. It quickly became apparent that New Line preferred the stereotypically traditional studio way of doing a "new" take on *Phantasm:* completely re-cast all the roles, including that of the Tall Man. I was lifelong friends with *Phantasm* stars Angus Scrimm and Reggie Bannister and honestly could not face up to telling either of them that they would be replaced in the franchise, even though they were both still vital working actors. So while the New Line offer atrophied, other, more interesting funding suddenly appeared.

Jack Turner, previously our advocate at United Artists, was now forming a company to produce independent films with actor Dwayne "The Rock" Johnson and his insightful manager and wife, Dany Garcia. I had a friendly breakfast meeting over at Barney Greengrass in Beverly Hills with Dany and Jack. They told me Dwayne was a fan of *Bubba Ho-tep* and they all loved the *Bubba Nosferatu* script; they felt it would make for a great first film for their company. And even better, they could provide six million dollars of independent funding from Miami investors to fund the film. Awesome! We were going to make a movie together!

Until we were not. I had sent the finished screenplay to Bruce to read and it had been almost a month with no response from him. Bruce finally got back with an email telling me he had some major problems with the script. He told me he was moving to Florida to appear in a new television series and he wouldn't have much time to discuss this subject. What followed were some really dark times for me.

Over several long phone calls Bruce told me he did not like the direction of our screenplay. He stated that his major concern was that by showcasing the supernatural adventures of Elvis in his younger days, it would somehow undermine what we had achieved with *Bubba Ho-tep*. He believed you could make a movie about Young Elvis kicking undead ass, or a movie about Old Elvis kicking undead ass, but you could not combine them into one. Try as I might, I never really understood his position—it's common knowledge that the real Elvis had an obsession with the occult and in *Bubba Ho-tep* we had him fighting a mummy, so who's to say he never came face-to-face with it, in his youth or old age? Bruce offered a series of other concerns with the draft. I was extremely amenable to accommodating his wishes—after all, we had a great relationship collaborating on the first film and he was absolutely brilliant in it. But something was different here.

I offered fixes for many of Bruce's other concerns. But he was resolute that if my story featured young Elvis having supernatural adventures prior to the events of *Bubba Ho-tep*, in the same film with old Elvis, he would not participate. Despite the fact that a year or so earlier Bruce and I had been out pitching this storyline together at MGM, he now did not want to do this movie. In our final call about it at the time, I asked him to trust in me: I had a vision for a good film and would do anything I could to solve his creative concerns along the way. Bruce stuck to his guns and his answer was a firm no.

For an indie filmmaker it is an extremely rare confluence of events when one has a script they believe in, a brilliant and critically lauded costar like

Paul Giamatti eager to participate, and bona fide investors ready to fund a multimillion-dollar production. This opportunity was now gone and I must admit that it stung. Our new producer Jack tried to intercede, approaching Bruce's representatives with a new financial offer. Again, no joy: they told Jack that Bruce wanted to focus on directing his own projects.

For several years after, along with Paul Giamatti and his producing partner Dan, we doggedly tried to resurrect the project. We approached Kurt Russell and Nicolas Cage to star, both with histories in regard to Elvis, but neither joined up with us. A few months later, I also pitched it to Hugh Jackman's manager, with no luck. At one point I even imposed on Paul to call up Dwayne Johnson and personally ask him if he would like to play the King (which in retrospect would have been utterly amazing!), but Dwayne politely declined. The King of Rock would not be played by the Rock. Ultimately, Paul reached out to acclaimed actor Ron Perlman, who responded very favorably. I believe Ron would have made a superlative star for *Bubba Nosferatu,* but by then the funding had evaporated.

A few years later, Bruce accepted my invitation to join Paul Giamatti and me at dinner. It was a very pleasant evening and everybody got along really well. Bruce ultimately told us that he would consider participating in a sequel, if it was written by original author Joe R. Lansdale. I reluctantly agreed to put aside my sequel screenplay and approached Joe, suggesting that maybe he could write us a sequel story with the idea that if it was not used, he could always release it as a book. With Bruce's and my wholehearted support, Joe started writing, but due to his busy career, including not only novels but his excellent *Hap and Leonard* television series, well over three years passed before he presented us with a full-length novel entitled *Bubba and the Cosmic Bloodsuckers.*

As I read through Joe's book I appreciated the panoply of new characters he created, and especially his very transgressive vampires. Though preferring the screenplay I had written with Stephen Romano (naturally), I reached out to Bruce to see what his opinion of the new novel was, and his thoughts on how we might adapt the Lansdale story. Bruce surprised me by responding that he would bow out of any future *Bubba* movies for financial reasons, and it became clear that it was time for me to accept his decision as final. In Hollywood, they say "never say never," but I believe now that a sequel to *Bubba Ho-tep* starring Bruce is just not in the cards.

However, science has proven that Elvis is eternal. His legacy will always be with us and his fans will always want more of him. Perhaps one day I'll come across another unique actor able to embody the spirit of Elvis, who could fill those white boots and energetically kick undead ass. The King may return one day, but as of this writing, Elvis has left the building.

"INCIDENT ON AND OFF A MOUNTAIN ROAD"

t was intended to be my feminist movie.

I was raised by two feminists. My mom introduced me to Gloria Steinem's *Ms. Magazine* when I was in my early teens and we always had copies of it around my house to read. My sister Anne brought the cause forcefully to our high school with her acclaimed and award-winning speech "Equal, But Not the Same," which she delivered so powerfully at interschool competitions. I always intended to explore this issue in a film one day, but when you are pigeonholed as a horror director, a genre that has spawned an entire subgenre devoted solely to misogynistically slashing up women, it is not exactly the obvious fit.

When I acquired the film rights to *Bubba Ho-tep,* I had also been a fan of Joe R. Lansdale's short story "Incident On and Off a Mountain Road," which was published in the same collection. In my mind "Incident" brilliantly laid out the bones of a potent polemic on feminism cloaked in the traditional male fantasy of the "damsel in distress." Except this was not your typical damsel; it took that very traditional trope and turned it right on its freakin' ear. I saw it as a mash-up of a horror monster / slasher film with a very mean feminist streak. "Incident" was a tight fourteen pages and told a harrowing survival story pitting a lost young woman against a vicious beast of a serial killer. At the time, I optioned the film rights for "Incident On and Off a Mountain Road" along with *Bubba Ho-tep* but was never able to get a movie based on it funded. After a year and a half of effort I let the rights lapse. Then, a decade later, pal Mick Garris came calling.

After the friendly success of Mick's Masters of Horror directors dinners, he approached me to participate in an idea of his to create a horror anthology television series anchored by the "Masters." Mick had cleverly raised the funding to create thirteen one-hour episodes with a genuinely novel plan. Each "Master" could select their own story and as long as the project stayed on schedule and budget, there would be no creative constraints whatsoever. Mick said he hoped the episodes would be visceral and chilling and earnestly suggested they could be as bloody as we wanted.

As Mick explained his plan to me, Joe's short story immediately popped in my head as a suitable candidate. Though it was very short at just fourteen pages, over the years I had been ruminating on how to extend and amplify the themes. I asked my *Bubba Nosferatu* cowriter Stephen Romano to join me and collaborate in fleshing out a teleplay.

"Incident On and Off a Mountain Road" tells the story of Ellen, a young woman driving through a wilderness area at night who crashes into a car abandoned in the road and finds herself stranded. As she searches for the driver of the other car, she finds the injured woman in the clutches of a vicious serial killer called Moonface. Ellen flees into the woods and it becomes an epic struggle for her to simply survive the night.

I was lucky to pull together a superb cast for the show. Bree Turner gave a ferociously subtle performance as newlywed Ellen, and the versatile Ethan Embry played her conflicted and explosive husband. Romano and I created a fabulous role for Angus Scrimm as the crazed captive Buddy, which he threw himself into with total abandon. Rounding out the cast was six-foot-ten-inch John DeSantis as Moonface, complete with prosthetic face and shiny metal teeth courtesy of the extraordinary Howard Berger of KNB EFX.

I moved up to Vancouver for a month to shoot the show. Vancouver is a beautiful place to live and work and the Canadian crews are superb. When I arrived, director John Landis had just finished his episode, which he cowrote with his talented son Max. John left me a funny greeting card at the hotel wishing me luck; it depicted several comic chimpanzees in a row with the handwritten inscription, "MASTERS OF HORROR?"

As I was preparing my shoot, the great Italian director Dario Argento was filming his episode. I heard rumors coming from the set that Dario's episode was particularly gory, featuring a female creature with a taste for male human flesh. I think Mick was just doing his job as executive producer, but he alerted me that some of the other directors, including Takashi Miike, were also planning hyperviolent episodes, which really goaded me to raise the violence quotient. I had planned to keep it restrained but hell, I didn't want to be the slacker of the bunch. So consequently I decided to really let loose with the sequences in which Moonface uses his industrial drill press on the eyeballs of his unfortunate victims.

As a boy I always enjoyed reading O. Henry stories with their delicious twist endings. "Incident" featured a great twist ending, although I would not characterize it as delicious in any way. This was my first time directing a film that ended with a shock twist and it bedeviled me throughout shooting. I was constantly paranoid of making a wrong decision and prematurely telegraphing the ending. It was a fascinating and novel challenge to devote so much energy to protecting the integrity of the final minutes of the film and made me appreciate the work of great filmmakers like M. Night Shyamalan who successfully managed to stun audiences with the endings of their films. I think my greatest relief was learning that the surprise ultimately did work and, thank God, no one saw it coming.

It was extremely gratifying when the Showtime network selected "Incident On and Off a Mountain Road" as the premiere episode to lead off the series. When my show aired it received possibly the best reviews of anything I had ever worked on. Lots of mainstream press showered it with praise, even the *National Enquirer* tabloid, which, amazingly, labeled it a "TV Pick of the Week."

I think the most satisfying compliment came from my lead actress's father. Bree's performance in "Incident On and Off a Mountain Road" moved her dad so profoundly that he said it was the first time in her career that he could genuinely understand why she had chosen the difficult path of an actress. High praise indeed!

STARTING A FIFTH AND FINISHING
A SIXTH *PHANTASM*

After *Phantasm Oblivion* I ultimately made two more *Phantasm* movies. One took over seven years to produce and the other was shot in a single day.

I met Brad Baruh when he was a senior executive producer at cable network E! Entertainment. Brad was the only horror fan on the E! staff and had generously offered to cover *Bubba Ho-tep* during our theatrical distribution phase. Brad created a full twenty-minute video segment about our film that included interviews with myself and Bruce, and he managed to get it into heavy rotation on *E! News*. It played over and over for an entire week on their national cable channel and was a huge boost to our release.

We became friends and I mentioned to Brad that Stephen Romano had written a spec *Phantasm* sequel script a few years back that I liked. What was cool about Stephen's screenplay was that it was 90 percent dialog. Imagine Angus Scrimm as the Tall Man performing multiple pages of dialog when in the original *Phantasm* he just uttered twenty-eight words. Since *Bubba Nosferatu* had fallen apart and nothing was going on with *Phantasm* at that time, Brad suggested we get the *Phantasm* actors together and film a table read of this new script as a tool to raise funding for a film. Brad offered to produce and pull together a small crew and I agreed. The project would come to be known as *Phantasm Forever*.

On a blustery day in March, the *Phantasm* family converged on the Laurel Canyon Stages in North Hollywood. The core team from the original film were there: Michael Baldwin, Bill Thornbury, Reggie Bannister, Kat Lester, and of course the inimitable Angus Scrimm. There was a sizeable role for Gloria Lynne Henry from *Phantasm III,* reprising her role of Rocky. The Romano script also featured a character who was referenced in *Phantasm II* but never depicted. The character was Celeste, Reggie's deceased wife, and Ashley Laurence of *Hellraiser* fame kindly offered to come to the stage for the day and help us out.

It was a party atmosphere, like a family reunion, yet hard work at the same time. On most movie sets you are doing well if you shoot four to five pages of script in a day's work. On this day we needed to shoot ninety. The actors were assembled around a black table against a green screen backdrop. Brad's idea was that if the reading turned out well, perhaps one day we could release this promo by compositing in some backgrounds to add some reality to the actors' performances. I really enjoyed the fast pace. It was a new way of working as we shot with two Panasonic VariCam video cameras. I enjoyed watching the action from the two large video monitors.

In the years since, I have assembled the sequences into a feature-length narrative. It is a fascinating detour in the *Phantasm* world. The actors were all on their game and in their prime. There's a show-stopping scene in which Angus, in character as the Tall Man, ruminates in solitude on his very existence, building into a fury as he rails against the forces allied against him. Fans of the series would love this project and I hope to figure out a way to share it with them one day. The *Phantasm Forever* experience spurred me to open my eyes to new ways of continuing the *Phantasm* story. Enter David Hartman.

PHANTASM RAVAGER

David Hartman was a brilliant animation director and illustrator and had been a key collaborator on the visual effects of *Bubba Ho-tep*. He was responsible for the amazing and hilarious animated hieroglyphics that tumbled out of the mummy's mouth. "Eat the dog dick of Anubis!" He and his artistic wife Kathleen also created the massive *Ben-Hur*–like art title sequence for the movie. I had always admired Dave and his work, especially the fact that he seemed to go out every weekend with friends and relatives and shoot a new short film. He had an artistic work ethic that inspired me.

One day Dave rang me up and asked if I would be amenable to him shooting a short film based on *Phantasm*. He had an idea in which Reggie would meet a young woman hitchhiking and things would not end well for her. I had so much fun working on the *Phantasm Forever* table read that I sparked to Dave's idea right away. I immediately called up Reggie Bannister and asked him if he would be up for shooting an experimental short film and he said to count him in. His wife, Gigi, who had worked on *Phantasm Oblivion* supervising makeup effects, volunteered her services as well. I checked in with Brad and he offered to come along and shoot it using his brand-new 1080p HD video camera. So along with my son and a local friend of the Bannisters this was our entire crew. Six people!

The weekend's shoot took place far up in the San Bernardino Mountains outside of Los Angeles. We actually shot in the mountain cabin where

Reggie and Gigi lived as they were kind enough to volunteer their own house. We had so much fun! It was as if I had been transported back to my student film days with this tiny crew and a small cast working together.

Everybody did everything. I did the lighting, sound, logistics, and helped out with the blood work. We had one major sphere-drilling/blood-splattering sequence, which we shot not only in the Bannisters' bedroom, but right in their bed. God love 'em! These were some of the truly fun aspects of filmmaking that had been denied me once I started directing larger productions.

I have always treasured the student film mentality in which a small group of creative, like-minded filmmakers come together to collaborate on a creative work. In this manner, in addition to being creatively satisfying, filmmaking can be a joyous experience. It's typically not like that in the traditional American union process of filmmaking. Job descriptions are legally stratified and woe be to the energetic crew member who attempts to help out a crew member from a different department. Sadly, it is just not allowed. I remember being stunned my first time on a studio set when it was explained to me that the Teamster drivers are responsible only for driving the trucks to location, and once parked there, they must sit and wait for the entire shooting day to pass and are not allowed to join in and work with the rest of the crew. Of course they are very capable in moving around the big rigs, and paid very highly for that service, but I couldn't help but feel sad that they were not allowed to experience the fun of filmmaking: painting a set wall, helping with a camera rig, or even throwing out a creative suggestion to the director.

The weekend shoot was so much fun that a few weeks later we did it again. And then again, and then again. When we finished up the first series of weekends, Dave was able to edit together almost twenty minutes of footage. But what could we do with it? It did not seem feasible to shoot an entire feature this way, nor did we ever really have a script. The process was more, "Let's go out this weekend and Reggie picks up a cute hitchhiker on a road." Then it was, "Let's shoot a scene where they talk at the hitchiker's cabin and she's killed horribly." And then on to, "Reggie encounters the Lady in Lavender."

While he was directing these weekend shoots, Dave held down a day job as supervising director on a Disney cartoon series entitled *My Friends*

Tigger & Pooh starring young actress Chloë Grace Moretz. As we went on hiatus from shooting *Phantasm Ravager,* Dave embarked on a new job creating the 3D-animated *Transformers: Prime* series for Hasbro. Around this time a robot came calling . . .

ZOMBIES AND ROBOTS

*J*ohn Dies at the End was the first film project determined by a robot. This is a true story.

Well before *The Walking Dead* became a cable TV juggernaut, I was a rabid fan of zombie fiction. It started back in the early nineties when I read a great short story anthology entitled *Book of the Dead,* which contained a brilliant story by Joe R. Lansdale entitled "On the Far Side of the Cadillac Desert with Dead Folks." This interest continued over the years and included the *Walking Dead* comic book series.

For a brief moment it seemed I had an opportunity to get involved with *The Walking Dead.* I emailed creator Robert Kirkman in 2008 to inquire about its availability for a television show. It turns out Robert was a *Bubba Ho-tep* fan and he said it looked like rights to *TWD* just might be available again in the next few days and his managers would call me. Well, those few days passed with no response and try as I might I was unable to get in contact with him again about it. I tried to recruit some director friends and every other month I would drop Robert another email trying to tantalize him, like "Stuart Gordon wants to get in on TWD," or "I just ran into George Romero's manager and he says George would love to get involved with TWD." A few months later I read about AMC and Frank Darabont being involved and that was the end of that.

During my infatuation with zombie fiction I forced myself to treat it as a guilty pleasure and set a self-imposed limit of no more than a couple zombie novels per year. I think what appealed to me most about these books was that all of them were about survival in an unfamiliar landscape and the challenge of being alone in a depopulated world.

One day, completely unsolicited, I received an email from a bot at Amazon.com. This robotic A.I. email told me that if I liked that last zombie novel I had ordered, then I would love a new novel that Amazon was selling entitled *John Dies at the End*, written by first-time writer David Wong. This Amazon bot certainly got my attention. Just the title hooked me. Here was an author with the audacity and sheer balls to announce in the title how his book ends. At the same time his title felt like a challenge. *Go ahead, read my book, I'm not afraid to tell you how it ends.*

The bot's description of the *John Dies at the End* storyline was even better:

> *It's a drug that promises an out-of-body experience with each hit. On the street they call it Soy Sauce, and users drift across time and dimensions. But some who come back are no longer human. Suddenly a silent otherworldly invasion is underway, and mankind needs a hero. What it gets instead is John and David, a pair of college dropouts who can barely hold down jobs. Can these two stop the oncoming horror in time to save humanity? No. No, they can't.*

David Wong and the kind folks at St. Martin's Press have allowed me to quote the original hardcover edition's dust jacket. That way, those of you who have not seen or read the book can get a flavor for *John Dies at the End*'s clever and subversive style.

> *STOP. You should not have touched this flyer with your bare hands. NO, don't put it down. It's too late. They're watching you. My name is David Wong. My best friend is John. Those names are fake. You might want to change yours. You may not want to know about the things you'll read on these pages, about the sauce, about Korrok, about the invasion, and the future. But it's too late. You touched the book. You're in the game. You're under the eye. The only defense is knowledge. You need to read this book, to the end. Even the part with the bratwurst. Why? You just have to trust me.*

The important thing is this: The drug is called Soy Sauce and it gives users a window into another dimension. John and I never had the chance to say no. You still do. I'm sorry to have involved you in this, I really am. But as you read about these terrible events and the very dark epoch the world is about to enter as a result, it is crucial you keep one thing in mind: None of this was my fault.

I immediately ordered the book and counted the days in anticipation. Upon its arrival I started reading and was thrilled by the audacity of Theseus's paradox, which was presented so uniquely in the prologue. Wong distilled the paradox thus: Hero chops off bad guy's head with axe and while doing so breaks axe handle. Hero replaces axe handle with new one, then chips axe blade while killing a creature he finds in his kitchen. Hero replaces axe blade with a new one and then is confronted by reanimated bad guy who has stitched his head back on. Zombie dead guy sees hero brandishing axe and says, "That's the axe that slayed me." Hero is stumped as he ponders whether that statement is true.

In addition to elevating absurdity into an art form, Wong's book is also hide-under-the-bed scary and laugh-out-loud funny at the same time. *John Dies at the End* introduced two great protagonists in slackers John and Dave, and as their supernatural adventure began, I could immediately see it as the basis for a badass film. That Amazon bot was right!

I learned that David Wong had started the book as a series of horror stories that he would release online every Halloween. By the time these stories reached novel-length, some seventy thousand people had read the entire book online. He already had a fan base! Oh, and David Wong was not his real name. Like the lead character in *John Dies at the End,* David Wong was a name the author assumed ostensibly to protect himself and his privacy. His real name was Jason Pargin. I wrote him an email explaining who I was, the films I had made, and how much I loved his book. I did not hear back. A couple of weeks later I wrote to him again.

After four long weeks a response finally popped up in my inbox. It started with, "I'm not ignoring your email, I'm just a little stunned. Assuming you are who you say you are, and if not, I'm equally stunned that someone would be bored enough to make up such a thing." Jason went on to tell me how his mom had taken him to see *Phantasm* at a midnight show when he was a boy and it scared the shit out of him. We set up a phone call and started talking about how to make a movie of *John Dies at the End*. I told him that my typical process was to take the project out to major studios and producers I had relationships with and if none of them had interest, then I would try to figure out a way to make the film independently. A month or two later we signed an agreement.

Even though I had little hope of getting industry interest due to its edgy nature, once I had finished writing the screenplay adaptation, I felt compelled to submit it to the major producers and studio executives I was acquainted with. An indie filmmaker just cannot leave any rock unturned. Their polite rejections were not a surprise.

When I was younger, I took these rejections personally. But over time—after experiences with *Phantasm, The Beastmaster,* and *Bubba Ho-tep,* all of which ultimately proved to be highly valuable commodities that in retrospect only a fool would ignore—I now approached these rejections differently. Sure it stings. And sure it creates a helluva lot more work and risk when I have to go out and scrape up funding independently. But I finally came to the realization that the problem was not with me. It was with them. And that revelation was liberating.

Rejection is such a major part of the entertainment business. Competition is so intense. One needs to develop a very thick skin to it. Everyone wants to direct, write, or star in movies, and the harsh fact is that there are very few slots available. I think my basic nature is to bounce off rejection, like a bumper car at the arcade, and try to find a way around it. To try to just keep moving forward even if it's not the exact path you imagined.

There are a lot of shortsighted, herd-mentality people out there whose only skill is in working their way politically up the studio executive ladders. Many of these "gatekeepers" control the movies and television shows we watch, and some are fairly clueless. So often their only concern is what their immediate boss thinks of them. (And by the way, if you are a film executive who has taken the time and effort to buy and read this book, you are different. You are one of the visionary few and I will be contacting you soon about a very cool new project I know you will love!)

My attempts to place my *John Dies at the End* screenplay with a traditional major studio or producer having failed, I headed back down that hard indie road. I had such faith in David Wong's unique work that I was prepared to again sink a chunk of my own money into a film despite the risk. I needed two more things to make this work. I needed another chunk of investment and some star casting to make the project viable.

After my friend Brad Baruh had left E! Entertainment he joined forces with Andy Meyers and Roman Perez in a company called M3 Creative. Using Brad's excellent marketing skills M3 quickly became one of the top boutique creative content production companies in Hollywood, with clients including Marvel and Disney. I told them about my plan to make a feature film of *John Dies at the End* and they eagerly offered to invest some money and, even more exciting, to put the resources of M3 at my disposal during production. This was a fantastic offer, as not only were they good friends and would be great to work with, but M3 could also provide all kinds of production assistance.

Bubba Nosferatu for the time being was dead in the water, so I reached out to Paul Giamatti to see what he thought of the screenplay. After reading the script, Paul told me it was one of the most insane things he had ever read and he generously volunteered to play anything in it I wanted him to. I told him that from the outset I had imagined him as playing the writer, Arnie Blondestone, who interviews our protagonist and propels the story with his questions. Paul agreed to join in with us and, as a bonus, to executive produce with his business partner Dan Carey.

I was extremely fortunate to land four other actors for key supporting roles in *John Dies at the End*. I had been a fan of Glynn Turman since he broke through decades previously in *Cooley High,* and was especially fond of his Emmy-winning performance in HBO's *In Treatment.* We were so lucky to get Clancy Brown to portray the role of Dr. Albert Marconi. Clancy was an outstanding film actor and a great guy who had created so many memorable roles over the years in classic films such as *The Shawshank Redemption, Starship Troopers,* and *Highlander.*

Good friend and skilled actor Daniel Roebuck was offered the odd role of Largeman, a ringmaster from another world, with over a dozen pages of fascinating dialog. The downside was that this character wore a freakish mask at all times and Dan's face would never be seen. Dan took one for the team and still created one of the most memorable characters in the film.

I was struggling over who to hire for the strange role of Roger North. He needed to be a unique and compelling actor who could believably manifest himself as a being from another dimension. A few years earlier at Crypticon, a horror convention in Seattle, I sat at an autograph table meeting fans, and actor Doug Jones was signing at a table across from me. I personally witnessed Doug as he interacted with his fans. There was always a long line of people waiting to meet him and Doug got up from his seat and hugged each and every fan. This genuine personal warmth and the fact that Doug always worked in heavy prosthetic makeup intrigued me. His signature creature roles in Guillermo del Toro films as aquatic man Abe Sapien in *Hellboy* and as the Pale Man in *Pan's Labyrinth* showed what he could do with prosthetics, but what would Doug be like stripped of makeup? Doug kindly volunteered to read for the part and he was simply wonderful. I cast him on the spot. After finishing *John Dies at the End,* Doug went back to full creature makeup and anchored the cast as the Amphibian Man in Guillermo's Oscar-winning Best Picture *The Shape of Water.*

With these four great actors on board, we now needed to solve the central conceit of this low-budget undertaking. Could we find two unknown actors who would be willing to work for minimum pay yet have the acting chops to creatively anchor an entire film? We could and did. Finding Chase Williamson and Rob Mayes was a complete blessing, and it was on the backs of these two actors' talent that we were able to make a good film.

Chase had just graduated from college and had never appeared on-screen in anything. Literally. Can you believe that on Chase's first day of shooting he found himself faced with performing six pages of dialog with one of the greatest actors on the planet in Paul Giamatti? As I arrived on production designer Todd Jeffery's amazing Chinese restaurant set, I was mortified that Chase might wilt under the pressure. The kid was a champ and went toe-to-toe with Giamatti, and that day, those two created some of the best scenes in the film.

While Rob generated an easygoing charm, he also possessed a natural facility for comedy. His ability to channel John directly from the pages and to find and emphasize the absurd moments of humor was a great asset to our film. Best of all, both guys were hardworking, unflappable, and a joy to work with. These two actors were one of the key reasons we were able to pull off such an ambitious film for such an insanely low price and I will always be grateful to them.

Sometimes filmmaking involves surprisingly bizarre choices. An iconic sequence in the *John Dies at the End* book indicated that this unique story would be going places others never dared. In this scene our hapless protagonists John and Dave are trapped in a mysterious girl's basement by a strange entity with a dark sense of humor. As John flees up the basement stairs and reaches for the basement doorknob, he stops dead in his tracks when the knob suddenly and shockingly morphs into a flaccid male penis. John instantly jerks his hand away. "THAT door cannot be opened!" he cries out.

I explained to Bob Kurtzman, our makeup effects supervisor, what I needed for the gag and he promised to ship out a prosthetic penis to the set for our shoot. When we were unwrapping the shipment from Kurtzman, boy did we find a surprise. Inside the box was a ten-inch prosthetic, only we were stunned to find that it was *fully erect*. In explaining my problem with it to Bob, it was a challenge to put into words my theories about why a flaccid dick was funny and a raging hard-on was not. Not the kind of philosophic queries one learns about in film school.

The effects got even more interesting as that sequence progressed. The boys hear a banging from a nearby chest freezer and suddenly dozens of slabs of meat come hurtling out of it onto the cement floor. The pieces of meat begin sliding together and assembling themselves until finally a towering creature made of meat parts stands and confronts our heroes. This was the Meat Monster, which would become a singular image from our film. David Hartman had created an early illustration of what the creature might look like that ultimately Bob Kurtzman refined and fabricated. Kurtzman's Meat

Monster suit was designed to fit the tall and slim frame of a friend of mine, Cesare Gagliardoni, whom I drafted to perform the role. Bob created an absolute work of art in this meat suit, and I am just so sorry that in the dark basement of the set some of the great detail in his design was never visible. One of the Meat Monster's hands was made to look like an entire ham, with slices of pineapple sculpted into it. The surface texture on the suit came from all different shapes and sizes of meat parts including eight-packs of wieners, bacon strips, and even a whole trout.

To create the effect of the meat coming together, I went back to my roots and we did it the old-fashioned way. Over two full days, with just our cameraman Mike Gioulakis, producer Brad Baruh, and another crew member, we were on our hands and knees dragging and puppeting rubber meat pieces around the basement floor. Our go-to tool to animate these pieces of "meat" was trusty ol' fishing line. We then enhanced the meat movements with various frame rates and shutter angles. Shooting this scene was ridiculous fun, but the finished sequence is marvelous.

Over the years I had learned a lot about making reasonably high-quality films on a tight budget. In the production of *John Dies at the End* I brought every one of these lessons to bear. For the aspiring filmmakers out there I am finally going to get down to brass tacks and list some of my tenets of indie filmmaking, in no particular order.

DON COSCARELLI'S FIVE-MINUTE FILM SCHOOL

- Don't even think of starting a movie unless your passion for its story is so strong that you cannot envision a life in which you are not making that movie. You may very well be working on this project for years on end and that level of dedication requires true love of your material and the story you want to tell.
- Unless you happen to have that rare gift of writing dialog like Joe R. Lansdale, David Wong, or Quentin Tarantino, never shoot a dialog scene longer than two pages.
- Like the Boy Scout motto, "Be Prepared!" It's critical that you do your homework and know your script better than anyone else and be able to run your entire movie in your head, before you expose a single frame. You must maximize every available second of your allotted production time. I guarantee that crises and disasters will strike your picture; you must be able to turn on a dime and shift directions at any moment. Be Prepared!
- Cast unknowns. Young actors are so much fun to work with! They are thrilled to get the gig and generally will do almost anything you ask of them. Since they are hoping your film will be their big breakout, they will be around after shooting and eager to help you. Unlike stars, after your shoot they won't immediately dye their hair blond and jet off to London to shoot another movie and be completely unavailable to you.

- You will be better served if you shoot your interiors in a warehouse and not a stage. Movie soundstages are a trap. Most cost at least a thousand dollars a day to rent and there are a whole lot of peripheral costs from stage managers to air-conditioning that can easily double that price. A warehouse leased for an entire six-month production period will generally cost much less than shooting on a stage, plus you can keep your sets standing, just in case. Sure, stages are big, soundproof, and feel professional to shoot in, but if you run over your schedule, or forget a shot, or want to come back and reshoot something, my friend you are SOL.

- Try not to shoot five-day and definitely never six-day weeks. It's just too brutal with not enough time for prep. Shoot intermittently where you can. I perfected this technique on *John Dies at the End* and never shot longer than a four-day week. On a lower-budget movie those "off days" are critical for preparation, logistics, budgeting, viewing, and editing your footage and simply clearing your mind. When you don't have money, you definitely need time to make a good movie. Which leads to my next rule:

- Try to get as many shooting days as possible. Every single financial decision on a film must be aimed at pushing your resources to provide you with more shooting days. It is a very simple equation. More time equals a better movie. Nice office for preproduction? Or, working out of your apartment and spending that money on three more days of shooting? You already know my answer to that one.

- Avoid assholes in your cast and on your crew. The late, great Mike Nichols once said it best: "No assholes. It's amazing what a difference it makes." There's nothing that destroys the morale of an enthusiastic team of cast and crew working toward a shared artistic goal than a lazy, entitled naysayer with a loud mouth. I've been following Nichols's advice since before he even formulated it. Life is simply too short to work with assholes. Believe it.

- Find key collaborators you can trust and depend on. It is crucial to put together a team you can rely on to loyally assist you with production. Even if it is just one key person, such as your producer or your cameraman. Every filmmaker needs a team.

- Take your time and get the best cast possible. Casting errors destroy movies. Other than your story, there is nothing in the filmmaking process that is more important. The right cast elevates your film to levels you cannot even imagine. Don't let a casting director bully you into choosing an actor you know is not right for the role just because of their timeline. Don't rush this. Get it right.

- Shoot as many takes as you can. But don't overshoot your coverage as you will put yourself in a scheduling hole. Those two sentences may seem totally contradictory, but you need to follow both. Shooting as many takes as possible will pay off later in the editing room big time. But always be mindful to stay on schedule so you can make your day.

- Edit thoroughly. Take the time to get the film right. The editing process is where the film is made, or lost. Show your cuts to trusted friends. Listen to their criticism. A shortened postproduction schedule equals doom.

- Reshoot like crazy. From the outset, plan for reshoots and build in a budget for pickup shots and don't let anyone else spend it. Keep all the key props, wardrobe, and set walls you might need and stick them in your own garage if you have to. Before you cast key actors ask them to swear to keep their hair the same length for a couple of months after shooting. Sometimes in editing an absolutely brilliant idea will occur that might literally save the movie, and all you need is an hour with an actor to shoot it. Plan ahead so you can do this.

- Don't follow the herd. Take creative risks. The audience is smarter than most Hollywood big shots give them credit for. Be daring creatively. Otherwise, why are you even making the damn thing in the first place?

SUNDANCE MEMORIES

had learned a nice trick on *Bubba Ho-tep*. Have you ever seen those portable office trailers located on construction sites? I had one delivered to my house on the driveway in my backyard. It made for a terrific editing room and the location was fantastic—just twenty paces from my kitchen and refrigerator. For under a hundred and fifty dollars a month, a spacious editing room delivered to your house? Hard to beat.

I had been editing *John Dies at the End* for going on two months and one day in early December the phone rang. It was Trevor Groth from Sundance. First some backstory . . .

We had submitted an early cut to the Sundance Film Festival but since Thanksgiving weekend had come and gone, and Sundance had already announced in the press the list of lucky entrants, we figured it was another lost cause—until that surprising call.

"Don, it's Trevor from Sundance. We would like to add *John Dies at the End* to the Midnight Program at this year's festival." There was a long silence on my end. Trevor probably thought my mind was moving slow that morning, but in actuality the neurons in my brain were firing faster than the speed of light.

Oh my God, are we really in? Wait! Can we finish the movie in time? How many days to the festival? We haven't even started the music score! What about visual effects . . . hundreds are unfinished! How will I get there? Audiences might hate this movie. Are the hotels sold out? Which actors will come? We need a pub-licist! Why didn't he invite Bubba Ho-tep? *Is this a prank?*

"Hi, Trevor, uh . . ."

"Don, are you there?"

"Yes. Yes. That's great news, Trevor. Thank you. I've got a lot of work here to finish."

"You *will* have your film finished in time then, yes?"

I was tempted to be honest, but my throat suddenly constricted as I realized how important it was that I answered that casual question correctly. So, I coughed. "Yes, shouldn't be a problem. Thanks, Trevor. We'll see you up in Park City."

What civilians never know, but most Sundance veterans are quite familiar with, is that an invitation to the most important film festival in the world entirely destroys your holiday season. When an invitation comes in for this mid-January festival, you are forced into a nightmarish forty-day schedule of excruciating and relentless pressure to get your film finished in time. No Christmas dinner, no New Year's celebrations—just a cycle of editing rooms, sound studios, visual effects meetings, composer consultations, and color correction. And it costs a ton of money. Yet dozens of underfunded filmmakers who win entry have no choice but to immediately pony up the tens of thousands of dollars required to get their films finished on time. We managed to finish just in time and I actually hand-carried the final film with me up into the snowy mountains of Utah.

For the first-timer it's an out-of-body experience. They treat you really well; in fact, on arrival I was given a free coupon to visit the Timberland suite in the festival hotel, which entitled me to a free parka and some cool snow boots. Paul Giamatti had been through it several times before and it was fun watching him chaperone our two young stars, Rob and Chase, as they were inundated with swag. All the luxury brands were there, falling over each other to give free stuff to the actors. They were not as generous to directors but nevertheless watching Chase, Rob, Clancy, and Paul score swag was fun.

The day before my premiere I had the pleasure of attending the Filmmakers Luncheon hosted by Sundance founder Robert Redford up at his Sundance Mountain Resort. They loaded all the directors in buses and we drove from Park City up through a snowstorm to the resort. I happened to sit next to filmmaker Rodney Ascher, who was to become one of the bright lights in creative documentary filmmaking. I found him to be a brilliant and funny guy, and his entry, *Room 237,* would go on to great acclaim. Redford made an appearance and gave an inspiring speech about staying true to your indie roots and making films that no one else makes. Afterward, Rodney and I tried to meet Redford, but every other filmmaker crowded around him and we couldn't squeeze our way in before he was ushered out.

As the clock ticked toward midnight we arrived at ground zero of the festival, the Egyptian Theatre on Main Street. I saw a line of people snaking down a flight of stairs on the side of the theater, waiting in the cold. I had the actors with me and figured it might be a nice gesture to say hi, so I led them over and down the stairs. As we descended the steps the folks in line went nuts when they saw Paul, Clancy, and Glynn. Like veteran politicians, the three of them each started pressing the flesh with fans. It was a raucous crowd of a couple hundred festival-goers, and as we worked our way down the line Paul was bumming cigarettes from fans and posing for selfies. Pretty soon a chant erupted: "Paul! Paul! Paul!" I was high as a kite, figuring that with this crowd in attendance, our movie was a surefire bet to play through the roof. We said goodbye to everybody and went inside. Little did I know that the downside to Sundance being the greatest film market in the world was that an audience of industry insiders had already grabbed all the seats inside the theater: none of those hundreds of enthusiastic folks in the standby line ever got into our screening.

Trevor Groth gave *John Dies at the End* a warm and generous introduction, even including sincere praise for *Bubba Ho-tep,* and then he brought Paul Giamatti up onstage. I know Paul said some very kind things about me, but I was so nervous about the upcoming screening that I have only a vaguely ephemeral memory of it. It was like my body was there, but my mind was on Mars. I came on after Paul's introduction and mumbled out a few forgettable words and the screening began.

As I took my seat, the first thing I noticed was that the theater screen was so tiny in proportion to the size of the theater. The Egyptian dated back to the silent days and was constructed for both vaudeville and movies; consequently screen size was not much of a priority back then. I remember thinking how strange it was that the flagship theater for the festival would be such a poor venue for a visual film.

The film started. The opening scene with our Nazi-tongued zombie played like gangbusters. The audience was laughing with the movie, what a relief! Then I noticed something. Twelve minutes into the movie, a schlubby silhouette stood up from his seat and moved to the aisle. Damn! We had our first walkout. Nothing is more soul-crushing for a filmmaker than having audience members walk out of your screening right in front of you, especially at its world premiere. It turned out to be a fairly significant indie distributor—Bob Weinstein, from what is the now defunct and ignominious Weinstein Company—trundling toward the exit. Despite my nerves, I was absolutely certain of one thing: there was absolutely *nothing* wrong with the first twelve minutes of my movie. Only a self-absorbed, entitled ass would jump to the head of the ticket line and take a seat from all of those nice folks waiting out in the cold of the standby queue when they knew they probably were only going to stay for a couple minutes.

After the screening I was showered with praise for the film, and though we did receive some solid interest from several important independent distributors, to my disappointment, we did not end up closing a distribution deal up in Park City. *John Dies at the End* went on to become a film festival favorite, hitting the trifecta of indie filmmaking by receiving invitations to the top three film festivals in the world: Sundance, South by Southwest, and the Toronto International Film Festival. I was gun-shy about personally doing another independent theatrical release like *Bubba Ho-tep* due to the sheer grunt labor and uncertainty that path requires. Consequently, a few months later, after SXSW, we made a deal with an enthusiastic distributor, Magnolia Pictures, for worldwide release.

Billionaire Mark Cuban owned Magnolia, and part of his entertainment portfolio also included the Landmark theater chain. Magnolia pitched us on what they considered a cutting-edge distribution strategy, which they had named "Ultra Video-on-Demand." Magnolia's premium VOD service would premiere *John Dies at the End* on cable and Internet VOD services at a premium rental price of $9.95, and then thirty days later release it into Landmark theaters across the country. It seemed counterintuitive that a movie could be available on your television thirty days before it was in theaters, but Magnolia professed to have had success with the strategy. This style of release has now fallen out of favor and in retrospect might have been a poor choice by us for our film. In hindsight we probably could have done better with the film by barnstorming an independent release like we did with *Bubba Ho-tep*. In any case, *John Dies at the End* did play successfully in theaters all around the country and the film garnered great reviews and a passionate fan base along the way.

FINISHING *PHANTASM*

*P*hantasm Ravager kept nagging at me. For several years I had been sitting on twenty minutes of amazing *Phantasm* scenes already in the can that I knew fans would love to see. But we never told a soul about it. However, *Phantasm* fans continued to badger me about making another *Phantasm* film. It slowly dawned on me that this footage could possibly be the basis of it. Once the distribution of *John Dies at the End* was finished up, I finally made a decision that we needed to take the *Ravager* material and finish it as a feature film. It was simply too good to ignore.

I started meeting with director Dave Hartman every Saturday morning for a coffee shop breakfast and we would brainstorm ideas about how we might take the disparate sequences we already had in the can and assimilate them into some kind of coherent *Phantasm* story. It was a huge challenge and as we worked, it reminded me a lot of the story challenges I faced when I made the original film.

Over the years, as our *Phantasm* characters aged and their battle against the Tall Man continued, I jokingly would tell friends that one day our heroic Reggie might end the series in a wheelchair, maybe with tricked-out weaponry, still fighting the Tall Man to the very end. Reggie's dogged loyalty and relentless pursuit of the Tall Man was one of the themes I cherished in the series. I may have mentioned this to Dave, and in one of our brainstorming sessions, the concept of dementia came up. We started asking each other rapid-fire questions about how this devastating illness might affect the mind of our intrepid hero. It immediately became apparent that this concept could form a logical conclusion to the series. In the first film we meet young Michael, at the beginning of his life, trying to comprehend the reality of death, and in the fifth and final film we could have Reggie as an older man facing these same implications as well. In the first film, Mike's dreams are penetrated by the Tall Man, and in the last, Reggie's delusions. And best of all, we could link all the scenes we had previously shot together by filming new sequences of now adult Michael's conversations with Reggie, who would be stuck in an old folks' home . . . trapped *in a wheelchair*. Perfect!

With newfound vigor we started making plans to make the final push to shoot the new connective tissue. Instead of some short films or webisodes, David Hartman would now be directing the final, full-fledged *Phantasm* conclusion.

The budget on *Phantasm Ravager,* by necessity, was almost half of the original. We were making a targeted film, by fans, for fans. By nature, it had to be the lowest-budget *Phantasm* on record. How could we possibly do it? The short answer—the same way we shot the earlier short segments, with that microcrew of five or fewer people. We called in favors everywhere, including from the wonderful actor Derek Mears (who played Jason in the *Friday the 13th* reboot), who spent an entire day masked in a brown cloak shooting a crazy sequence as a seven-foot-tall "giant dwarf-creature," which was unfortunately cut from the film in the final edit.

Our wives made huge contributions. Kathleen built many of the sets and the critical hand props. Shelley handled all of the wardrobe and much of the other logistics. I'll never forget the day she pulled up to the house driving a five-ton truck loaded with set dressing, her wide grin barely visible over the dash. Gigi Bannister, Reggie's wife, handled makeup effects. There was more grunt labor involved for everybody than I care to remember. But the process was genuinely fun, both exhilarating and exhausting. We had no one lording over us, we just set out to shoot interesting sequences every shoot day. We also imposed on a lot of our friends to come out on a rotating basis and help us for free. Since we had no release date, there were no time demands. Sometimes we would spend an entire month just prepping for one weekend shoot.

The final sequence of the screenplay called for Mike's long-lost brother Jody to make a dramatic appearance as a battle-hardened survivor of the war versus the Tall Man. As scripted, Bill Thornbury would come roaring into the story driving an armor-plated "Battlecuda," a weaponized version of the Plymouth muscle car the brothers drove in the first film. For the past thirty years I had held on to the *Phantasm II* car and eagerly volunteered it to make a reprise appearance in the new film. I drove the car out to Dave's house and we pulled it into his garage. Over the next two months Kathleen went to work on her "art project." Using a variety of tools and textures, including chain-link fencing and even peanut oil and cocoa powder, she transformed my car into the thundering beast of a battlewagon our heroes would drive.

One of Dave's superb choices was to bring his family friend Stephen Jutras into the *Phantasm* world to portray the badass warrior character of "Chunk." Dave's inspired idea was that Chunk would be a hard-core tough guy who could pull Reggie's ass out of the fire time and again, yet the actor portraying him would be diminutive in stature. This made for a unique on-screen buddy pairing that was rooted firmly in *Phantasm*'s offbeat sensibility. I was thrilled to include this new character and actor because for years our series had been pushing the edge of political correctness in our depiction of little people as scary monsters. Now we had a great actor, who also happened to be a little person, who could rival Reg's heroics and could battle the dwarf-creatures side-by-side with him. A personal favorite scene of mine is when Chunk blasts a dwarf-creature just as it's about to chow down on the hapless Reggie. Stephen's line as his character kicks the creature's corpse: "I hate those little motherfuckers." It's priceless.

Since no one was getting any younger and it was becoming apparent that this was probably Angus's last *Phantasm* film, Dave suggested that we shoot a coda sequence in which we offered up a ray of hope to *Phantasm* fans that some of our younger cast might one day carry the franchise. The scene involved the irrepressible Chunk battling his way back from certain death and meeting up with a long-lost *Phantasm* favorite, Gloria Lynne Henry reprising her signature role as Rocky from *Phantasm III*.

We returned to the desert where we began the project several years before. In the intervening years, the collapsing house where we filmed the opening scenes of the film had been burned to the ground by vandals; now it made for the perfect postapocalyptic setting for the final scene with Rocky and Chunk. It was pretty cool that we stayed true to our roots and shot that entire scene with just our traditional five-person crew.

The final day of shooting with our original actors called for two memorable scenes. First up was the melancholy death scene of our never-say-die hero Reggie. The scene called for him to take his last breaths confined to a hospital bed with his two best friends Mike and Jody at his side. To watch Dave brilliantly direct this tender moment, one we will all face one day, was simply heartbreaking. Actors Michael Baldwin, Bill Thornbury, and Reggie Bannister were at their finest and brought such subtlety and empathy to the scene. A bit of *Phantasm* serendipity occurred during the last take of Reggie's death scene: on the street outside the set a random ice cream truck drove by, and the tinkling bells of "Three Blind Mice" added a poignant live musical score to the scene. I had worked together with these fine actors for almost four decades, and their performances that day had me weeping and beaming with pride at the same time.

We then went on to shoot what would be Angus Scrimm's final scene in a *Phantasm* movie. The scene found Reggie coming awake, years in the past, in a strange vintage hospital with Angus portraying the alter-ego character of Jebediah from *Phantasm Oblivion* in the bed beside him. Actress Kat Lester appeared dramatically at the end of the scene and was delightful. Watching Angus play this scene while confined to a bed was astonishing. Even though he was battling advanced age and serious illness, I watched this still-powerful actor conjure magic right in front of us.

The music of *Phantasm* has always been a key component of its success. We were so lucky to be able to enlist veteran *Phantasm* composer Christopher L. Stone to score *Ravager*. Chris was there at the very beginning on the original *Phantasm* as a young sound designer, in an uncredited role, personally creating the guttural dwarf-creature voices using his analog Roland SVC-350 vocoder. Fred Myrow began collaborating with Chris musically on subsequent films including *Phantasm II* and *Phantasm III*. Chris then single-handedly scored *Phantasm Oblivion*. For *Ravager* Chris created the ultimate *Phantasm* score while staying true to Myrow and Malcolm Seagrave's original musical themes. It is a soaring, moving, and majestic score that carries the viewer through the triumph and heartbreak at the *Phantasm* saga's core.

We premiered *Phantasm Ravager* at Fantastic Fest in Austin. The Alamo Drafthouse South Lamar was packed with *Phantasm* fans eager to witness the unveiling of the final chapter in the series. From the opening images the screening was a great success; the fans loved the movie. I was so relieved for Dave. He had stuck through the long years of our unconventional production and labored for thousands of hours, alone, working on the film's expansive visual effects. After the screening, there was a hosted Q&A with Dave, myself, and the cast. It immediately became apparent that we had done well with *Ravager* when the first audience question was asked. "What are your plans for *Phantasm 6?*"

A BAD ROBOT THIS WAY COMES

While I was editing *Bubba Ho-tep* I received a call from a self-professed *Phantasm* fan. He introduced himself to me as a television producer who had recently completed a series entitled *Felicity* and was working on a new show. His name was J. J. Abrams and he described in enthusiastic detail how he had seen *Phantasm* when he was in his teens and that it had a lasting impact on him. Even though I had no idea who he was, I found his comments about *Phantasm* to be very thoughtful and incisive. On the spur of the moment I invited J.J. to come over to my little editing trailer on my driveway and watch the cut of my new film with the intent that he might give me a fresh view of the material.

I played *Bubba Ho-tep* for him and he gave me some valuable notes. Afterward, while we were hanging out in the trailer he casually mentioned that he was working on a new spy series for ABC. He even played the pulsing new theme music for me on his laptop, which he had just composed himself. On a lark I tossed out a suggestion that he should really meet Angus Scrimm. I told him that not only was he a great guy, but that he was a great actor and maybe they could find a way to work together one day. J.J. eagerly took Angus's phone number from me and departed. Within just a couple of days I heard from Angus that he had a very pleasant conversation with "a nice young chap." He told me they discussed J.J.'s new show and it appeared there might be a featured role in it for him as an interrogator named McCullough. The show was *Alias*.

Angus was so excited to get the role. He had toiled in the trenches of low-budget indie films for most of his career and I know he relished the opportunity to appear in such a mainstream network show of high quality. And more importantly, Angus loved working with J.J., who treated him with such respect and kindness.

Over the years J.J. and I stayed in touch as he created some impressive work in both television and film. Just as I was finishing up *John Dies at the End* I received an email from him asking if I would be interested in bringing *Phantasm* over to his production company, Bad Robot Productions, to screen for his coworkers. Several of his team had never seen the film. I told him that would be great, but the only problem was what to screen. I had a single 35 mm print in my possession but it was pretty scratched up. The only alternative was a standard-definition commercial DVD. Neither was optimal. J.J. was surprised we had no high-definition materials for a film like *Phantasm,* but I explained that the distribution license with the current distributor was coming to an end in a couple years so they had no incentive to invest in a new HD version. J.J. told me we needed to fix this and he would get me over to his company to meet with Ben Rosenblatt, his head of postproduction. He was sure Ben could find a way to solve the problem.

A week later I arrived in the vicinity of the Bad Robot world headquarters and was unable to find it! I was at the address, but there was no Bad Robot, just a company called the "National Typewriter Company." I went into an office next door and they informed me that the National Typewriter Company was in fact the Bad Robot offices and that people came in their office by mistake all the time. I walked back over and peered through a window and all I could make out inside were vintage printing presses and typesetting machines. I approached the heavy steel door and noticed a tiny sign over the doorbell. It cryptically read, "Are You Ready?" I knew I was in the right place.

Ben Rosenblatt had a plan. Bad Robot was producing the newest feature film incarnation of *Star Trek* along with several television series and had brought a lot of postproduction resources in-house. In particular they had recently invested in a high-end Spanish film finishing system called Mistika, which they were using on all their big projects. Ben suggested we start with a full-frame 4K scan of the original *Phantasm* negative at Bad Robot's film lab of choice, FotoKem. Ben intimated that since they ran so much Bad Robot television series work through FotoKem, he believed they would give us an excellent price for the scan. Ben proposed that if I could cover the cost of the scan and the hourly cost of the technician, Bad Robot could provide everything else we would need as long as I wouldn't mind working around their other projects.

Decades ago I had attended a seminar at the Directors Guild hosted by director Martin Scorsese about long-term storage of film elements and the peril that our collective motion picture history was in as film negatives degraded over time from improper storage conditions. I learned that to preserve the color integrity of a film negative, it needed to be stored at a constant temperature of around forty degrees Fahrenheit with very low humidity. When film goes bad, you can smell it. It reeks of vinegar. They call this vinegar syndrome. Independent films were at the most risk as they frequently had no major studio behind them to monitor and protect their valuable negative materials. A couple of years after that seminar, I decided to move the original *Phantasm* camera negative over to a high-security, long-term cold storage vault. It cost some money, but in the long run it proved to be well worth it. The Bad Robot restoration project was a terrific opportunity to make a permanent digital record of my film in a pristine version, and essentially protect it forever.

Moving the precious *Phantasm* camera negative from the cold storage vault over to FotoKem was a terrifying prospect. What if it was lost or damaged along the way? It just didn't feel right to trust it to some delivery guy with a truck. I remembered reading a story about director Stanley Kubrick and how once when he was forced to change film labs he personally picked up his negative and instructed his driver to not exceed thirty miles an hour on the drive to his new lab. Following in the master's footsteps, I engaged in a similar process of personally picking up just one reel of negative at a time, driving it slowly over to FotoKem, and not bringing them another until the previous reel was successfully scanned. (Unlike Kubrick, I did not have a chauffeur.) Everybody thought I was crazy to do it this way, but god forbid *Phantasm* was incinerated in a car crash!

Once the negative was scanned, over the next year and a half, it would go something like this. Ben would ring me up, "Hey Don, are you free tonight at eight p.m.? We've got four hours available." And I would go over to Bad Robot and work with their in-house colorist, Juan Cabrera, on the restoration. Juan did a fantastic job using the Mistika and together we created a version of the film that I believe is better than the 35 mm prints originally screened in theaters.

Once Juan was finished, Nate Orloff came in to assist with the grunt work of the restoration. For months on end I would sit with Nate as we went through the entire film and removed every scratch or ding in the image. He was also able to fix some serious original flaws in the film. In the third act, our heroes Mike, Jody, and Reggie enter the white room—and on the floor, in the shadows, sat a yellow bucket that was accidentally left in the shot. For decades, no one else noticed it, but I had been groaning every time I saw that damn bucket. With a few quick keystrokes it disappeared forever. I was extremely careful not to fall into the trap that some directors have in which they alter important and meaningful sections of their classic films. The only other alteration I allowed was to a less than one-second-long profile shot of the sphere. The new effect, composited by VFX wizard Andrew Kramer, blends seamlessly, and in my mind is now perfect.

After color-correction and restoration were complete I stopped by Bad Robot to take a final look and bumped into J.J. in the hallway. He wanted to know what we were doing about the audio. I was very clear with him that I did not want to overstay my welcome at Bad Robot; he had been so extremely generous in supporting the visual restoration, but J.J. insisted that if the visuals were perfect, we needed to make the audio perfect also. He got with Ben and they brought in their resident Bad Robot audio wiz, Robby Stambler, who it turned out just happened to be a huge *Phantasm* fan like J.J. Robby went to work with his teammate Lindsey Alvarez. They took the original mono tracks, ripped them apart, and put them together again with enhanced sound effects and clever mixing. They turned it into one blistering, kickass soundtrack. Fred Myrow and Malcolm Seagrave's music was now so present, warm, and powerful that I think this new soundtrack may be my favorite part of the entire restoration. Hats off to others in the Bad Robot crew including Mike Silver, Phil Hoang, and Josh Tate for all their hard work on the restoration.

Later that year and early the next, *Phantasm Remastered,* as it was now called, had its first two major screenings, coincidentally both in Austin, Texas. The first one, stealth and off-the-radar, was held at Harry Knowles's now defunct twenty-four-hour Butt-Numb-A-Thon festival as a special surprise screening. It was a powerful and vivid premiere at the state-of-the-art Alamo Drafthouse South Lamar theater. The audience loved it and the film had never looked so spectacular or sounded so clear and brilliant. As actor Michael Baldwin and I entered the theater to surprise the audience, it turned out that Alamo impresario Tim League had turned the tables with a special surprise for us. Above the audience, two flying spheres (modified model drones!) flew in over the crowd in unison and hovered in the auditorium. Specially designed just for the screening, these actual flying spheres buzzed over the audience to their delight.

Thanks to senior film programmer Jarod Neece, the official premiere of *Phantasm Remastered* was held a few months later at the South by Southwest Film Festival. J.J. was at SXSW and very kindly introduced the film to a warm response from the assembled crowd of *Phantasm* fans. They loved it.

Subsequently I have attended over a dozen screenings of *Phantasm Remastered* around the world, and the film has looked and sounded absolutely gorgeous. Aaron Lea created an impressive new reimagining of the original poster and I was honored to have *Phantasm Remastered* subsequently selected for inclusion in Art House Theater Day, and the restoration played nationwide in a hundred art house cinemas around the country.

I am honored and grateful that J. J. Abrams and his dedicated Bad Robot Productions staff would so generously offer their talents and resources to archive *Phantasm* in such a pristine form in perpetuity. I, along with *Phantasm* fans around the world, definitely owe them a sincere debt of gratitude.

A TALL MAN

Phantasm Remastered had not yet been announced and we received an invite from the Alamo Drafthouse Richardson, just outside Dallas, to screen the original film. As the *Phantasm* cast and I would be attending the nearby Texas Frightmare Weekend horror convention, we decided it would be fun to all attend the screening and do something different. The event was billed as the last 35 mm screening of *Phantasm* along with a live commentary of the film by the cast and me. We didn't know it then, but this would be Angus Scrimm's last appearance with us at a horror convention.

The fans loved to meet Angus in person. Once, while we attended Mike and Mia Kerz's highly attended horror convention Flashback Weekend in Chicago, I watched a line of fans clamoring to meet, hug, and kiss this frightening icon of death. It puzzled me as to why, and I finally just chalked it up to a strange mix of both Angus's warm, genteel nature and the fans' desire to confront their fears in the flesh.

With the rigors of the requisite air travel it had become difficult for the eighty-nine-year-old Angus to satisfy all the convention requests he received. On several occasions I would arrive at a convention and not learn until the last minute that Angus was unable to attend. Angus truly felt bad about disappointing his fans, but since he was blessed with a mischievous spirit, he came up with a plan. During my panel discussions at the convention Angus would gamely ring up my cell phone right in the middle of it. I would make a fuss and pull out my phone, grumbling about who would have the temerity to call and interrupt during such an important conversation with the *Phantasm* fans. Then with feigned surprise, "Oh, look. It's Angus Scrimm calling. Gee, would you mind if I answered it?" The fans would always roar and I would hold my cell phone up to the microphone and Angus could broadcast a greeting directly to the assembled crowd. The fans loved this and would always demand that I keep Angus on the line. They would bombard us with questions, with me onstage and Angus answering from the comfort of his own home.

One of the last screenings that Angus attended was a very small cast and crew showing of *Phantasm Ravager* at a postproduction house in Santa Monica. He was not driving anymore so Dave offered to swing by and pick him up on his way in. During the drive, Angus asked who would be driving him home. Dave, half in jest, told him that if Angus liked the movie, he would be driving him home, but if he didn't like it, then Don would drive him home. This was Dave's first feature film and I didn't blame him for not wanting to endure a long drive alone with an unhappy star. After the screening Angus was rather inscrutable as to his opinion of the film. Dave couldn't contain his anxiety and curiosity and finally blurted out the question on everybody's mind: "So Angus, what did you think of the movie?"

In his mischievous way, Angus averred, "David, you will be driving me home tonight."

Angus was a lifelong movie lover, and had started his showbiz career in his teens as a theater usher at the Paramount Theater, a grand movie palace in downtown Kansas City, Missouri. Watching Karloff and Lugosi in that theater is where he developed a love of horror films that would serve him so well in later life. He moved to Hollywood to pursue his dream of a career in movies and studied at the University of Southern California under William DeMille, who was legendary director Cecil B. DeMille's brother. His best classmates were (director-to-be) Sam Peckinpah and (humorist-to-be) Art Buchwald. Before his acting career took off, Angus always supported himself as a writer. He wrote for *TV Guide* and worked as an associate editor at *Cinema* magazine alongside future Academy Award–winning director

Curtis Hanson. (Angus had a featured role in one of Hanson's early films, *Sweet Kill.*) For most of his career, Angus supported himself between acting gigs as an author of liner notes for Angel, the classical division of Capitol Records. Angus never won an Oscar for acting, but in 1975 he did win a Grammy Award for writing liner notes on an Erich Korngold album. Along with notes for legendary artists such as Miles Davis, Sinatra, and Itzhak Perlman, Angus also wrote the liner notes for the first record album I ever purchased when I was just ten years old, *Meet the Beatles!* As a kid I remember reading those notes on the back of that album over and over while listening to that classic first Beatles record. Yet when the executives at Capitol Records asked Angus if he wanted his name credited with his liner notes on the back cover of the Beatles album, he demurred, as he had no faith this youthful British pop band would have any longevity.

Over our forty-year friendship Angus taught me so much about the movies. He introduced me to the work of many of the great stars and filmmakers of the thirties and forties. Over the years, as a benefit of his side job at Capitol Records, he gifted me with literally hundreds of soundtracks of the great movie composers, many of which he had worked with on their records. Over the years, as I married and had children, Angus became part of our family, and this was a genuine blessing. Even my dogs loved him: he had a practice of always carrying a small bag of dog treats in his pocket, and when they would spot this tall man walking up the front path to our house our entire pack would erupt in howling joy.

As Angus progressed into his late eighties, he had been in declining health for some time. Shelley and I were concerned that he had not been getting the best health care. Angus could be a very stubborn individual and despite his protestations that his doctors were treating him well, he just seemed to be continually getting weaker. Finally Shelley set up an appointment with a reputable gerontologist for a complete health exam. I picked him up and drove him over and sat with him during the appointment. The doctor declined to make any diagnosis until the medical tests were completed. The results were not good.

Angus was suffering from a blood cancer and had been living with this condition, completely undiagnosed, for some time. We were referred to a specialist and Shelley and I took him in for a consult. The doctor then told us about some excellent new treatment options that could easily extend the survival rate to five years or more. Angus made the decision to pursue the new treatment option, and with great hope he received a delivery of the very expensive medication. The plan seemed to be going well for several months, but on a subsequent trip to the doctor's office he collapsed and suffered a calamitous event. Angus was admitted unconscious into the intensive-care unit of the adjoining hospital. The prognosis was grim.

As we raced over to the hospital and arrived in the ICU waiting room I witnessed something truly amazing. This small room was packed full of Angus's neighbors. These were people who knew him not as a horror icon, but as their kindly neighbor who met them in the nearby park every evening as they walked their dogs together. I heard story after story as these nice people related to me how much they valued Angus's gentle kindness, how much they relished sitting in the park in the evenings with him listening to the humorous stories he would tell about simple things like his youth in Kansas City. In turn, they were astonished as Shelley and I explained to them how beloved Angus was by horror fans worldwide and what an impact his work had made over the decades. Many of them were completely unaware that Angus was a celebrated horror movie star.

After several excruciatingly long days of no improvement in his condition, the doctors and family decided it was time to remove Angus from life support. The doctors asked us if anyone would like to be there as it happened, and I volunteered to accompany one of the family members into the room to attend to Angus in what might be his final moments. Angus had been such a prominent fixture in my life over so many years—professionally involved in key successes from *Jim The World's Greatest* to the *Phantasm* films, and personally as a cherished family member—that I felt a duty to see him through to the end.

It was hard not to weep as the ventilator was removed and this strong man took his final breaths. I drew some comfort in appreciating this amazing and surprising life we led, a life in which Angus and I made our stock-in-trade exploring death and dying in the horror movie world, and yet here we would be together at the end of his life. I had never witnessed the intimacy of a person actually dying in front of me and the irony that my first experience with death would be with the Tall Man from *Phantasm* was not lost on me. However, it was strangely fitting that I would be there as my good friend made passage. In so doing he would give me strength for that one day in the future when I make that same journey.

THE SHAPE OF THINGS TO COME

P eople always ask me what film I am making next. What they are probably unaware of is that, in this business, there is never any guarantee
one will ever make another film. Sure, a very few mega-directors will
always be able to make the films they want for the rest of their lives. But for
the rest of us, there is no guarantee at all. Every opportunity to make a feature film must be treated as a genuine gift.

The traditional indie film business appears as if it might be in its death
throes. It is getting tougher every day to earn enough to return investors'
money, let alone make a profit. The international market for indie films from
the United States is extremely difficult and the ranks of independent distributors overseas are shrinking every year. I wish I had better news.

In contrast, the cost of entry for filmmakers has dropped tremendously
with the advent of digital cameras and postproduction software tools. The
means to make a movie could be in your back pocket. Anybody can make
a movie now, even with that cell phone camera, and with some creativity
and skill it can look as polished as a studio feature. But getting it seen and
into profits is the true challenge. I used to caution aspiring filmmakers to
keep their indie film budgets to under a million dollars. Now my warning
threshold tells them to keep it to a maximum of a hundred thousand dollars,
otherwise risks of financial loss will be huge.

I certainly intend to direct more feature films and have written several
brilliant (of course!) screenplays that I am currently seeking funding for. I

have also been surprised with the interest in channeling some of my previous films into reboots and series. Who knows, perhaps one day a *Phantasm, Bubba Ho-tep,* or *John Dies at the End* series, sequel, or remake will be in your local theater or streaming on your TV. That would be cool.

In any case, what I am most excited about right now is this book. It is my sincere hope that some visionary young filmmakers are reading these very pages right now and planning to ignore most of my advice and find their own path to success in movies.

I will be waiting and watching for your films. Good luck! I'm rooting for you.

HOLLYWOOD FOREVER CEMETERY

August 10, 2008

I t was the night we returned to the graveyard. Everybody was there—the terrifying Tall Man, Angus Scrimm; the luscious Lady in Lavender, Kat Lester; and everyone's favorite ice cream man, Reggie Bannister.

As we arrived we saw a line down Santa Monica Boulevard with an eclectic mix of horror fans, teens, and some tricked-out hearses. A sold-out audience was sprawled on blankets on the lawn directly adjoining the graveyard. As the sun went down, the bottles were being surreptitiously passed around and the joints were firing up. The crowd was a thousand strong, and if you accounted for all the souls in the vicinity there were probably a hundred times that number. All to watch *Phantasm*. At night. Under the stars. In the graveyard. It would be a screening to remember.

The summer screenings in the Hollywood Forever Cemetery, run by the group Cinespia, are projected against the massive white marble wall of the mausoleum of original superstar and heartthrob Rudolph Valentino. A stellar lineup of Hollywood luminaries were guaranteed to be in attendance, even if they were no longer living. Many of these movie greats who had a huge influence on me were entombed on the premises of Hollywood Forever and would be directly in viewing distance of *Phantasm*. How strange and wonderful! Douglas Fairbanks Sr. was right there in the lavish memorial built by his grieving wife, the epitaph reading, "GOODNIGHT, MY SWEET PRINCE." Peter Lorre, who scared the hell out of a young Don Coscarelli in his astonishingly creepy *The Beast with Five Fingers,* was there. Also in attendance would be one of the great screen actresses of all time, Janet Gaynor, star of the silent classic *Sunrise,* one of the best films ever. And great directors would be there too including John Huston, Cecil B. DeMille, and Victor Fleming. Even Shelley's grandfather Max had a great view from his nearby crypt.

It might have been the best place ever to screen *Phantasm* and the perfect venue for a reunion with cast and crew. We had practically lived in graveyards and mortuaries during the shooting of *Phantasm*. Now decades later we were all returning to one to share our film with its longtime fans.

There was also something fitting and remarkable about this venue for me personally. When I started writing *Phantasm* as a very young man, its themes came from my deeply rooted childhood fears of death. Now, decades later, I realized that in making *Phantasm,* in putting those fears up on screen for all to see and working on a daily basis with the tools of the death trade— coffins, funeral coaches, embalming rooms—it served to desensitize me to my fears and allow me to come to grips with them. I cannot in good conscience tell you that I am now completely fearless of the prospect of one day entering that dark void, but the entire process is a hell of a lot less terrifying after having made *Phantasm*. Today, I find cemeteries some of the most relaxing and genuinely peaceful places on the planet.

Before the film started we spread out our own blanket and I was thrilled to find beside us the venerable movie star Clu Gulager, who had brought his folding chair and blanket to watch *Phantasm* in the graveyard. This was profoundly meaningful to me because as a young filmmaker I was so keenly influenced by *The Last Picture Show,* and here was one of its stars attending a retrospective screening of my film. It was a true honor and it made me feel like I had come full circle.

Along with these wonderful actors, my entire *Phantasm* phamily was there. Surrounding me were loyal friends who had been there from the beginning. Paul Pepperman, who had done so much in getting *Phantasm* made, including casting his own fingers as prosthetics for young Michael to hack off. By his side was his wife, Jacalyn, whom he met when she was an earnest young camera assistant on *Phantasm*. Seated nearby was Daryn Okada, our sixteen-year-old grip on *Phantasm* and subsequently full-fledged cinematographer on *Phantasm II*. Beside Daryn was his wife, Cean, who had a featured acting role in *Phantasm Ravager,* and their charming son Evan, who gripped on the fifth *Phantasm* just like his dad had on the first film. My wife, Shelley, who had become a key player in the later sequels, designing the costumes on both *Phantasm Oblivion* and *Ravager,* was on my blanket, as was my son Andy, who had worked tirelessly on the crew of *Ravager* as well as many of my other films, for which I am eternally grateful.

Darkness had enshrouded the cemetery, the moon was on the rise, and it was time to start the show. As they brought the cast and me up onto a makeshift stage right in front of Rudy Valentino's tomb, the graveyard was filled with applause. The few words we spoke were greeted with warmth and enthusiasm from these loyal and, many of them, longtime fans. Our Tall Man, Angus Scrimm, finally took the stage and spoke for all of us when he slyly intoned, "I have been in a lot of cemeteries, but this do beat them all. Many of my cherished ones are here. My mother Pearl, my father Alfred, my two older sisters Lucille and Marie. But they are all interred. So for me this is a family reunion. Also with my *Phantasm* family and my new family here, as we all watch this landmark movie."

Angus was right. It was a family reunion. Decades previously I had been privileged and blessed to make a small horror film with some actors and crew who became my lifelong friends. Somehow we came together, pooled our collective talents, and this indie movie of ours went on to receive worldwide adulation. *Phantasm*'s success allowed us to keep working together throughout most of our lifetimes. Not many have been the recipient of a gift such as this, and I now understood how rare and valuable this experience of mine has been.

The lights went down, a hush fell over the graveyard, and *Phantasm* began to play. And what was the response to the movie that night? Let me tell you. It was a real scream.

EPILOGUE

Our *Phantasm* stuntman, George Singer, skidded the black Barracuda to a stop and leaped out of the driver's seat to help me, then suddenly stopped dead in his tracks. "Dude, your face is on fire."

The burning wadding and fiery debris that had been spit out of the shotgun barrel was now embedded in the camera pad that was taped securely to my face. George and Paul and Roberto jumped to my aid, desperately trying to tear the burning camera pad loose from my head. After several sharp tugs it ripped free before my skin could catch on fire. My vision was so obscured that I had been completely oblivious to the danger I was in, due to all that aluminum foil wrapped around my head.

So we got the shot. And that's all you're trying to do on an indie film . . . get the shot. However, we couldn't rest on our laurels, we had a movie to finish. Next up, we needed to crash that hearse into a tree. But how in hell could we do that? On a regular studio movie your rigging effects team would lay down a cable track which would guide the driverless car directly into the tree with no risk to any stuntman. Of course, we didn't have those kinds of resources when we made *Phantasm*. But we did have a bunch of young, resourceful indie filmmakers who wouldn't take no for an answer, including George Singer. "Hey George, do you think if we put our truck behind the hearse and pushed it up to like thirty miles an hour, that you could then steer the coach from the backseat and into that tree and maybe just before impact drop down into some stunt pads to protect yourself from impact?"

"Sure thing, bro. Let's go for it."

FIN

MUSIC UP

ROLL END CREDITS:

THIS MEMOIR WAS

WRITTEN

AND

DIRECTED

BY

ME.

MY PRODUCER: was my enthusiastic editor at St. Martin's Press, Peter Wolverton, and it was his original inspiration that I should embark on this path of memorializing my experiences in the indie film world. Peter's solid guidance and passion for the project galvanized me to get this book done.

THE EXECUTIVE PRODUCERS: of this story are my loyal parents, Donald "Dac" and Kate Coscarelli. Thanks to Uncle Sam, they were forced to travel to Tripoli, Libya, to bring me into this world. Back in the States, in addition to giving me access to my first cameras, they unwaveringly supported every single creative effort of mine and my sister's. I learned from them that there is no higher calling in this life than nourishing your children's talents. Try it. The world will be a better place for it.

CO-PRODUCERS: are several longtime friends: Paul Pepperman was an important collaborator on my first four films and was my brother-in-arms and loyal consigliere in the impossible challenges of making those movies. Jeff Conner has provided sage advice in the editing of this book and has recently been my favorite collaborator on new work. Roberto A. Quezada worked in many capacities on four of my films and has been an extremely valuable collaborator over the decades both creatively and logistically. I have known Roger Avary since he was eighteen years old and am so proud of the world-class filmmaker he has become. Brad Baruh in many ways was responsible for getting *John Dies at the End* made and I look forward to working with this talented filmmaker on exciting new projects to come. David Hartman made important contributions to *Bubba Ho-tep* and *John Dies at the End* and his creativity and talent made it a pleasure to work with him on his directorial debut, *Phantasm Ravager*. And, of course, high school pal Mark Scott Annerl, who was there at a critical juncture on *Phantasm* and also, back in the day, helped us almost bring home that *Iron Man* trophy for Woodrow Wilson High when our backs were against the wall versus Long Beach Poly.

CO-EXECUTIVE PRODUCERS: Charles Champlin, Sidney J. Sheinberg, and Peter Saphier supported my first film and without their contributions my career as a filmmaker might have ended right there.

ASSOCIATE PRODUCERS: are my literary agent, Alyssa Reuben, and her dedicated assistant, Katelyn Dougherty, who so capably closed the deal with the publisher.

CINEMATOGRAPHY: credit goes to the talented photographers whose excellent photos populate this book, including: Scott Redinger-Libolt, Bill Richert, Paul Pepperman, and Robert Raphael. I would also like to send out my heartfelt thanks to these great cinematographers whom I have so enjoyed working with through the years: John Alcott, Daryn Okada, Chris Chomyn, and Michael Gioulakis.

MUSIC: by Fred Myrow, Malcolm Seagrave, Christopher L. Stone, Lee Holdridge, and Brian Tyler. These brilliant composers and friends have scored all of my films and are unheralded collaborators in their successes. It was an honor and a pleasure to collaborate with these great talents.

ASSISTANT PRODUCER: duties were diligently supervised by Jennifer Donovan.

PUBLICITY: for this book was expertly handled by the terrific Kristopher Kam, with marketing by Paul Hochman and Sara Beth Haring.

STORY CONSULTANT: was meticulous copy editor Bill Warhop.

ART DIRECTOR: was the fabulous Rob Grom, who designed our mind-blowing cover.

ASSISTANT ART DIRECTORS: were our interior and photo insert designer Steven Seighman and production team Eric Gladstone and Ryan Jenkins who laboriously designed this book.

CATERING: by ChefChloe.com—Damn that girl can cook!

SOCIAL MEDIA: services by Crush Social.

TRANSPORTATION: provided by 1971 Plymouth Hemicuda—of course!

THE PLAYERS: Gregory Harrison, Robbie Wolcott, Marla Pennington, Dan McCann, Jeff Roth, Terrie Kalbus, Ralph Richmond, Michael Baldwin, Bill Thornbury, Reggie Bannister, Kat Lester, Ken Jones, David Arntzen, Mary Ellen Shaw, Myrtle Scotton, Marc Singer, Tanya Roberts, Rip Torn, John Amos, Josh Milrad, Ru, Charak, Kodo and Podo, Ronnie James Dio, Lance Henriksen, Mark Rolston, Dermot Mulroney, Catherine Keener, Ben Hammer, Dominic Hoffman, Steven Antin, Traci Lind, Paul Provenza, James LeGros, Paula Irvine, Samantha Phillips, Kenneth Tigar, Mark Major, Gloria Lynne Henry, Kevin Connors, Heidi Marnhout, Bruce Campbell, Ossie Davis, Ella Joyce, Bob Ivy, Edith Jefferson, Larry Penell, Solange Morand, Bree Turner, Ethan Embry, John DeSantiis, Chase Williamson, Rob Mayes, Paul Giamatti, Clancy Brown, Glynn Turman, Doug Jones, Daniel Roebuck, Fabianne Therese, Jonny Weston, Jimmy Wong, Tai Bennett, Allison Weissman, Bank Lee, Cesare Gagliardoni, Dawn Cody, Stephen Jutras, Daniel Schweiger, and Angus Scrimm as the Tall Man.

WWW.PHANTASM.COM

WWW.FACEBOOK.COM/PHANTASMMOVIES
TWITTER: @DONCOSCARELLI
INSTAGRAM: @DON_COSCARELLI

FADE OUT:

CUE EXIT MUSIC

DON COSCARELLI FILMOGRAPHY

1975   *Jim The World's Greatest*—cowriter, codirector, producer
          Universal Pictures

1976   *Kenny & Company*—writer, director, producer
          20th Century Fox

1979   *Phantasm*—writer, director
          Avco Embassy Pictures

1982   *The Beastmaster*—cowriter, director
          MGM

1984   *The Last in Line*—writer, director
          Artist: Dio
          Warner Bros. Records

1988   *Phantasm II*—writer, director
          Universal Pictures

1990   *Survival Quest*—writer, director
          MGM

1994   *Phantasm III: Lord of the Dead*—writer, director, producer
          Universal Pictures

1998   *Phantasm: Oblivion*—writer, director, producer
          MGM/Orion